Quality
Food Plots

YOUR GUIDE TO BETTER DEER
AND BETTER DEER HUNTING

Kent Kammermeyer
Karl V. Miller
Lindsay Thomas Jr.

Editors

A Publication of the
Quality Deer Management Association

Quality Food Plots

YOUR GUIDE TO BETTER DEER AND BETTER DEER HUNTING

Published by the Quality Deer Management Association
Bogart, Ga.

To purchase additonal copies of this book, contact the
Quality Deer Management Association:
(800) 209-3337
www.QDMA.com

ISBN No. 0-9777104-1-6

Printed in the United States of America

Cover photo (feeding bucks) by Charles Alsheimer. Additional cover photos by Charles Alsheimer,
Tes Randle Jolly and Lindsay Thomas Jr. Cover design by Cindy Adams.

ACKNOWLEDGEMENTS

The editors of *Quality Food Plots*, along with the staff of the
Quality Deer Management Association, are grateful to the following
for contributing chapters of this book:

Craig Dougherty, Ph.D.   Carroll Johnson III, Ph.D.
Phil Freshley, CPSSc   Jim Wills Jr., Ph.D.
Craig Harper, Ph.D.

We would like to thank the following individuals and groups
who also contributed to the success of this project:

Charles Alsheimer   Bill Lea
Phil Anderson   Bill Marchel
John Andrae, Ph.D.   R. Larry Marchinton, Ph.D.
Brad Bailey   David Morris
Doug Bastian   David Osborn
Blaine Burley   Chris Pevey
Ken Burnette   The Phosphate and Potash Institute
Mark Buxton   Tal Robertson
John Carpenter   Steve Scott
Don Carter   Bill Sell, Ph.D.
Bobby Cole   Brian Sheppard
Chris Cook   Kevin Smith
William Cooper   Robert Smith
Wilbur Dellinger, DVM   Ed Spinazzola
Ryan Foster   Todd Stittleburg
Bill Gray   Roger Stout
Steve Gulledge   Jeff Sturgis
Tommy Hunter   The Forage Information System
Tommy Jenkins, M.D.   Paul Svetz
Tes Randle Jolly   Rans Thomas
Roger Kingsley   H.W. Williams Aerial Photography
Bryan Kinkel   Grant Woods, Ph.D.
Patrick Kinney   Forestry Images

SPONSORS

Quality Food Plots was made possible in part by the generous
financial support of the following companies, agencies and individuals.
The QDMA, a nonprofit organization, would like to thank these supporters
for helping us accomplish our educational mission.

Bass Pro Shops
www.basspro-shops.com

Evolved Habitats
www.ehoutdoors.com

Georgia Forestry Commission
www.gatrees.org

International Paper Co.
www.internationalpaper.com

Kammermeyer Consulting
www.deerclovers.com

Modern Habitat Solutions
www.thefirminator.com

Mossy Oak BioLogic
www.mossyoakbiologic.com

NorthCountry Whitetails
http://northcountrywhitetails.com

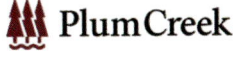

Plum Creek Timber Co.
www.plumcreek.com

Pogue Agri-Partners
http://pogueagri.com/

Roy O. Martin Lumber Co.
www.martco.com

ED SPINAZZOLA

QDMA Board member
and author of
Ultimate Deer Food Plots

Star Seed
www.gostarseed.com

**USDA Forest Service, Southern Region
State and Private Forestry**
www.southernregion.fs.fed.us

Weekend Warrior
www.weekend-warrior.com

JEFF STURGIS

Whitetail Habitat Solutions
www.whitetailhabitatsolutions.com

Wildlife Specialties
www.amcomfg.com/brushmaster.html

QUALITY FOOD PLOTS

EDITORS
Kent Kammermeyer
Karl V. Miller, Ph.D.
Lindsay Thomas Jr.

ART & DESIGN
Cindy Adams

PUBLISHING COORDINATOR
Cindy Herndon

TECHNICAL EDITORS
Craig Harper, Ph.D.
Brian Murphy
David Osborn
Grant Woods, Ph.D.

Quality
YOUR GUIDE TO

Food Plots

BETTER DEER AND BETTER DEER HUNTING

FOREWORD

Four million years of fine tuning have created the perfect animal, the noble white-tailed deer. The geographic range of the species bears testimony to its adaptability and therefore its presence in habitat and climate extremes from the Everglades of Florida to the deserts of the Southwest and from the tropical regions of South America to the ice box conditions of northern Canada.

Follow a deer around for a day and you will gain an appreciation of just how selective it is while feeding — a nibble here, a few steps, and a nibble there. Follow a deer for a year and you will gain respect for the seasonal nutritional demands on an animal and how it responds to those demands within a relatively small home range, usually less than a square mile.

Researchers have done just that. They have accompanied captive whitetails, conditioned to human presence, into natural habitats and have recorded the species and amounts of plants eaten. Related studies have involved an analysis of the plant species and their nutritional values collected from the stomachs of hunter-harvested deer. In addition to identifying hundreds of plant species eaten by deer, researchers have discovered that deer exhibit an uncanny ability to select the most nutritious leaves or portions of individual plants.

How do deer *know* the difference? Is it their exceptional sense of smell, or is it something more? Just like scientists are discovering more and more about the senses of white-tailed deer, is there a yet-to-be-discovered process for discerning the nutritive value of foods? Or, do deer simply use an acute sense of smell or touch in selecting the most tender and therefore most nutritious parts of plants? Such questions, yet to be answered, provide the impetus for research. What we have learned is that whitetails are a reflection of what

they eat, and a myriad of conditions determines their diet — not the least of which is high-quality, agricultural food plots provided by hunters.

The practice of Quality Deer Management (QDM) has given rise to a group of individuals best described as deer stewards who seek to produce and grow the highest-quality plants for increased deer health and attraction. These hunters-turned-managers have launched into the disciplines of agronomy, nutrition, climatology, agriculture, horticulture, silviculture, animal husbandry and habitat manipulation to provide optimum conditions for whitetails in the form of small, "personalized" agricultural food plots.

The Quality Deer Management Association (QDMA) exists in part to show these dedicated deer managers the way to produce these high-quality plants. The QDMA provides a guiding light for QDM throughout our nation and abroad. This international scope involves the promotion of better deer and better deer hunting for an increasing number of deer stewards committed to balancing the needs of whitetail populations and those of our diverse society. Uniquely suited to do this, the QDMA has assembled a cadre of experienced and accomplished managers to write the most comprehensive guide to producing high-quality plants, *Quality Food Plots: Your Guide to Better Deer and Better Deer Hunting*. Contained within the covers of this book are detailed discussions of the aforementioned disciplines related to the biology and management of white-tailed deer and their habitats. The QDMA and its author-members are to be commended on the production of an invaluable management tool. This book is destined for the library of conscientious and dedicated deer stewards around the world.

R. Joseph Hamilton
Founder of the QDMA

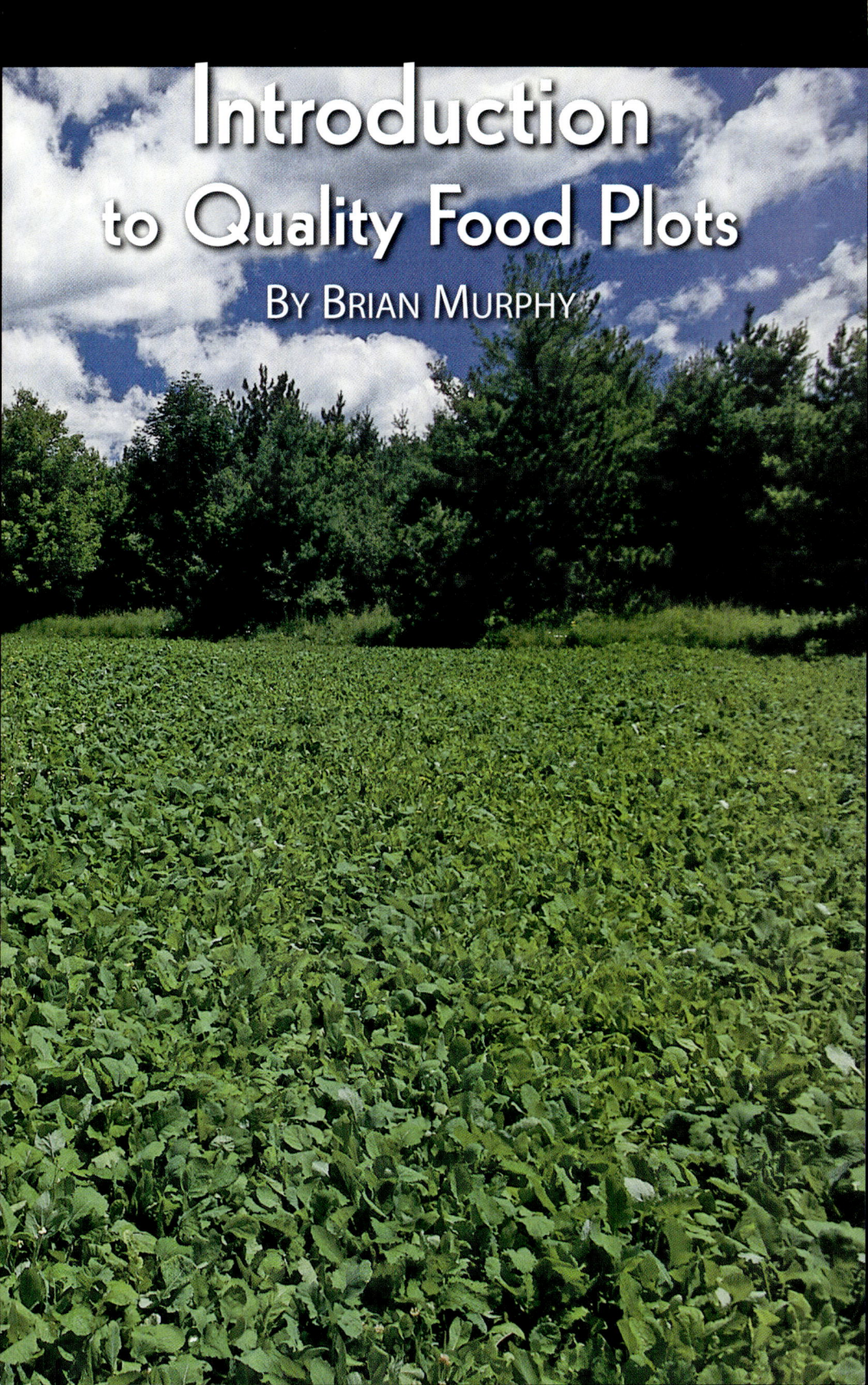

Introduction
to Quality Food Plots
By Brian Murphy

INTRODUCTION

one

Food plots are the hottest topic among whitetail hunters today. From Texas to Maine and everywhere between, hunters and managers are hungry for information on what they can plant to improve the quality of their deer herds and hunting experiences. With a few notable exceptions, the widespread interest in food plots is a recent phenomenon, dating back to the late 1980s in the South and the mid-1990s in the North. Other areas, such as the Mountain West and Canada, are just beginning to jump on the food plot bandwagon. Food plot topics once unknown to deer hunters now dominate hunting magazines, Internet chat rooms and seminar halls across North America. The tremendous interest in food plots has even spawned a flourishing new industry of seed providers, equipment manufacturers and food plot consultants.

While the primary purpose of this book is to provide you with cutting edge information on food plots for white-tailed deer, it is important to step back and review the history of food plots in North America and their role in deer management.

ORIGIN OF DEER FOOD PLOTS IN NORTH AMERICA

Whitetails have taken advantage of agricultural crops since American Indians began farming. The fragile, often contentious relationship between deer and farmers continued with the arrival of European settlers. It is even more pronounced today with whitetail populations at record levels in many areas. The big difference between then

BLENDING IN
Bagged seed blends are now big business. The food plot industry has helped hunters advance from simple cereal grain plots to higher-protein legumes and specialized mixes.

GOOD ENOUGH FOR GOVERNMENT WORK
By the mid-1970s, many state wildlife agencies were experimenting with plantings for wildlife openings — as well as experimenting with building materials for browse exclosures. These planted wildlife openings were becoming common on managed public hunting lands.

and now is that today many thousands of acres of crops are planted specifically for deer, a once unimaginable practice. Deer can no longer be considered simply a by-product of the forest.

So when did hunters and managers begin planting crops specifically for deer? While the exact starting point is not well documented, historical records indicate that food plots were being planted as early as the 1930s in Pennsylvania, Michigan and Wisconsin. This period coincides with the growth of the wildlife management profession and with the intensive restocking efforts that followed the extirpation of whitetails from many areas of North America around the turn of the 20th century. During the 1940s and 1950s, researchers developed a better understanding of the seasonal dietary needs of whitetails. Armed with this information, biologists responsible for restocking programs soon recognized the importance of wildlife openings, particularly in the "big woods" areas where many initial restocking efforts were focused. This was a critical turning point for many restocking programs. By the mid-1970s, wildlife openings and agricultural plantings were common on intensively managed state lands, and whitetail populations were flourishing.

Landowners and farmers also played a role in the origin of food plots. As restocking programs began to scatter deer across the country, whitetails began showing up in farmers' fields. Given the scarcity of deer in most areas, farmers initially considered whitetails a novelty and allowed them to graze undisturbed on their crops. As early as the 1970s, a few landowners even began leaving small portions of their

INTRODUCTION

crops unharvested or planted small, isolated areas specifically for deer. These early food plots typically contained wheat, oats or rye in the fall or soybeans, peanuts or corn in the spring. These plantings represented some of the first privately planted food plots for whitetails.

RISE OF THE COMMERCIAL FOOD PLOT INDUSTRY

During the late 1970s and early 1980s, interest in food plots for deer began increasing, especially in the southern United States. As a result, sales of cereal grains and clovers for wildlife food plots increased, and seed companies began taking note. While a few seed companies began promoting deer mixes at the local or regional level, the birth of the nationwide commercial food plot industry unquestionably began in 1988 with the launch

THE WHITETAIL INSTITUTE

NEW ADDITION

In 1988, B.A.S.S. founder Ray Scott (left) launched The Whitetail Institute and introduced a new product, Imperial Whitetail Clover — it was the birth of the commercial food plot industry.

of Imperial Whitetail Clover by The Whitetail Institute. This product was the brainchild of Institute founder and well-known bass fisherman Ray Scott. Two years earlier, Ray, also an avid deer hunter, noticed that the deer on his hunting property preferred white clover to rye and oats when planted side by side. Intrigued by this discovery, Ray hired plant geneticist Dr. Wiley Johnson to develop highly desirable and nutritious clover varieties that would grow in the widest range of locations and soil types. Dr. Johnson tested numerous clover varieties for seedling vigor, nutritive quality, drought resistance and many other factors and eventually settled on a blend that soon became known by hunters and managers as "Imperial Clover" or "Whitetail Clover."

The launch of Imperial Whitetail Clover also marked the turning point away from simple "green fields" of cereal grains such as wheat, oats or rye to perennial, legume-based plots that were higher in quality and could last several years without replanting. The success of Imperial Whitetail Clover and other Institute clover varieties such as Advantage and Insight led many other seed companies and hunters to add perennial clovers to their typical cereal grain fall mixes. The results were positive and, as they say, the rest is history.

Despite the success of Imperial Whitetail Clover and other Whitetail Institute products, for nearly a decade the only other national seed companies aggressively marketing food plot products were Pennington Seed Company and Antler King Trophy Products.

Founded by Brooks Pennington in 1945, Pennington Seed Company is among the largest seed companies in the United States. Interestingly, Pennington produced its first wildlife seed catalog in 1988 – the same year Imperial Whitetail Clover was launched. Pennington is best known for its high-quality, reasonably priced, region-specific seed blends. More recently, Pennington made a big splash with the introduction of Durana clover. Developed by researchers at The University of Georgia, Durana is a persistent variety of white clover that performs well under intense grazing pressure, grass competition, heat and drought conditions and even in cool northern environments.

Antler King Trophy Products in Wisconsin is considered one of the early food plot pioneers in the northern United States. Founded by Todd Stittleburg in 1988, the company initially specialized in quality deer feeds and mineral supplements for captive and wild deer. However, in response to the growing demand for food plot products by northern hunters, they introduced their first food plot blend in 1992. Antler King quickly gained a reputation for hardy, cold-tolerant blends that performed well in northern climates.

In 1998, Haas Outdoors Inc., makers of Mossy Oak camouflage, launched BioLogic Wild Game Blends. What distinguished BioLogic blends was the inclusion of rape and kale – members of the brassica family, which also includes turnips. These plants were included at the recommendation of biologist Dr. Grant Woods. While conducting research in South Carolina in the late 1980s, Grant documented improvements in deer weights and antler size with as little as 1 percent of the property planted in high-quality food plots. Wanting to research this relationship further, Grant approached Toxey Haas, president of Mossy Oak, for financial assistance. Toxey agreed, and Grant eventu-

ENTER BRASSICA

Biologist and researcher Dr. Grant Woods (right) was instrumental in importing and testing brassica varieties — including rape and kale — for Mossy Oak's Biologic brand during the early 1990s. On the left is Bobby Cole, vice president of Biologic.

1

INTRODUCTION

ally served as the lead researcher for BioLogic. During the early 1990s, Grant imported numerous varieties of brassicas used in New Zealand to maximize body and antler growth in farmed red deer for testing at numerous locations across North America. This research continues with nearly 40 plant varieties tested annually.

Founded in 1993 by Gary Schwarz, Tecomate Wildlife Systems (formerly Tecomate Seed Company) specializes in food plot seed mixes for wildlife. Gary, an oral surgeon, developed an innovative food plot

TECOMATE WILDLIFE SYSTEMS

FILLING THE WARM-SEASON GAP

Innovative food plot programs designed by Gary Schwarz (left) and David Morris (right) of Tecomate Wildlife Systems put an emphasis on warm-season nutrition for deer health and antler growth. Gary and David are shown here with Gary's daughter, Rebecca, who killed this 173²/₈ net Boone & Crockett buck.

program that greatly increased antler size on the bucks on his south Texas property – Tecomate Ranch. Soon, demand for his ideas and products were so great, Gary had no other option but to enter the wildlife seed business. In 2000, Tecomate became a national company when Gary partnered with David Morris, whitetail book author and previous co-owner of *North American Whitetail* magazine. Interestingly, prior to their partnership, Gary and David spent nearly 20 years independently perfecting almost identical food plot programs. Gary perfected his program at the Tecomate Ranch, and David worked on his program at his Burnt Pine Plantation in Georgia and later at his magazine partner Steve Vaughn's Fort Perry Plantation in Georgia. Unlike previous food plot programs that focused on cool-season plantings, their programs maximized year-round nutrition with a focus on spring and summer nutrition. As a result, Tecomate is most noted for its productive, nutritious, and drought-tolerant warm-season legumes such as lablab, Buckbeans and ebony pea. Tecomate also was largely responsible for raising awareness of the value of warm-season food plots and the need for comprehensive, year-round food plot programs in whitetail management.

Another company deserving mention is Olds Seed Solutions (formerly Olds Seed Company). Dating back to 1888, it is one of the oldest seed companies in the United States. Olds introduced its first deer forage blend under the Brier Ridge brand in 1998. However, for nearly a decade before, Olds had been custom-mixing deer blends for local feed stores throughout the Midwest. Since the late 1990s, many other companies, both large and small, have introduced food plot blends for white-tailed deer. Perhaps some of these companies will help shape the next chapter in the history of food plots in the United States.

ROLE OF FOOD PLOTS IN QUALITY DEER MANAGEMENT PROGRAMS

In many respects, the rise in popularity of food plots was predictable. As deer populations began to flourish in the 1970s and early 1980s, hunters became preoccupied with harvesting a buck – any buck – and took advantage of the growing body of information on deer rubs, scrapes, movements and behavior to hone their hunting skills and maximize their success. However, by the mid-1980s, many hunters began noticing that decades of intense buck harvests and inadequate doe harvests had produced overabundant deer herds with skewed adult sex ratios favoring does, and few bucks were surviving beyond their first set of antlers. These astute hunters began questioning traditional management approaches and exploring alternative management strategies. This desire provided the basis for the Quality Deer Management (QDM) movement and the formation of the Quality Deer Management Association (QDMA).

JIM SHAEFFER, TECOMATE WILDLIFE SYSTEMS

HUNGRY FOR FOOD PLOTS

With the spread of QDM, hunters are hungry for information about deer nutrition and food plots, and the QDMA is responding. This field day hosted in 2005 by QDMA's Northeast Michigan Branch featured a 4-acre demonstration site including 17 different plantings. Nearly 500 Michigan residents attended the full day of seminars and field tours.

INTRODUCTION

Coincidentally, the birth of the modern food plot industry in 1988 occurred the same year the QDMA was founded in South Carolina by wildlife biologist Joe Hamilton. Thus, it is safe to say that 1988 was the formal beginning of the modern QDM movement, at least outside of Texas.

Not surprisingly, the growth of the food plot industry and the QDM movement have followed similar patterns – slow starts during the late 1980s followed by accelerated growth in recent years. This is common for practices that challenge traditional paradigms. In fact, today it would be nearly impossible to separate food plots from discussions on QDM – they are inextricably connected. However, this connection has led to the misconception by some hunters who believe that QDM is simply the practice of planting food plots for deer.

Comprehensive QDM programs involve four common building blocks – herd management, habitat management, hunter management and herd monitoring. In many situations, food plots play a key role in QDM. Research has shown that even a small percentage (1 to 3 percent) of a property planted in high-quality food plots can increase deer body weights, antler size and fawn recruitment. However, food plots alone are not QDM, and they are not a quick fix for chronically mismanaged deer herds. In fact, in areas of deer overabundance and inadequate antlerless harvests, food plots can exacerbate the situation by boosting herds further above what the natural habitat can support. This is unhealthy for both the deer and the habitat and the reason why food plots should never be considered replacements for natural forages.

When combined with appropriate population management, food plots should reduce browsing pressure on native vegetation to the point where natural regeneration, including highly desirable deer forages, can occur. Fortunately, this balance between deer herds, food plots and native vegetation is becoming more common as more hunters embrace the total QDM concept.

Although food plots are only one tool in the QDM bag, they do provide a deeper and more

THE FOUR CORNERSTONES OF QDM

Food plots alone are not QDM, but they can play a key role in a successful QDM program. QDM involves four building blocks:

Herd Management; harvesting an appropriate number of does to reduce or stabilize a population where necessary, and restricting the harvest of young bucks. A reasonable starting point for most QDM programs is protecting 1½-year-old bucks.

Habitat Management; improving available nutrition. The two most common methods include food plots and natural vegetation management.

Hunter Management; educating hunters so they fully understand the benefits and costs of QDM before they become active participants. Ongoing education helps committed hunters achieve QDM objectives.

Herd Monitoring; collecting harvest and observation data to track improvements, document QDM success, and fine-tune future management.

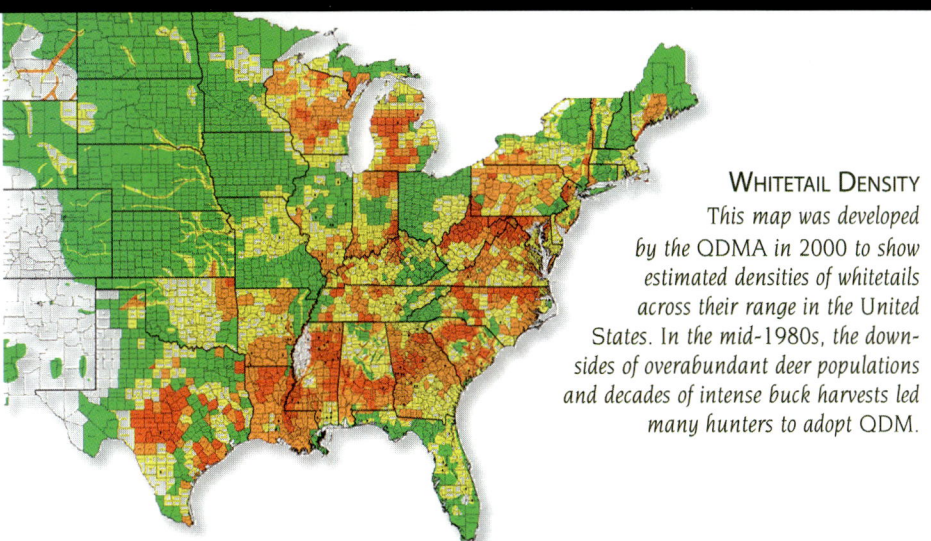

unique connection to the land than most other QDM practices. Numerous QDM practitioners have commented on the almost spiritual connection with the land that planting food plots provides. In fact, many hunters now spend more time planting and maintaining food plots than they do hunting. Perhaps this activity fills an important void in the relationship between man, wild animals and the Earth that has largely been lost in our modernized world.

Another benefit of the food plot revolution is the awareness by hunters that they can actually make a difference on the lands they hunt. When correctly planted and maintained, food plots provide an active, tangible way to improve deer herd quality and deer hunting success. Previously, passing young bucks and harvesting does were about the only ways that hunters could participate in deer management at the grassroots level. But, unlike deer populations that are affected by hunters on surrounding properties, the success or failure of food plots is largely controlled by the hunter – except of course when Mother Nature has other plans.

In many respects, food plots provide a natural medium through which hunters can test the deer management "waters." While some never progress beyond the "green field" stage where their plots are simply used to help harvest deer, most eventually become more involved in deer management and intensify their quest for knowledge on deer biology, ecology and behavior. In essence, food plots serve as the first step for many hunters on a journey that ultimately transforms them from deer hunters to deer managers.

While once nearly impossible to find, information on food plots now abounds in popular magazines, books and other outlets. However, in many cases, this information is incomplete, outdated, or region-specific. The purpose of this book is to provide practical, comprehensive and biologically sound information on food plots for white-tailed deer. Collectively, the authors of this book have more than 150 years of research and on-the-ground experience with food plots and habitat management. We believe *Quality Food Plots* is the most complete and user-friendly food plot reference ever produced, and we are confident it will lead you on a path to better deer and better deer hunting.

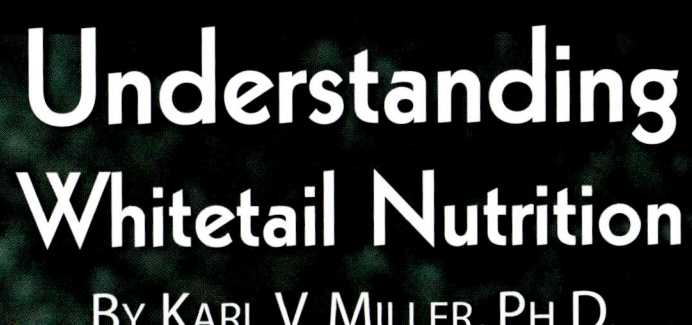

Understanding
Whitetail Nutrition

By Karl V. Miller, Ph.D.

UNDERSTANDING WHITETAIL NUTRITION

two

Any assessment of deer nutritional requirements must consider local habitat conditions. However, an adaptation of the old military adage is appropriate for deer – "A deer herd runs on its stomach!" Good nutrition is the key to having a deer herd in good physical condition with high reproductive rates, high fawn survival and optimum antler quality. Supplemental plantings should provide high-quality forages at times when natural food resources are limited or when deer nutritional requirements are high. Therefore, a basic understanding of deer nutrition is crucial to developing a food plot program.

WHITE-TAILED DEER FOOD HABITS

Deer forage selection can be highly variable and is based in part on seasonal changes in forage availability, the relative abundance of different plants in the particular region or habitat, and forage palatability. Nutritional requirements of deer also vary seasonally and among differing age and sex categories of deer.

Although deer are generally classified as browsers, their food habits extend well beyond the eating of buds and leaves of trees, shrubs and woody vines. In fact, a wide variety of other plant materials make up the bulk of their diet. Grasses, fruits, nuts, forbs (annual and perennial herbaceous plants), agricultural crops, and mushrooms likely are more important in the diet of deer than woody browse, although this is dependent on habitat type. In fact, some studies have indicated that deer will occasionally use half or more of the plant species occurring in a given area. However, usually about 10 percent or fewer of the plant species comprise the bulk of their diet on an annual basis.

UNDERSTANDING TERMS RELATED TO DEER NUTRITION

Preference: Choice or selection that a deer makes when provided alternative forages. Typically, preferred forages occur in the diet in greater amounts than would be expected based on their availability in the deer's habitat.

Palatability: Relative acceptability of feed as influenced by taste, smell, structure, or other plant attributes such as toxic properties, thorns and fiber content.

Digestibility: Ability of forages to be transformed into basic nutrients that can be assimilated by the digestive system. It is generally viewed as the feed consumed minus undigested materials in the feces.

Carrying Capacity: The number of deer a habitat can support for a long-term period without a reduction in habitat quality. Carrying capacity can be increased through habitat improvement and food plots.

FEED THE NEED
Optimizing the health and physical condition of a deer population means providing adequate nutrition when deer need it most, such as when antlers are growing.

Instead of classifying deer as browsers, biologists more accurately describe them as "concentrate selectors," meaning that their diet selection concentrates on the most nutritious and palatable forages. When given a choice, deer have an uncanny ability to select higher-quality forages.

Not all plants are equally nutritious or palatable. Some plants have inherently higher nutrient content, whereas others provide poor nutrition or are not easily digested. However, even some plants that would otherwise be highly nutritious can have adaptations that deter browsing. Many plants contain chemicals such as phenols, tannins and terpenes that can make them less palatable and less digestible. Quality not only varies among species but also among individual plants, within parts of individual plants, or over the life stage of the plant. This means that a deer's diet can vary tremendously from area to area and season to season.

Biologists often classify deer forage plants as primary choice, secondary choice

UNDERSTANDING WHITETAIL NUTRITION

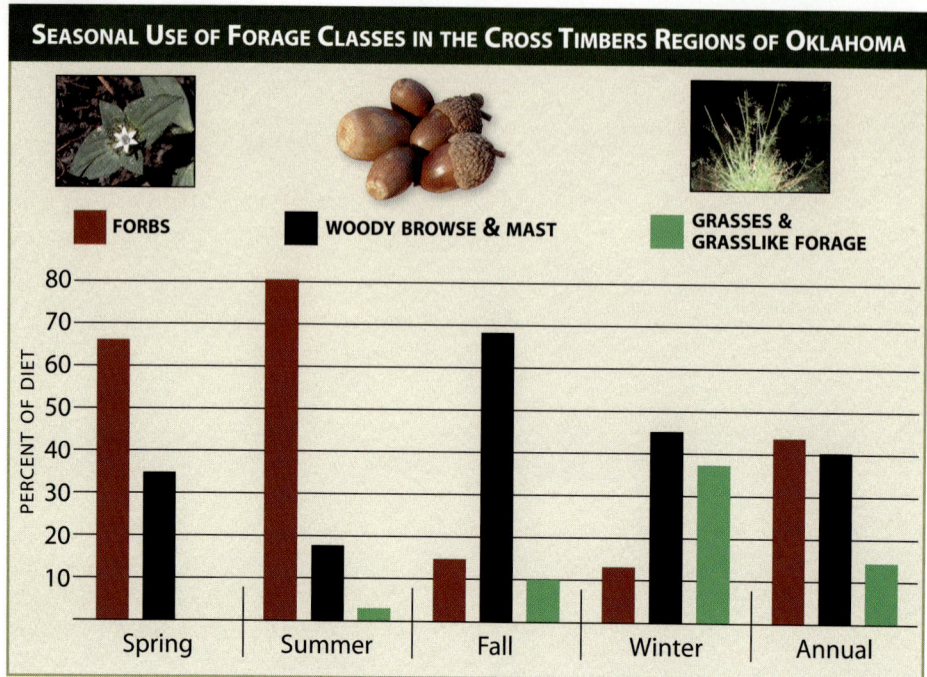

Adapted from *White-tailed deer: their foods and management in the Cross Timbers*, 1991, by K. L. Gee and others.

or starvation plants. In most areas, when deer densities are kept well within the carrying capacity of the range, primary choice plants are abundant and make up the bulk of the deer's diet. In these conditions, deer can benefit from the optimum nutrition available. However, when deer density gets too high, or in some poorer quality habitats, primary-choice plants are scarce. The deer's diet then shifts to secondary-choice plants that provide lower forage quality. Biologists often assess habitat capability and relative herd density based on browsing pressure on primary and secondary forages. However, these assessments must be based on experience with local plant communities and the food habits of local deer. Nevertheless, a low abundance of primary-choice plants coupled with significant browsing pressure on secondary-choice plants is a strong indicator that deer densities are too high.

Seasonal shifts in forage availability and the nutritional requirements of deer also impact deer diets. Although complete food-habits studies of deer have not been conducted in many areas of the country, several studies have illustrated these dietary shifts. For example, in Oklahoma, deer diets in spring and summer were dominated by succulent forbs (*see the chart on this page*). However, they typically made up only about 15 percent of the diet in fall and winter. In this study, the browse category included the leaves and fruits (mast) of woody vegetation such as trees, shrubs and vines. During spring and summer, leaves and mast were much less important than forbs. However, during fall, leaves and mast composed more than 65 percent of the diet. Acorns were an important component of the fall and winter mast category, but the leaves and fruits of other woody plants were likewise important. Grasses were little used during spring and summer, but they became important during winter when forbs and acorns became less available and native or planted grass species increased in availability.

Similarly, a study in Mississippi illustrated the seasonal dynamics of deer diets (*see the chart at the bottom of this page*). Mast consumption peaked in fall at the time of greatest acorn availability, although fruits and berries were commonly consumed during summer. Use of browse and grasses peaked during the late-winter months, and forb use was highest during spring and summer.

It's important to understand some of the biases in the methods that biologists use to assess deer diets. Most food-habits studies have focused on the rumen contents of harvested deer or on microscopic examination of poorly digested plant fragments in deer feces. Although these studies can provide a reasonable assessment of a particular deer's recent diet, they typically can only provide a relatively coarse assessment of an entire deer herd's overall diet. Deer diets can shift dramatically over a short period of time, even within a season. Because different types of plants and plant parts have different degrees of digestibility, food habits based on rumen or fecal analyses tend to underestimate the importance of some highly digestible plant materials such as fruits and mushrooms. Coarse, poorly digestible material tends to stay in the rumen longer, and its importance may therefore be over-represented.

Continued on page 20.

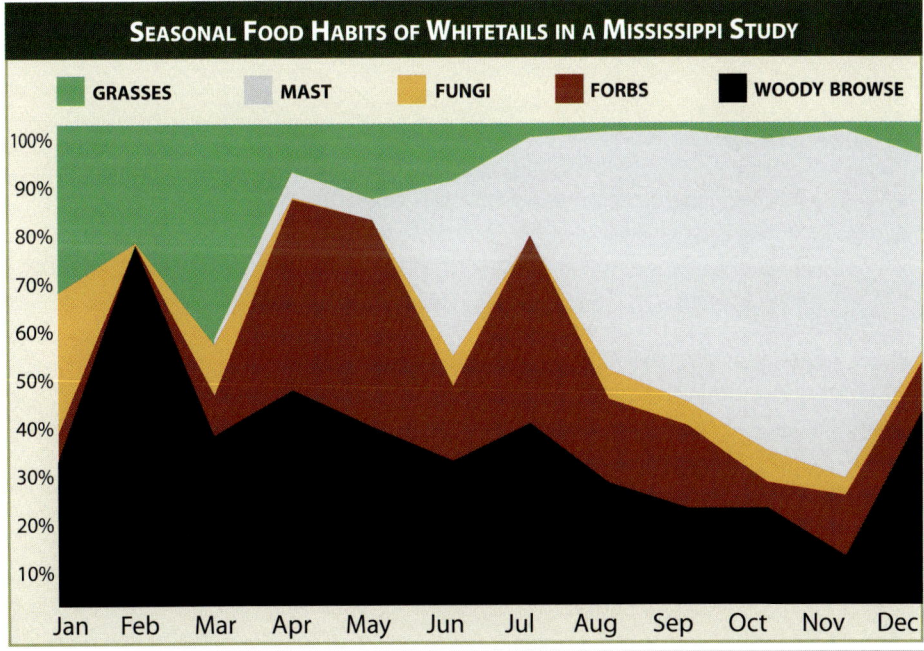

Adapted from *Evaluation of white-tailed deer and cattle diets in two southeastern pine forests*, 1980, by W.A. Mitchell, a Ph.D. dissertation at Mississippi State University.

UNDERSTANDING WHITETAIL NUTRITION

A LOOK INSIDE THE
WHITETAIL DIGESTIVE SYSTEM

After being swallowed, food enters a large compartment called the rumen, which makes up about 80 percent of the stomach. In the rumen, trillions of bacteria and protozoa help the deer digest the high-fiber diet. This provides much of the deer's energy requirements in the form of volatile fatty acids that are absorbed by thousands of finger-like projections lining the rumen wall. Materials in the rumen are constantly mixed by strong contractions. Interestingly, this fermentation also produces a lot of gas, so deer must belch frequently.

PHIL ANDERSON

The rumen lining.

At birth, fawns have a very poorly developed rumen. In fact, because milk is totally digestible by enzymes in the stomach, fawns have a mechanism called the reticular groove that allows milk to move directly from the esophagus to the true stomach, bypassing the rumen. Once fawns begin experimenting with green vegetation, the rumen develops quickly and is fully developed by the time of weaning. However, because a fawn's rumen is smaller than an adult's, it is less efficient. Therefore, fawns continue to require a higher quality diet than adults.

PHIL ANDERSON

The reticulum lining.

The next part of the deer's digestive system is the reticulum. The inside of the reticulum has a honeycomb appearance, and one of its functions is to help bring boluses of food back up to the mouth for rechewing. It also serves as a receptacle for heavy foreign objects that are accidentally ingested.

After materials in the rumen and reticulum are reduced in size by chewing and digestion by the microorganisms, they pass through a third compartment called the omasum. This portion of the deer's stomach is sometimes called "the book" because the folds resemble the pages of a book. Here more volatile fatty acids are absorbed, as well as other nutrients such as potassium and sodium. In addition, the omasum further reduces particle size and reduces the water content of the material

before it is passed to the final compartment, called the abomasum. This is the deer's true stomach, and it functions very similarly to a human's stomach. The walls of the abomasum secrete enzymes and hydrochloric acid. The pH of the material entering the abomasum is usually around 6.0 to 7.0, but it is quickly lowered to about 2.5 by the acid to allow the appropriate digestive enzymes to work. The most important function of the abomasum is to partially break down proteins from the feed and the microorganisms coming from the rumen.

The small intestine is the primary location of digestion by enzymes and absorption of nutrients. After food materials leave the stomach, secretions from the liver, pancreas, and other organs contribute various enzymes that complete the digestion of proteins, fats and sugars. These secretions also raise the pH back above 6.0. Finally, the large intestine concludes the digestion process by completing the fermentation of materials, absorbing water along with water-soluble nutrients, and serving as a site for bacterial synthesis of some vitamins.

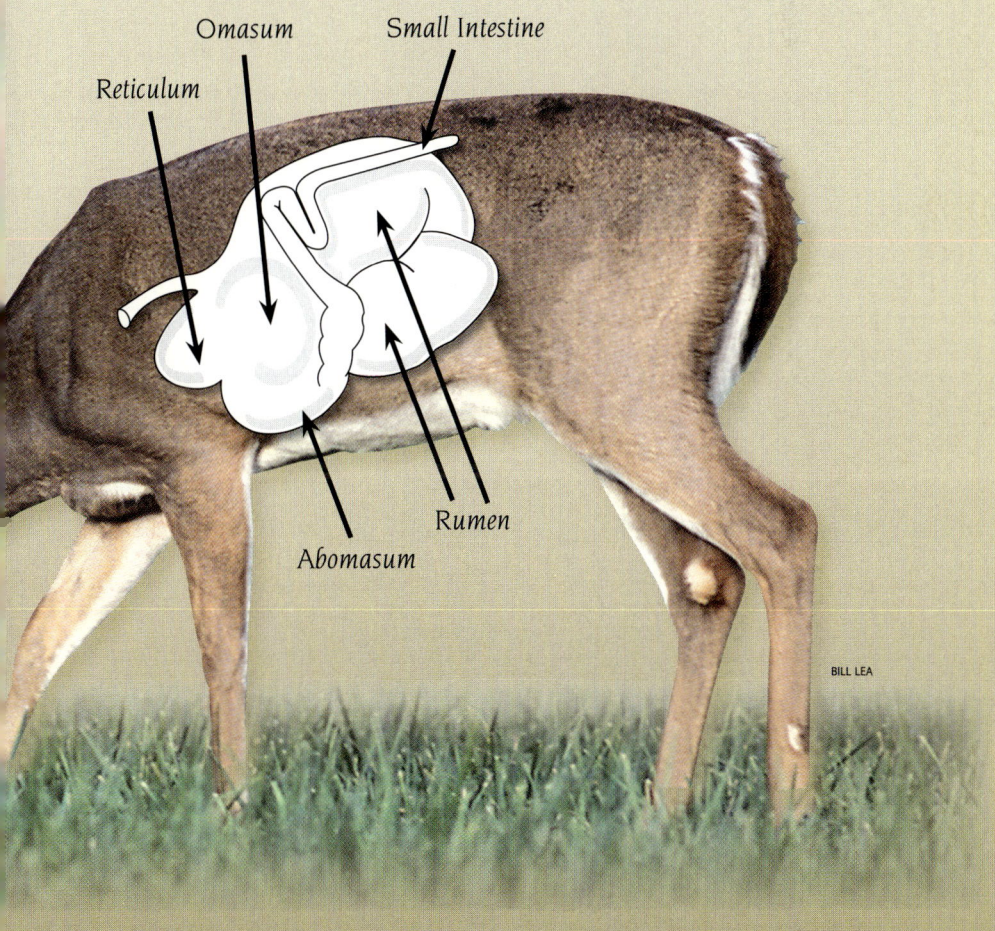

Omasum

Small Intestine

Reticulum

Abomasum

Rumen

BILL LEA

UNDERSTANDING WHITETAIL NUTRITION

Continued from page 17.

THE DIGESTIVE SYSTEM

The deer's digestive system is superbly adapted to provide the maximum nutrition from a diet composed of a wide variety of plant materials. Deer are a member of a group of animals called ruminants that have a specially designed digestive system. This group includes cows, sheep and goats – but not horses. Like all ruminants, deer have stomachs composed of four parts designed to maximize foraging efficiency (*see the previous two pages*). In good habitats, deer can fill their rumen quickly and then retire to more secretive environments to chew their cud and avoid danger.

To understand deer nutrition, it is important to realize that the amount of time that food materials remain in the rumen is directly related to forage quality. Tender, succulent vegetation such as fruits or young forbs and leaves with thin cell walls are easily broken down into smaller particles that pass through the rumen faster than mature leaves or coarse grasses. Therefore, deer foraging on tender vegetation benefit not only from the higher nutritional quality of these forages but also from the ability to eat greater quantities because of limitations on rumen capacity. This emphasizes the importance of high-quality food plots in areas of inherently low-quality natural forages or at specific times of the year when forage quality is low.

BASIC NUTRITIONAL REQUIREMENTS: PROTEIN

Protein is required for normal body maintenance as well as for growth of muscle and bone. Protein requirements for deer depend on the time of year and the life stage of the animal. However, research has identified some general baseline requirements. For an adult to maintain body condition, protein levels in the diet must be at least 6 to 10 percent. However, for body growth, yearlings need protein levels of at least 11 percent and

BILL MARCHEL

PREDATOR AVOIDANCE

The digestive system of deer and other ruminants allows them to feed quickly then return to heavy cover. There, bedded in a safer area, they can regurgitate and chew food more thoroughly. When easily digestible forages are more abundant, deer feed more frequently – their total nutritional intake is higher, and they may be more visible to hunters.

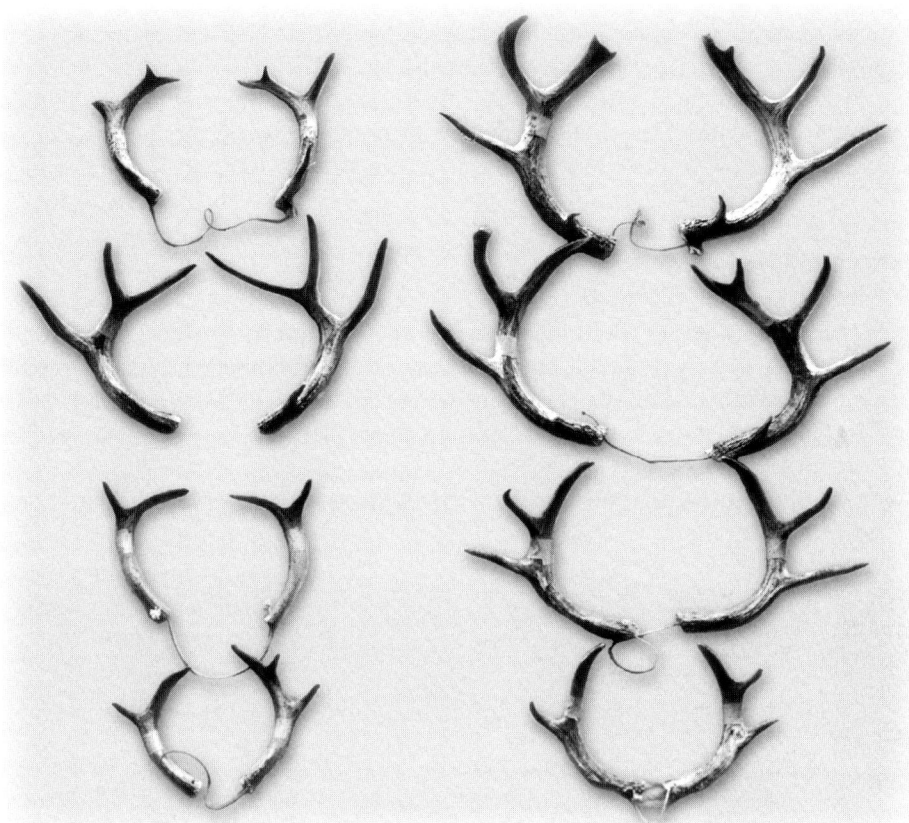

PROTEIN AND ANTLERS

These antler sets are representative of the results of a study at the Kerr Wildlife Management Area in Texas that investigated the importance of nutrition in antler development. The deer on the left was from a group of bucks fed a low protein diet (10.5 percent during the first year and 8 percent thereafter) whereas the deer on the right was fed a diet composed of 16 percent protein throughout the study. Study by D. E. Harmel, J. D. Williams, and W. E. Armstrong. 1989. Texas Parks and Wildlife Department.

fawns after weaning need 14 to 22 percent or more.

More recent research in Texas has indicated that post-weaned fawns require a minimum of 14 to 18 percent protein in their diet for average growth and future antler development, whereas 16 to 20 percent will provide for excellent growth and antler development. Minimum requirements for optimum antler development of yearling and mature bucks is between 13 and 16 percent.

Protein requirements also vary by season. For example, protein demands rise during the spring and summer periods of body growth. Pregnant and lactating does also require a high protein diet to provide adequate milk for their nursing fawns. Adult females require a minimum of 11 to 15 percent protein in the diet during late gestation, but requirements rise to 14 to 22 percent for optimal milk production.

Doe milk provides 36 percent or higher protein, so protein restrictions during lactation certainly can impact milk production and fawn nutrition.

Protein requirements during a deer's first year are particularly critical. Studies in Pennsylvania and Texas indicate that restrictions in protein intake can severely impact body growth during the first year of life as well as the size of a yearling's first set of antlers (*see illustration on page 21*). The effects of inadequate nutrition during the first year can persist for several years, even when adequate protein is subsequently provided.

Many food plot plantings are very high in protein, and when used to supplement natural forages they can raise the average protein level in the diet. For example, legumes such as clovers, alfalfa, soybeans, cowpeas, lablab and jointvetch can have protein levels in excess of 30 percent during portions of their growth. If high-quality food plantings constitute 50 percent of a deer's diet in areas where natural for-

CHARLES ALSHEIMER

EATING FOR TWO (TO FOUR)

A doe's requirements for protein and digestible energy rise significantly during gestation and while nursing fawns. If nutrition is inadequate during this crucial time, fawn health is reduced, and survival rates drop.

ages average 15 percent protein or less, food plots can raise the average protein intake to well above 20 percent.

DIGESTIBLE ENERGY

Although most discussion on forage quality focuses on protein levels, the energy content is equally important. Energy is needed for body maintenance, body-temperature regulation, reproduction, growth and activity. Deer derive energy from the digestion of fats and carbohydrates, although excess protein can be used as an energy source as well.

Like protein, energy requirements vary seasonally and according to the life stage of the animal. For example, during winter, particularly in northern regions, deer decrease their activity as an energy-conserving measure. Because of these varied energy requirements it is difficult to establish specific baseline energy requirements for deer. However, in general, mature does require about 25 kilocalories of digestible energy per pound of bodyweight each day (kcal/lb./day). These requirements rise to about 33 kcal/lb./day during the peak of lactation. As expected, fawns have much higher energy requirements – approximately 70 kcal/lb./day – although these requirements are provided by the doe. Requirements for adult

PROTEIN LEVEL VS. PROTEIN INTAKE

A wide variety of plant materials make up the whitetail's diet. Even where high-quality food plots are available, deer will still select from many different food sources, and a deer's average protein intake will be based on this diverse diet. Plant testing can reveal a food plot crop's protein level at the point in time when the sample was taken. However, deer feeding on this crop do not have an equivalent overall intake of protein. For example, a plant may test at 30 percent protein, but deer likely are not receiving 30 percent protein in their diet because most natural forages have much lower protein levels. However, the availability of quality food plots with high levels of protein certainly helps raise the average protein intake. When habitat management is used to increase the quality of native forages at the same time, the effect is further enhanced.

BILL LEA

bucks likely are similar to those of non-lactating does, although requirements may rise following the breeding season when bucks attempt to restore body condition lost during the rut.

Lipogenesis, or the building up of fat reserves in the fall, also requires a high

UNDERSTANDING WHITETAIL NUTRITION

CHARLES ALSHEIMER

ENERGY BAR

Left standing in the fall, corn can provide critical energy in the form of carbohydrates that help deer build fat reserves before winter's arrival.

energy intake. During the fall, the deposition of fat reserves in anticipation of winter takes precedence over body growth. In fact, studies in Michigan indicate that fat production is under photoperiodic control. Regardless of diet quality, fawns stopped growing during November and shifted resources to fat production. However, fat reserves of fawns on a high-quality diet were significantly greater than poorly fed fawns.

Many of the common deer foods in the fall, such as acorns and other fruits, have high fat or carbohydrate contents that allow deer to establish fat reserves before the onset of winter. Interestingly, acorns from the white oak group tend to be high in carbohydrate content, whereas those of the red oak group tend to be much higher in fat content. Certain food plot plantings can similarly target the energy needs of deer during fall and winter. In particular, corn and grain sorghum are high-energy forages. If left standing into the fall and winter, they can provide critically needed energy, especially during years of poor acorn production.

CALCIUM AND PHOSPHORUS

Calcium and phosphorus are the major mineral constituents of a deer's body and are primarily associated with bone formation and maintenance. Mature antlers are composed of approximately 22 percent calcium and 11 percent phosphorus. In addition, calcium is important for nerve function, blood clotting, muscle contraction, and other functions, whereas phosphorus is important in virtually every aspect of metabolism.

Early research on white-tailed deer suggested that dietary requirements for optimal antler growth were 0.64 percent calcium and 0.56 percent phosphorus. However, later studies suggest that 0.40 percent calcium and 0.30 percent phosphorus, or lower, were sufficient. Unquestionably, growing deer and lactating does require higher calcium and phosphorus levels.

The production of antlers is a significant drain on a buck's calcium and phosphorus reserves. Bucks can store some excess minerals in their skeleton for later use. At the time of antler mineralization, bucks undergo a form of osteoporosis and mobilize minerals from the skeleton for production of the antlers. After antler mineralization is complete, the minerals lost from the skeleton are replaced from the buck's diet.

In most areas, dietary requirements for calcium and phosphorus are met in the deer's natural diet. However, calcium and phosphorus can be deficient in some soils, and concentrations of these nutrients can be well below levels required for optimal antler production or lactation. For example, in areas of the Southeast Coastal Plain, phosphorus concentrations in some important deer forages such as greenbrier and gallberry may average only 0.12 percent or less. Although mushrooms can provide adequate calcium and phosphorus, they are an inconsistent and unreliable source. High-quality food plots in these areas can increase calcium and phosphorus availability. In particular, legumes such as clovers tend to be high in calcium, whereas grains, such as sorghum and corn, tend to be high in phosphorus.

SODIUM

Sodium (salt) helps maintain water balance and the passage of nutrients into cells. Because of the intake of a high-water-content diet in the spring and early summer, coupled with sodium demands for lactation and antler development, deer diets often are deficient in sodium at this time of year. Although deer have mechanisms to "recycle" sodium, sodium often must be obtained from other sources such as salt licks. Not surprisingly, peak use of salt licks in spring and summer coincides with nutritional demands for sodium.

OTHER NUTRIENTS

Relatively little information exists on a deer's requirements for other minerals. Minimal dietary concentrations have been established for a few trace elements, such as iodine (0.26 parts per million, or ppm) and selenium (0.2 ppm). Iodine deficiencies, although rare, can result in enlargement of the thyroid gland and general poor health.

Similarly, our understanding of the vitamin requirements of deer is also limited. However, vitamin deficiencies are uncommon among deer because most vitamins are supplied by the plants consumed by deer (vitamins A and E), produced by the microorganisms in the rumen (vitamins K and B-complex), or produced by the deer themselves (vitamins D and C).

PUTTING IT ALL TOGETHER

The selection of plants or plant mixes for deer food plots must consider the seasonal fluctuations in forage quality and availability in a particular habitat as well as the times when nutritional demands are high.

Throughout much of the whitetail's range, there are basically two periods of nutritional stress. Winter, with its low availability of quality forage coupled with nutritional demands to maintain body temperature, is a nutritionally stressful period. Obviously, winter stress is greater for deer in northern regions compared to many areas of the South that have a milder climate and a greater abundance of natural forages during winter. However, even in southern regions, particularly areas of the southern Appalachians, Ozarks, Ouachitas and the Gulf Coastal Plain, winter nutrition can be a significant concern. Targeting supplemental plantings to provide late winter forage before spring greenup of native plants, or to provide optimal nutrition during fall to allow deer to maximize fat reserves before winter, can provide significant benefits to a deer herd.

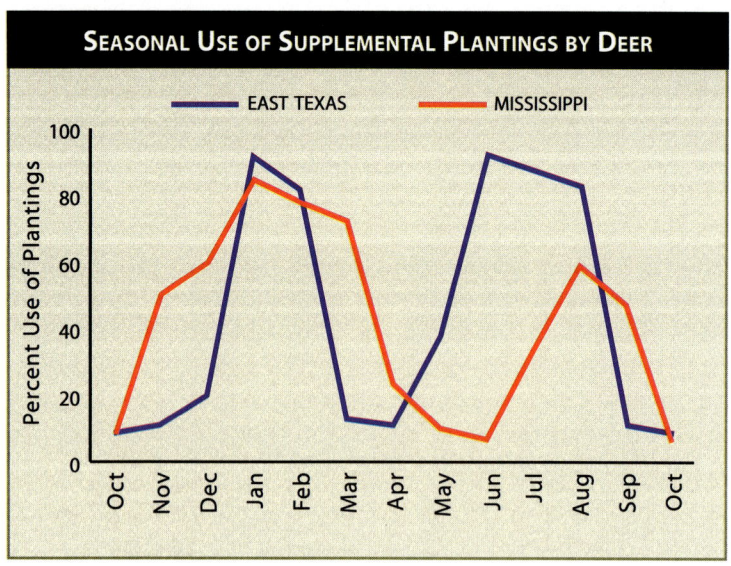

Adapted from *Food Plots and Supplemental Feeding*, 1995,
by James C. Kroll and Ben H. Koerth, and from *Food Plantings for
Deer in Mississippi*, 1994, by Bob Griffin and Harry Jacobson.

Perhaps just as important, at least in the South, is the summer/early fall nutritional stress period. This is a time of high nutritional demands by lactating does and recently weaned fawns. Although natural vegetation may still be abundant at this time of year, the quality of native forage declines dramatically as plant materials decline in digestibility and nutritional content.

The seasonal importance of high-quality food plots has been clearly demonstrated by two studies in East Texas and Mississippi (*see the chart on the facing page*). In both of these studies, deer used supplemental plantings heavily during the winter and summer/early fall periods of nutritional stress. Food plantings were little used during the spring flush of high quality natural forage, or the fall period of mast production.

The timing of availability of supplemental plantings must correspond to nutritional demands of the local deer herd. Although these general guidelines are applicable to most areas, knowledge of local conditions is extremely important. Consult with your state wildlife agency, state university extension wildlife program, or a consulting biologist to determine the specific requirements for deer in your area.

CHARLES ALSHEIMER

3

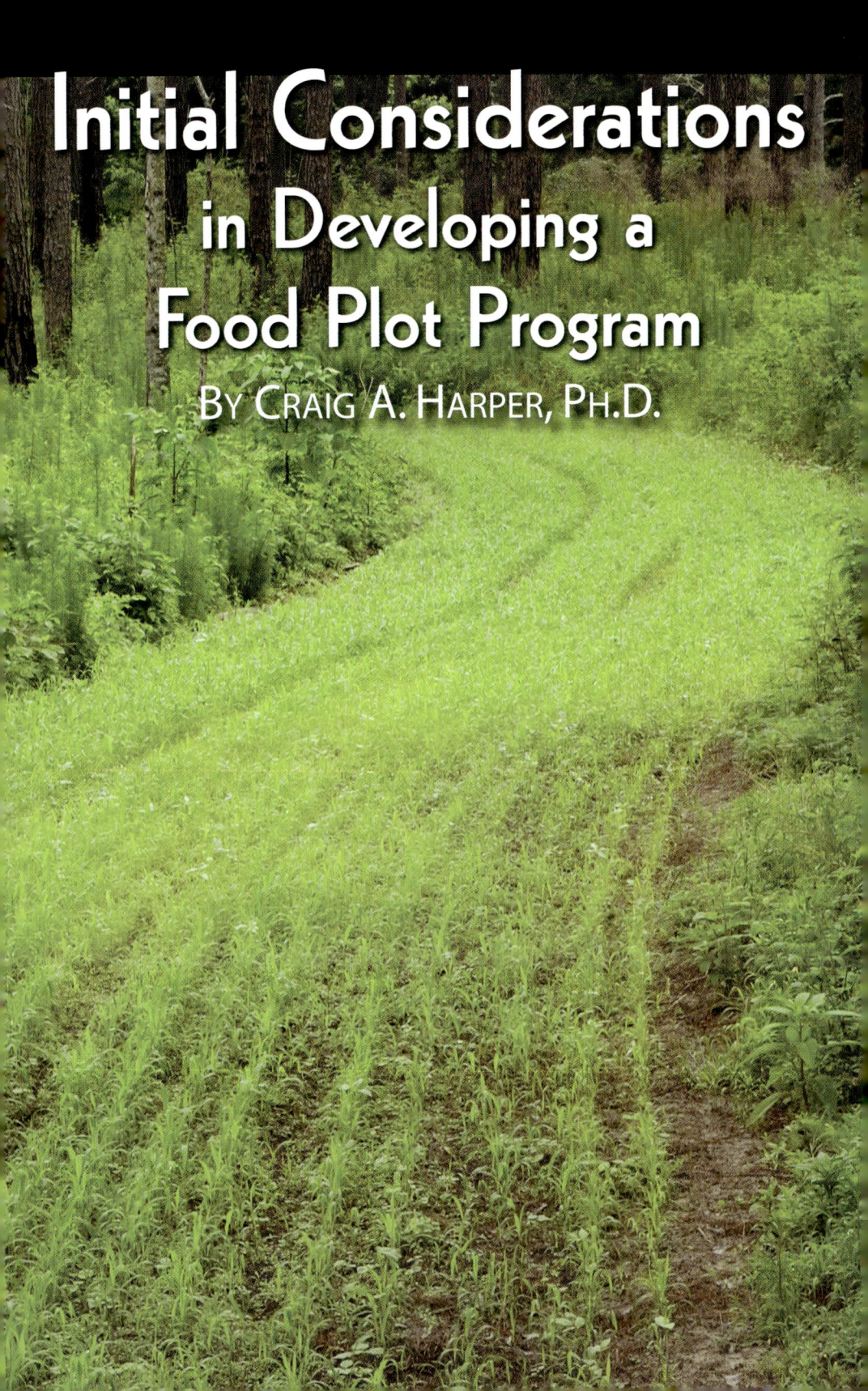

Initial Considerations
in Developing a
Food Plot Program

By Craig A. Harper, Ph.D.

three

When you consider establishing a food plot program, the primary decisions boil down to answering two basic questions:
- *What do you want your food plots to accomplish?*
- *What do you have to work with?*

Too many hunters and landowners look at food plot plantings as a one-size-fits-all proposition or continue to repeat the same thing year after year without evaluating the success of their efforts. Others jump on the latest fad planting without first evaluating a number of important considerations that will help determine the most appropriate planting.

Before ground is broken or the first seed sown, you can improve your odds for success by identifying your limitations and setting realistic objectives. This chapter will help you formulate a food plot program that will fit your specific needs. While no book can provide all the answers for every situation, this chapter will help you ask the right questions — the what, when, where and why of planting food plots. The first and most important question is, *Why?*

CRAIG HARPER

PLAN OF ACTION
Planting seed is not the first step in a successful food plot program. The work should begin long before planting time, starting with careful evaluation of goals, obstacles and available resources.

SIGN OF TROUBLE

A visible browse line like the one in this photo is a sign that available nutrition and habitat quality are low, deer populations are too high, or both. Planting food plots without controlling the deer population may only exacerbate the situation, delaying habitat and herd recovery even longer.

ESTABLISHING YOUR OBJECTIVES

No single food plot program is appropriate for all situations. Some hunters and managers want to increase the size or number of deer on their hunting property, while others simply want to use food plots to aid deer harvest. The first step in developing a food plot program is to clearly define your objectives. There are a number of questions that you need to ask before visiting the seed store or starting the tractor. These include:

- *Is your goal to enhance the nutrition available to deer during times of nutritional stress? Have the primary stress periods of the area been identified? Do you want to increase the carrying capacity of the property so your habitat can support more deer?*
- *Are additional body weight, antler growth and rapid fawn development primary considerations, or is winter nutrition more important?*
- *Do you want your food plots to make it easier to see and hunt deer?*
- *Are your food plots intended for deer alone, or are other species such as wild turkeys a major consideration?*

FOOD PLOTS TO FILL NUTRITION GAPS

Periods of nutritional stress for deer vary across the whitetail's range, as was discussed in Chapter 2. In northern regions, summer is usually a time of abundant, quality forage. However, harsh winter conditions can make life difficult for deer. Although deer reduce their activity during winter to conserve energy, they still need adequate forage to survive and maintain body weight until spring. If your objective is to minimize nutritional stress in these areas, food plots that provide abundant fall forage to aid in building fat deposits, or plots that persist into the winter or begin growth in late winter before native vegetation, can be critically important.

In southern regions, especially the Deep South, winter is not as stressful, but winter food plots still can be important to help maintain body condition until spring greenup. However, equally important is the late-summer stress period before oak mast is available. Although natural forages may still be abundant, forage quality declines significantly in late summer. This decline in forage quality, coupled with the demands of lactation in does and the high demands of fawns at weaning, can make summer food plots an important part of a complete food plot program. Choices for plantings in this situation must include forages that maintain high quality until natural foods such as acorns become available.

Some habitats simply do not have the natural forage abundance or quality to support as many deer as other areas. Because food plots can provide several tons of forage per acre, they can add significantly to the carrying capacity of the natural habitat. However, it is important to first determine if the natural carrying capacity is low because of inherently poor forage abundance or if the habitat has been damaged by a prolonged period of high deer density. If you are in a situation of chronically overgrazed habitat, food plots may only worsen the problem. Instead of food plots, a substantially increased doe harvest may be required to allow the natural habitat to recover. Food plots can aid in this situation by reducing pressure on the natural forages. However, this will only happen if, and only if, the population is kept under control while the habitat is recovering.

Food Plots to Maximize Body Growth and Recruitment

Most food plot programs are designed with the intent of enhancing antler size, body growth and fawn recruitment. If this is the objective, you must have an integrated, year-round food plot program incorporating both cool-season and warm-season forages. Care should be taken to provide a variety of high-quality forages that peak in production and attractiveness during different seasons.

Food Plots as Deer Attractants

Planting food plots to facilitate hunting is an appropriate goal and certainly can help achieve other QDM goals such as an adequate doe harvest. When planting food plots where hunting is the primary objective, bedding areas and travel corridors should be identified. With this objective, the main consideration is deer travel patterns. There is no need to attempt to pull deer into an area they wouldn't ordinarily move through when the food plot can be positioned where they naturally want to travel. Prevailing winds also should be considered. Food plots positioned in funnels where deer naturally travel are real magnets.

When planting food plots for hunting, choose forages that will be available and attractive during the appropriate hunting season. Warm-season plots typically attract and hold deer until the first frost. In most states, these are prime places to bowhunt during the early season. Cool-season plots such as clover mixes as well as

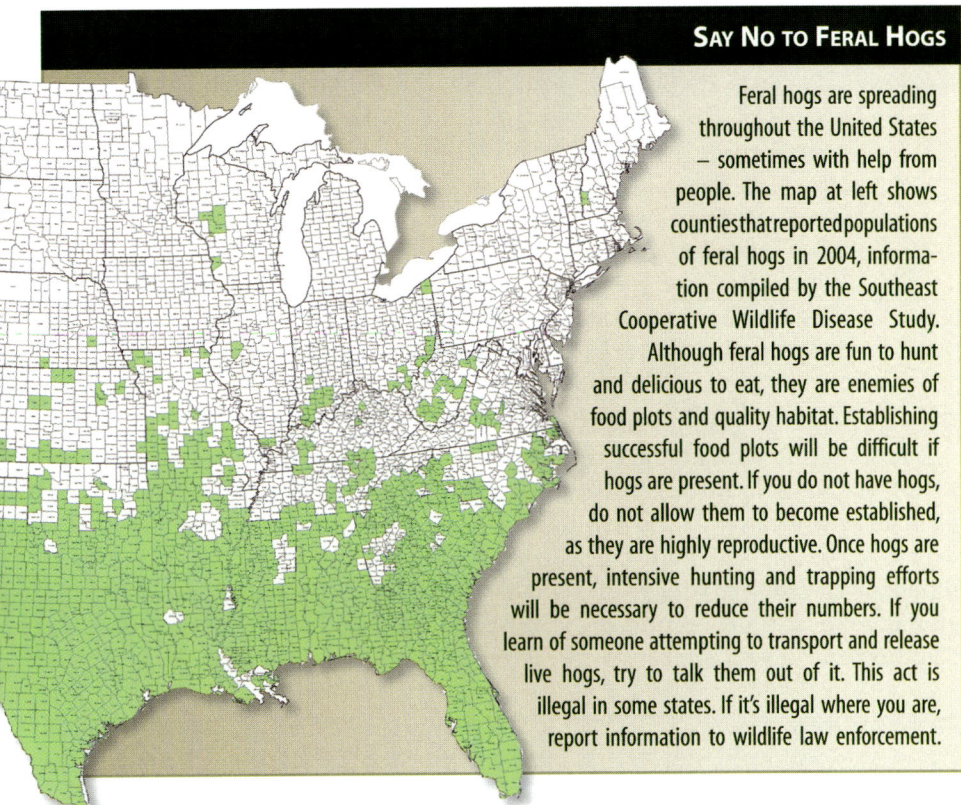

Feral hogs are spreading throughout the United States – sometimes with help from people. The map at left shows counties that reported populations of feral hogs in 2004, information compiled by the Southeast Cooperative Wildlife Disease Study. Although feral hogs are fun to hunt and delicious to eat, they are enemies of food plots and quality habitat. Establishing successful food plots will be difficult if hogs are present. If you do not have hogs, do not allow them to become established, as they are highly reproductive. Once hogs are present, intensive hunting and trapping efforts will be necessary to reduce their numbers. If you learn of someone attempting to transport and release live hogs, try to talk them out of it. This act is illegal in some states. If it's illegal where you are, report information to wildlife law enforcement.

grain plots such as corn and sorghum provide attractive forage throughout the hunting season. Chapters 7 and 8 will guide you through crop selection for food plots.

FOOD PLOTS FOR DEER AND OTHER SPECIES

Another consideration when planning a food plot program is the focal species. Are white-tailed deer the only focus, or do you also want to attract wild turkeys or mourning doves? Most plantings that benefit deer also benefit turkeys, which eat the green leaves as well as seeds produced in food plots. Certain plantings will also provide "bugging" grounds for young turkey poults. Grain plots also provide quality brooding cover, especially in plots allowed to go fallow for a growing season after maturity. Deer benefit from some dove fields, especially corn, buckwheat, sunflower and grain sorghum. When integrating the requirements of several species, select forage plantings that are beneficial to each. For example, a perennial food plot of ladino clover provides outstanding forage production and quality for both deer and turkeys as well as excellent insect production for turkeys.

Are wild hogs numerous where you hunt? If so, reducing their numbers through shooting and trapping should be a priority if you wish to attract deer and turkeys to food plots. Hogs can do major damage to food plots, not only destroying crops but rooting deep holes in fields, increasing wear and tear on your equipment.

CONSIDERING YOUR CONDITIONS

After your objectives have been determined, realistic opportunities and limitations should be identified. There are many things to consider including:

- *Is the deer density on your area too high, and has your habitat quality been impacted?*
- *How big is the property you are managing, and what is going on around you?*
- *What equipment and financial resources do you have?*
- *Where on your property can you establish food plots?*
- *How big should your food plots be?*
- *What are the best species to plant in your situation?*

DEER DENSITY AND HABITAT CONDITION

Your most important initial considerations before spending time and money on a food plot program are deer density and the current habitat conditions. It is futile to plant an acre of clover or cowpeas in the middle of 100 acres of mature hardwoods with a browse line. The most expensive crops planted in properly prepared and fertilized soil and sprayed with all the right herbicides are useless if they are eaten to the ground as soon as they germinate. Habitat management and herd management go hand-in-hand. If your average deer weights are low and most of the preferred browse

BE VERSATILE

Food plots are only one tool for increasing available nutrition. Other options include prescribed fire, timber thinning and other techniques to improve the abundance and quality of natural forages.

species are eaten to a nub, or absent, the deer density needs to be lowered. Evaluating the relationship of your habitat with deer density is a critical step in a QDM program. Food plots are often planted to make additional nutrition available. However, as we have already established, if the deer density is already beyond the carrying capacity of the habitat, food plots are futile unless complemented with appropriate herd management. Food plots are only one component of deer management and should be used to complement timber management, prescribed fire and old-field management. It is foolish to try to support a deer herd on food plots alone.

When evaluating available habitat, you should consider composition of habitat carefully before deciding where to

CRAIG HARPER

LIFE SUPPORT

Small timber cuts and "daylighting" roadways like this one can increase cover, forage variety and habitat diversity. With a diversity of intermixed habitat types on a property, food plots can serve as bonus nutrition rather than "life support."

plant food plots. Whitetails thrive in areas with considerable habitat diversity. Large tracts of mature hardwood forest, for example, may support 40 deer per square mile, but the deer will be in relatively poor shape, and forage quality may be quite low. On the other hand, an area containing hardwood forests in stands of various ages, interspersed with managed pine stands, row crop agriculture, old fields containing native forbs and grasses, and brushy thickets may support 40 deer per square mile in good shape with little impact on the natural forages.

By increasing diversity of habitat types, as well as thorough mixing or "interspersion" of habitat types across a property, an area can be made more productive for deer, enabling the additional nutrition provided by food plots to contribute more to antler growth and reproduction. When possible, locate food plots where several habitats come together. This normally corresponds with deer travel corridors and is often adjacent to bedding cover and other food resources. Food plots designed specifically for hunting are usually located in these areas. When maximum nutrition is your goal, be sure food plots are evenly distributed across the entire property — at least to the extent that soils, moisture and equipment access will allow. Also, make sure quality forage is available throughout the year, particularly during the late winter and late summer stress periods.

PROPERTY SIZE AND SURROUNDING PROPERTIES

Property size and the context of the property in relation to the surrounding area is an important consideration in any food plot program, regardless of deer density. Small properties usually do not have enough area to provide a wide variety of plantings, particularly crops such as corn and soybeans that are most appropriate for 3- to 5-acre and larger plots. However, when several landowners form cooperatives with common QDM objectives, food plot programs can be combined, ensuring a variety of plantings are available that provide nutrition throughout the year for the shared deer herd. This is also an excellent opportunity to share equipment and other costs. For example, buying lime, fertilizer and herbicides can be much more cost effective when neighbors share the expense because these products are often cheaper in larger quantities.

In areas with abundant row-crop agriculture, pay close attention to which crops are planted on adjacent properties, especially when the property you are hunting is less than 200 acres. Planting highly preferred crops that differ from those that farmers are already planting can help encourage feeding activity away from crop fields. For example, in areas where corn, soybeans and wheat are grown, planting other species such as clovers, lablab, chicory or American jointvetch provides something a little different. Typically, in agricultural areas, nutrition is not limiting for most of the year. However, during the interval between harvest and establishment of the next

A LITTLE HELP FROM MY FRIENDS

STEVE GULLEDGE

If you're managing small acreage, you're on a tight budget, or both, forming a "cooperative" with neighboring landowners and hunting clubs will be beneficial in many ways. When it comes to food plots, a group of cooperating landowners can pool and share equipment and effort. You take your equipment to their property to help plant their plots, and they return the favor to help plant yours. This way, each individual does not have to own several different pieces of equipment. Also, by buying some items in bulk, such as lime, fertilizer, herbicides or seed, the group saves money compared to purchasing smaller amounts individually.

Beyond food plots, landowners in a cooperative can also more effectively manage for a quality deer population across larger acreages. To assist you in forming a "QDM Cooperative" in your area, the QDMA has published a booklet with guidance on how to set up an effective and successful cooperative. Visit www.QDMA.com for information.

crop, food plots can provide valuable nutrition. In these situations, position food plots specifically to enhance hunting opportunities.

In many other areas, agriculture is limited and soils tend to be less productive. Here is where food plots can make a huge impact on both nutrition and deer movements. When deer find nutritious, palatable forage in an area where little quality forage is available, their daily movement patterns and core home range may shift significantly. In these areas, the impacts can be profound! Depending on deer density and size of the property, 5 percent or more of the area may need to be planted, along with other habitat management practices, before nutrition is not a limiting factor and deer can reach their potential.

EQUIPMENT NEEDS AND OTHER COSTS

Food plots can be expensive to establish and maintain, particularly if you plan to purchase all of the equipment. However, once the equipment and implements are paid for, the price per ton of forage produced decreases substantially. Who can put a price on watching a 150-class buck feed in a patch of clover they planted? Who thinks about how much money they spent on food plots when their mature-buck harvest doubles and body weights increase by 20 percent or more? There are certainly some things that money can't buy! Although there are ways to reduce costs, food plots are much less expensive than supplemental feeding, and the benefits are worth it.

In most situations, the greatest expense related to a food plot program is the cost of the equipment. The equipment needed to maintain a food plot program on a large tract may cost $50,000 or more. Certainly, small plots can be planted with ATVs and associated implements. However, an intensive food plot program requires serious equipment. In addition, some things, such as sub-soiling and breaking sod, cannot be done with a 4-wheeler. Other equipment, including plows, sub-soilers, disk harrows, cultipackers, planters, spreaders, spray rigs, and rotary mowers are necessary if a wide variety of plantings are to be established and maintained properly. A detailed discussion of the necessity and relative costs of these implements is found in Chapter 5.

Most soils in the eastern United States need lime and fertilizer to optimize plant growth. Fertilizers are needed where soil nutrients are limited, and it is not unusual for fertilizer costs to exceed $50 per acre. Liming is necessary to increase soil pH, improve nutrient availability, improve nitrogen fixation among legumes and increase herbicide effectiveness. Sites should not need liming every year, but initial liming costs can be considerable when soil tests recommend 2 or more tons of lime per acre. It is most cost-effective to contract a lime truck from a local agriculture supply dealer rather than buy bagged lime, although the dealers may require a minimum purchase of 4 to 6 tons. Bagged lime, especially pelletized lime, is expensive. It should be avoided unless plots are very small or inaccessible by truck. Bulk lime can also be purchased from agricultural supply dealers. However, "lime buggies" must be rented to spread the lime, which takes time, fuel, and additional effort. Chapter 4 will provide practical guidance on dispensing lime.

Other costs to consider include seed and herbicide. Seed is usually the most inexpensive item when planting. However, you can still expect to pay $25 to $80 per

INITIAL CONSIDERATIONS

acre when planting quality seed. Herbicides are also expensive but may be necessary for successful food plots, especially considering the amount of fertilizer, seed and time that can be wasted if weeds overtake the planting. For example, grass-selective herbicides often are needed in both warm- and cool-season plots at a cost of $10 to $14 per acre. That's a small price to pay to keep johnsongrass from overtaking a plot of warm-season legumes. Considering average costs for seed, lime, fertilizer, and herbicide, a quality food plot will average around $150 to $200 per acre, not including costs for equipment, fuel or labor.

> **DOLLARS AND CENTS**
>
> Considering average costs for seed, lime, fertilizer, and herbicide, a quality food plot will average around $150 to $200 per acre, not including costs for equipment, fuel or labor.

WHERE TO PLANT?

Matching a planting with the correct soil type is critical to food plot success. Don't expect plants adapted to well-drained sites to grow well on wet sites and vice versa. Similarly, most plants adapted to hot summers and mild winters shouldn't be expected to survive well in the Northeast or Great Lakes regions. Never plant a seed blend containing species that aren't adapted to your site. There is something that can be planted on virtually any site that will attract and provide needed nutrition for deer. Specific information on plant adaptation can be found in the Food Plot Species Profiles in Chapter 14.

Most food plots are planted in existing openings. These areas may include old agricultural fields, rights-of-way, log landings or loading "decks" from recent timber harvests, and firebreaks or woods roads. However, each of these choices requires some special considerations.

Old Agricultural Fields. Existing fields are the most commonly selected sites for planting food plots. However, because of the prior agricultural history of the site, the soil likely contains an abundance of weed seeds. In the South, any soil disturbance during spring and summer typically produces an abundance of sicklepod, or other persistent weeds, that may completely choke out a food plot planting. Seeds for this weed and a host of others may lie dormant in the soil for many years just waiting for you to initiate a food plot program. When considering old agricultural fields as planting sites, be sure to include weed prevention in your plans.

When probable competitors are identified before planting, food plot mixtures can be chosen based on herbicides that can be used to eliminate problem weeds. Grass-selective herbicides can be used to eliminate grass weed species such as johnsongrass without harming broadleaf crops like clover and cowpeas. Broadleaf-selective herbicides can eliminate broadleaf weeds such as sicklepod in grass crops like corn and grain sorghum. Chapter 10 will cover weed control in detail.

Rights-of-way. Utility rights-of-way also offer some unique possibilities and problems. These long, linear openings traverse a variety of habitats and can easily allow you to establish plots across the property. Perhaps most importantly, many

utility companies have cost-share programs that can significantly reduce your out-of-pocket costs. Contact the local office of the utility company to see if they have any programs that may assist you, or get in touch with your state wildlife agency's private lands biologist.

Rights-of-way traverse the landscape without respect for slope or soil type, so it is important to select areas with relatively flat ground and good soil. Alluvial soil in valleys often is the most fertile. Finally, be sure that your plantings are out of sight of any road to minimize potential poaching problems.

Log-landings. Many timber companies that lease hunting rights often allow hunting clubs to establish food plots on old log landings, or log "decks," remaining from recent timber harvests. However, heavy logging equipment often produces heavily compacted soils. Nevertheless, these sites may be the only sites where food plots are permissible, and if given proper consideration and soil amendments, they can produce high-quality food plots. Often, these areas will require some significant treatments such as subsoiling, liming and fertilizing. Choice of plantings, at least initially, should focus on species that are tolerant of poor site conditions, such as rye and crimson clover (cool season) or grain sorghum (warm season). Also, log-landings typically are too small to allow planting of highly preferred forages, such as soybeans, that are susceptible to overgrazing.

Firebreaks and Woods Roads. Trails and woods roads through forested areas provide some opportunities for forage plantings. Although these areas typically are quite narrow, they often extend long distances. Unfortunately, many woods roads receive too little sunlight to produce high-quality food plots. However, during winter in hardwood areas, or in all forest types where the canopy has been heavily thinned during timber operations, sufficient sunlight penetrates to the forest floor to allow some types of semi-shade tolerant plantings to do well. Small grains and perennial clovers, in particular, seem to do quite well in these situations.

Clearing a New Plot. In some areas, it may be necessary to create new openings. When doing so, the best soils should be located because lime and fertilizer requirements will be lower and production higher on these sites. Bulldozer and front-end loader operators typically charge about $50 to $100 per hour. An operator can usually clear a two-acre opening in about one day. At $80 per hour, clearing a 2-acre food plot would cost approximately $600 to $800. Constructing a woods road for access is a necessity. With a clear road, a lime truck can access the site, and equipment access is much easier. Also, a clear woods road makes it easier to get harvested deer out of the woods!

KENT KAMMERMEYER

SHADE TOLERANCE

Woods roads can make good food plots provided there is enough sunlight reaching the ground. Steps can be taken to kill or remove low-value tree species close to the road to admit more light. Also, select food plot species that tolerate moderate shade, such as clovers (shown here). Crimson, subterranean, white Dutch and ladino clovers are good examples.

Breaking Up Large Plots

Deer feel less safe using large, wide open food plots and may use them little or not at all during daylight hours. Piled windrows, like those seen in this plot, or planted hedgerows offer visual breaks that make large plots seem smaller.

Size, Shape, and Distribution

In areas where little forage is available and deer density is relatively high, larger food plots are required to withstand grazing pressure — although appropriate population control can certainly improve this situation. White-tailed deer, however, rarely venture too far from cover. When larger fields are planted, it often helps to break up these fields into sections using hedgerows planted in trees and shrubs that provide fruit and hard mast as well as visual breaks throughout the field. In large fields, a variety of plantings should be included. For example, a 10-acre field could be broken into a 4-acre section planted in corn, a 2-acre section planted in a warm-season forage, a 1½-acre section planted in a perennial cool-season forage, and a 1½-acre section planted in an annual cool-season forage. Hedgerows breaking up the sections would encompass about an acre. This provides considerable variety and a reliable food source throughout the year.

Unless deer density is high and overgrazing is a problem, 1- to 3-acre food plots are the optimal size. At this size, distance to escape cover is not a concern for deer, and plenty of sunlight is available for the plants. Smaller plots can be useful, especially in hunting situations, but attention has to be given to shade effects. If plots do not receive at least five hours of direct sunlight, plant production will be reduced. For small plots of ¼ to ½ acre, adjacent trees should be killed or removed to admit additional sunlight.

Designing food plots with irregular shapes may have advantages for enhancing hunting success, but this may also make it more difficult to maneuver equipment when preparing the seedbed, planting, fertilizing, liming, spraying, and cultipacking the plot. Obviously, this is less of a concern when an ATV is used to prepare a plot as opposed to a 50 hp tractor. Most programs need both larger "nutrition" plots that are easily managed as well as smaller "hunting" plots. More on food plot shape, particularly as it relates to hunting success, can be found in Chapter 12.

Food plots should be distributed fairly evenly to optimize nutrition across a property. To provide 1 to 5 percent of the property in quality forage requires about 2 to 8 acres of food plots for each 160-acre section. Special consideration should be given to areas on the property where little other forage is available. For example, if half a property contains considerable early successional cover, such as old-fields and agriculture, and the other half is wooded, additional food plot acreage should be devoted to the forested half.

CRAIG HARPER

DAYLIGHTING

Excessive shade limits food plot production. Most food plot plants require four to six hours of direct sunlight per day for optimal growth. This can be a problem when planting woods roads, firebreaks or edges and corners of fields bordered by woods. The solution is to fell or kill some trees, especially those with less wildlife value, and allow additional sunlight into the site. Examples of trees with low wildlife value include sweetgum, maples, elms, ashes, yellow poplar, sourwood and sycamore. Standing dead trees, or snags, provide food for woodpeckers and other birds. Woodpeckers create cavities for nesting, which are later used by other species, such as bluebirds, wood ducks, screech owls and many others.

Trees can be girdled with a chainsaw or hatchet by making a cut around the tree through the cambium layer, which is just inside the bark. If a chainsaw is used, don't cut too deep or the tree may fall during the next windstorm.

Some species will grow back from root sprouts after being girdled. Herbicides should be used in these cases. After girdling, the wound should be sprayed with an appropriate herbicide (Garlon 3-A or Arsenal AC). Refer to herbicide labels for rates and procedures. Girdling and spraying is best accomplished August through February. In late winter or early spring, strong sap flow will push the herbicide out of the cut.

When planning the distribution of food plots, it is important to dedicate separate acreage to both warm- and cool-season plots. It makes no sense to plow or disk a lush plot of cowpeas in August, when they are needed most, to plant clovers. Likewise, it is not wise to destroy a clover plot in April or May to plant warm-season forages. If only one field is available, plant half the field in a warm-season plot and the other half in a cool-season plot. For hunting purposes, especially in larger fields, a warm-season plot can be planted in the center of the field with a strip of cool-season forages around the edge. Deer will typically walk around the edge of the field during fall and winter instead of walking out into the middle of the field.

HOW MUCH AND WHAT TO PLANT?

A general rule of thumb is to establish 1 to 5 percent of the property in quality food plots. However, the specific requirements are related to the objectives, budget, deer density and overall habitat quality. If maximum nutrition is the objective and the overall habitat quality is good, with deer densities well within the carrying capacity, planting 1 to 2 percent of the property should be sufficient to meet most objectives. If habitat quality is low and deer density high, or if nothing short of maximum body and antler development is your goal, establishing 5 percent or more of the property in food plots, along with habitat and herd management, may be necessary to meet maximum nutrition objectives. If your density is high, it may be much more cost effective to reduce herd density.

Before the appropriate planting can be selected, choices must be made whether to use annual or perennial plantings and which season to target — warm season or cool season. In most cases, both warm- and cool-season plots should be established to ensure adequate nutritional benefit throughout the year. However, if an abundance of quality, warm-season forage is already available, such as soybean fields or abundant forb growth in woods and old-fields, cool-season plots should take precedence.

Virtually all warm-season plantings used in wildlife food plots are annuals. On the other hand, there is a good variety of both annuals and perennials available for cool-season plantings. The decision to plant an annual or perennial cool-season plot should be based primarily on soils and moisture regime and landowner objectives. Sites that are dry in summer should support annual clovers from early fall through late spring but may not maintain perennial clovers year-round. Re-seeding clovers, such as crimson and arrowleaf, may be good choices in these areas. Sites that are frequently flooded in winter may support warm-season plots planted in late May to early June and provide forage through early fall. Some clovers, including crimson, subterranean, white Dutch and ladino, will grow in mild to moderate shade, but best growth occurs where there is at least five hours of direct sunlight per day. Aspect, the compass direction that sloping ground faces, should be considered also. East- and north-facing aspects are cooler and retain more moisture. In southern latitudes, these sites are better suited for perennial clovers. In the northern latitudes, south- and west-facing aspects should be considered as they will be warmer in the winter and produce forage later in the fall and earlier in the spring.

Many people assume that annual forages require more work or cost more than perennial forages. This isn't necessarily true. Perennial cool-season forages, when managed correctly, require at least one annual fertilizer treatment, one or two mowings per year, and perhaps one or more herbicide applications each year. Fertilizer is normally applied in late summer and sometimes early spring. Herbicide applications may be needed at the same time. According to weed pressure, an early to midsummer application might be necessary also. Clover responds well to mowing, which is normally needed in late summer and in spring and fall depending on weed pressure. Annual cool-season forage plots are planted in late summer to early fall with a fertilizer application. Warm-season forages are planted in late spring and left through the summer. All things considered, the cost per ton of forage does not differ appreciably between annual and perennial plantings.

SOILS, GENETICS AND EXPECTATIONS

Many hunters think food plots are the key to growing monster bucks on their property. They soon find out differently. Age combined with enhanced nutrition provided by a high-quality food plot program can create quality bucks. Food plots are an important management practice intended to make nutrition available so deer can reach their potential, provided they live long enough. Although soils can be

amended and made very productive, genetics are not changed by food plots. What this means is landowners in Florida, for example, should not expect a food plot to produce a deer typical of Iowa or Saskatchewan. Hunters and landowners should not be concerned with trying to influence the genetics of a deer herd. However, serious nutrition problems can and do occur throughout the whitetail's range. Many of these are directly related to overabundant deer herds that have chronically exceeded the carrying capacity. There are other areas with extremely low inherent deer habitat quality. Both can be mitigated with proper herd and habitat management.

Realistic expectations are extremely important. Those who enjoy working with the land and watching wildlife benefit from their food plots are usually pleased with their efforts. Those who plant food plots merely to kill a trophy buck are often disappointed.

CONCLUSIONS

There are many factors to consider before planting a food plot. Many are based on agronomics, whereas others are related to economics. It is not wise to rush out and plant just any available open space with the latest "Big Buck Blend." The smart food plot manager has clear objectives, considers surrounding habitats and budget constraints, maps out locations for food plots with regard to soils and deer travel patterns, then plants according to forage limitations and predicted weed pressure. Most importantly, the smart land manager plants food plots to complement other habitat management practices while keeping the deer density in check with an appropriate doe harvest strategy.

CRAIG HARPER

SUMMER VACATION

Except where agricultural crops such as soybeans are abundant or high-quality natural forages are extremely lush, your food plots should not take a summer vacation. Both warm- and cool-season crops should be planted to ensure year-round nutrition. This photo shows a high-quality warm-season plot – lots of viny legumes climbing over plants that offer structure, such as sunflowers or sorghum.

Understanding Soils
and Soil Fertility

By Phil Freshley, CPSSc

four

Because agriculture is so important in the United States, many volumes have been written on soil classification and fertility. Although this chapter will only cover the basics of soil management, it should help you identify favorable conditions and pitfalls when establishing your food plot program. Soil conditions are a critical consideration when planting food plots. Remember, soil fertility and water combine to form the gas in the tank for the plant engine. Sunshine is the spark plug. When you're producing deer forage, the importance of soil fertility can be summed up in three sentences:

- *Nitrogen is the key element for plant protein production.*
- *Calcium and phosphorus are essential building blocks for antlers, bone, milk and body growth.*
- *Balanced plant nutrition provides the greatest forage yields.*

UNDERSTANDING NATIVE FERTILITY

The physical characteristics and fertility of soil vary widely from place to place. A soil's natural fertility is dictated by the minerals in the parent material and biological activity that formed the soil and the amount of weathering that has occurred over the life of the soil. Weathering is controlled by numerous factors such as climate and soil type, but water movement is the most important. When water moves down through the soil, it dissolves nutrients and carries these compounds and tiny mineral particles deeper into the soil. Eventually, a layer of clay forms below the topsoil. This process is assisted by the activity of plant roots and soil organisms such as bacteria, fungi, nematodes and worms. These organisms produce organic acids that break down soil minerals and convert organic material. As a result, the surface soils become more acidic, and nutrients and the smallest soil

VANISHING TOPSOIL

Due to historical erosion, food plot growers in many areas of the United States are working with less-fertile subsoils now that topsoils have been lost. This photo, taken in 1928 in Alabama, shows the devastating results of erosion associated with cotton farming in the South. When native soil fertility played out, many cotton farms were simply abandoned in favor of newly cleared land, and the cycle started over. The South's famous "red clay" is actually a subsoil layer exposed by human activity.

particles – clay – move out of the root zone. This happens in all soils, with the rate depending on rainfall and climate, and strongly influences natural fertility.

Understanding how soils develop in different areas of the country can help us identify sites that may be most fertile and what elements may be deficient in the soil. As a general rule, the more weathered a soil is, the less fertile it is. Weathering is a slow process from a human perspective. It may take up to 10,000 years for a significant clay layer to appear below the topsoil in eastern climates. Soils with several feet of clay accumulation below the topsoil are hundreds of thousands of years old. This is why most old soils have a loamy to sandy topsoil with high amounts of organic material that is very different than the underlying layer of clay. Beneath the clay, the soil takes on the structure of the original parent material. In a young soil, there is less difference between the topsoil, subsoil and parent material. This pattern of layering that develops is called the soil profile and is used to classify the soil.

The most confusing thing that you may encounter in looking at food plot soil profiles is that many areas have a recent history of erosion or other disturbance such as logging decks and grading. In many areas of the United States, the topsoil is significantly eroded or absent, and all you may have left is the subsoil. In these areas you can expect lower organic content, higher clay content and lower fertility at the surface than an undisturbed soil.

Soil scientists examine soil profiles and evaluate the factors responsible for its current condition. These factors are:
- *Climate* (historic temperature and rainfall)
- *Parent material* (structure and chemistry of the original rock)
- *Organisms* (plants, fungi, microbes, worms and other animals, especially man)
- *Topography* (slope, erosion and drainage patterns)
- *Time* (how long the first four factors have been in play)

Based on the soil characteristics created by these factors, soils are classified into 11 orders, seven of which are common in deer country. These orders are further classified into suborders, groups, subgroups, families and series. However, it's not necessary to know the details of the classification system to build a successful soil management program. Most areas have been mapped by United States Department of Agriculture (USDA) Natural Resources Conservation Service (NRCS). You can consult your local NRCS office for this detailed information and further advice on local soil conditions.

REGIONAL TRENDS IN SOIL TYPE AND PROPERTIES

Usually just a few soil orders dominate each climactic and physiographic region of the country because historic rainfall, temperature and vegetation are similar, and parent material consists of only a few types. Therefore, it's easy to make some generalizations about soil properties for various regions of the country. These general conditions will help you understand potential opportunities and limitations of your food plot program.

Subtropical Areas. Because warm temperatures and high rainfall increase weathering rates, the most weathered and therefore least fertile soils are in some subtropical and tropical landscapes such as the southeastern United States and Central America. Examples include the Piedmont of Alabama, Georgia, the Carolinas and Virginia. In these areas, soils are primarily Ultisols which are highly weathered with a red to yellowish-red clay subsoil. Native plants in these areas have adapted by having low nutrient requirements and by recovering the limited nutrients through litter decomposition. Pine stands can thrive on as little as 15 pounds of nitrogen per acre per year and very low levels of calcium. In contrast, our forage crops require five times as much.

When tropical/subtropical areas are cleared for agriculture without the addition of lime and fertilizer, they are productive for a year or so due to the nutrients stored in soil organic material, but they quickly become infertile. This is why the slash and burn agriculture in the tropics is so devastating. It is also why some areas of the southeastern United States lost 2 to 3 feet of topsoil during the cotton farming era. Therefore, food plots in the South generally will require more lime and fertilizer than other areas. However, the advantage of these climates is that the growing season is longer and winters are mild, so more forage can be produced on a yearly basis.

DOMINANT SOIL ORDERS OF THE *EASTERN AND CENTRAL UNITED STATES*

Illustrations courtesy of the NRCS Soils website at http://soils.usda.gov

MOLLISOLS: Moderate age soils similar to Alfisols that developed on grasslands in glaciated landscapes and have deep, black topsoil with high base mineral content and neutral pH.

ALFISOLS: Moderate age soils (1,000 to 200,000 years old) typically brown in color that are slightly to moderately weathered, developed under deciduous forest cover on old glacial deposits and have high base mineral content. They are productive for most crops.

SPODOSOLS: Moderate aged soils that are slightly to moderately weathered and developed under coniferous forests. They tend to be acidic and infertile. Sandy Spodosols are mineral poor.

ULTISOLS: Old soils (from 100,000 to more than 1 million years old) that are highly weathered and have low base mineral content. They have a moderately low capacity to retain additions of lime and fertilizer.

INCEPTISOLS: Young soils (less than 10,000 years) that are beginning to form distinct layers from weathering. Found in river bottoms, steep mountains or relatively recent marine deposits in the eastern and midwestern United States. Sandy types are usually mineral poor; loamy types can be mineral rich.

4

UNDERSTANDING SOILS AND SOIL FERTILITY

ANTLERS MADE OF DIRT

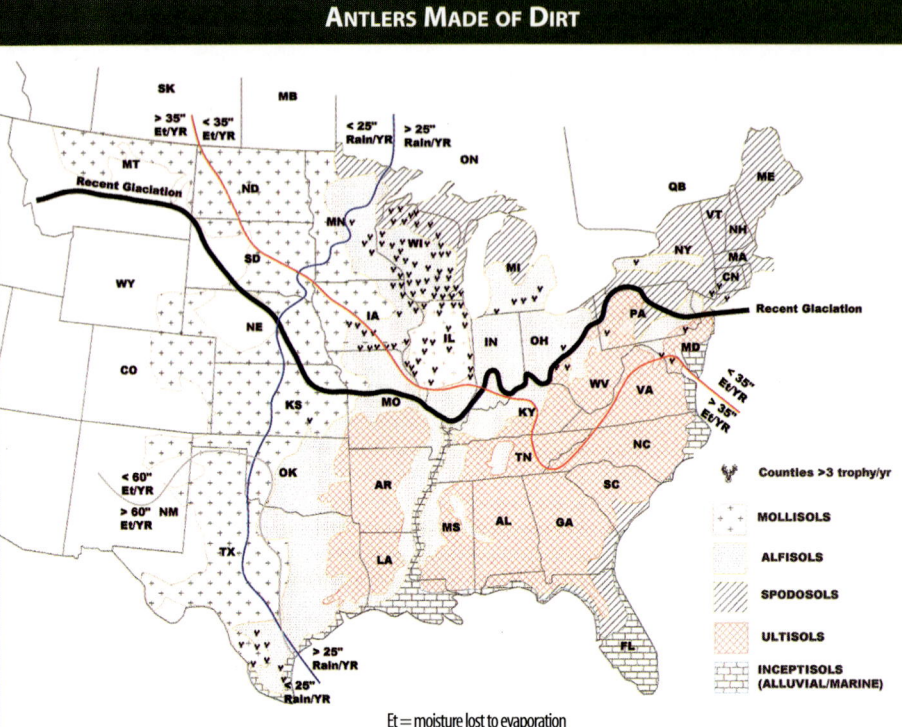

Et = moisture lost to evaporation

The map above compares dominant soil types around the United States with the top Boone & Crockett and Pope & Young producing counties from 1991 to 2000. Symbols on the map represent counties that reported 30 or more record-book whitetails during this time period. By far, the most productive soils for large-racked bucks appear to be Mollisols, Alfisols and Spodosols formed on recent glacial deposits in areas having adequate annual rainfall for plant growth during the growing season.

These are some of the youngest soils in the United States, and the younger a soil is, the less the process of weathering has leached minerals from the topsoil. In the upper Midwest and Northeast, the last glacial event occurred less than 15,000 years ago. The movement of glaciers over these landscapes ground rock into gravelly silt called glacial till. In terms of minerals, the native fertility of these soils is high.

Deer antlers are about half protein and other organic compounds and a third or more minerals, with calcium and phosphorus making up about 90 percent of the mineral weight. Soils with higher calcium, phosphorus, magnesium and trace minerals will produce forage – both natural and agricultural – conducive to antler growth.

The most glaring exception on the map above is south Texas. South Texas is arid. In arid climates, leaching of minerals is slow. In fact, parts of south Texas have mineral crusts at the surface – natural mineral licks. Combine this with intensive water management for both livestock and deer, as well as a larger average size of individually owned tracts of land and associated older age classes of bucks, and you can get awesome antler development.

Temperate Areas. The Northeast, and eastern portions of the Midwest, are cooler and slightly drier than the South. In addition, many of these areas were covered by glaciers in the past. By grinding up rocks and exposing fresh minerals, glaciers create "new" soils. Weathering is low to moderate. Most soils in these areas are Alfisols and Mollisols with some Spodosols. These soils are younger and browner than Southern soils and have deep, dark topsoil. As you would suspect, they are more fertile and usually have a higher pH and greater mineral content. Recently glaciated areas have some of the most fertile soils in the world, particularly the Mollisols that have developed in grassland areas. The limitations in these areas are shorter growing seasons, moderate rainfall, and sometimes long, harsh winters that may limit carrying capacity for deer.

Semi-Arid Areas. Weathering is very slow in areas having low rainfall such as the western United States except on western slopes of mountain ranges. Another exception is in areas of low to moderate rainfall and high evaporation such as the Southwest. Soil types in these areas include Alfisols and Mollisols. Because of low weathering rates, the nutrient and mineral content may be quite high, but the lack of water limits forage production. Where agricultural irrigation, cattle watering or river bottoms reduce the water limitations, deer may prosper and attain excellent growth on native and agricultural forages.

LANDSCAPES WITH UNIQUE SOIL PROPERTIES

Even within regions, there are some areas that have unique soils due to topographic influences such as mountains, river and creek bottoms, and coastal plains. These conditions need to be considered when selecting and evaluating your food plot sites.

Mountain Areas. The mountains in the eastern United States, including the Appalachians, Ozarks and Adirondacks, have varying levels of natural fertility. These are old landscapes, but because of steep slopes, some areas are unstable. Landslides and slope creep uncover less weathered material that may have high mineral content. This mixture of older and younger soils includes Entisols and Inceptisols in any region, Ultisols in the South, and Alfisols in the North. In general, mountains formed from rocks such as granite and schist are nutrient poor. These rocks weather slowly and soils arising from them are low in nutrients. In contrast, good soil fertility can occur in the vicinity of rocks containing limestone, dolomite and other sedimentary rocks. Soil testing is critical in these areas due to the variability that may be encountered.

In mountainous areas, river and creek bottoms where eroded minerals accumulate have the best native fertility and are therefore the best sites for food plots. However, broad ridges, benches and plateaus with slopes less than 10 percent also make decent food plots, if not too rocky, but will require more amendments. In mountainous areas, erosion can be severe on slopes greater than 10 percent, so steep slopes should be avoided.

River and Creek Drainages. When topsoil is eroded, much of it ends up being deposited along streams and rivers. These soils are typically classified as Inceptisols. The erosion and deposition process concentrates nutrients and often produces the most fertile soils in any area. The principal limitation for food plots in these areas is flooding or saturated soil conditions which can prevent tillage or drown roots.

Soils in bottomlands will always reflect the fertility of the landscapes upstream. Most of the time, fertility in bottoms is better than surrounding land because this is where much of the good topsoil eroded from the hills ends up. Along large rivers like the Mississippi, soil fertility may be almost as good as the upper Midwest where the river begins, even as far south as Louisiana. Areas along small streams will reflect the fertility of nearby landscapes. In most cases, these are ideal food plot sites where drainage is adequate, and they will require the least fertilizer for good forage production.

Coastal Plains. Soils in coastal areas are the product of encroachment and recession of ocean shorelines. Along the Atlantic and Gulf Coast, historical shorelines extended as far as 150 miles inland. Soils in these areas are dominated by marine deposits which are usually sandy but also include marine clays. Sandy soils are nutrient poor, and fertilizers are leached rapidly from the surface. These soils are younger than the adjacent Piedmont region and include Inceptisols and sandy Spodosols on Lower Coastal Plain sites, and sandy Ultisols on older, Upper Coastal Plain sites.

Sites on sandhills, which are old dunes, can be excessively drained and droughty, while nearby depressions may be too wet for planting food plots. The best sites are usually on moderately drained soils between the wetlands and sandhills. In these areas, plant roots can grow to water, but the water table is deep enough to allow good aeration. Even the best sites in these sandy areas will require regular fertilizer application to maintain forage production. Because fertilizers wash out of sandy soils quickly, smaller repeated applications usually are better than one annual application.

SOIL PHYSICAL CHARACTERISTICS

The physical characteristics of the soil, such as texture, color, structure, and pattern of layering, can tell you almost everything you need to know about water drainage, seed and root bed limitations, and potential fertilizer needs. Knowing how water, air, and nutrients move in the soil can be understood by examining the topsoil, subsoil and topography of the land. This understanding is critical for selecting the best site for food plots.

SOIL HORIZONS, TEXTURE, AND STRUCTURE

These properties determine the pathways of rain water as it enters and moves through the soil. Consequently, understanding soil texture and structure allows you to predict how much and where water and nutrients will be stored in the soil for plant use between rains.

Soil Horizons. As soils weather over time, distinct layers form called horizons.

The description of the soil horizons is called the soil's profile. Horizons differ in physical features and typically move water and air at different rates. Most commonly, soils have three layers named the A, B and C horizons that correspond to the topsoil, subsoil and parent material. In most soils, the subsoil (B horizon) has a higher clay content than the topsoil (A horizon) or parent material (C horizon). In old soils, the B horizon may be 50 percent or more clay while the A horizon is 50 percent or more sand.

Texture. The texture of a horizon is an indicator of how fast water will move through the soil and how much water the soil can hold. Soil particles are divided into four size groups: rock fragments, sand, silt and clay. Other than rock fragments, sand has the largest particle size, ranging in diameter from 0.05 to 2 millimeters. Silt ranges from 2 microns (a thousandth of a millimeter) to 0.05 millimeters in diameter. Clay is the smallest mineral with a diameter of 2 microns or less.

The proportion of each type of particle in a soil defines its texture. The texture class is defined by the U.S. Department of Agriculture using a textural triangle. It is not necessary to know the exact percentages of each particle type to evaluate the soil. Generally, a typical loam would be about 50 percent sand, 20 percent clay and 30 percent silt. If it had 10 percent more sand, it would be a sandy loam, or if it had 10 percent more clay then it would be clay loam, etc.

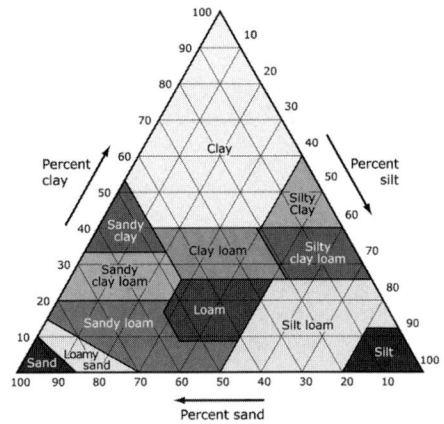

It is easy to check the texture of the soil in your food plots. Simply moisten a handful of soil, form it into a ball and gently toss it in the air several inches. If it won't stay together when you catch it in your hand, it is sandy loam or coarser, meaning loamy sand or sand. If it stays in a ball, it is usually loam or finer. If you can take a small, moist sample and make a 1-inch or longer ribbon between your thumb and forefinger, it is probably some type of clay, sandy clay or silty clay. If the ribbon forms but breaks at less than an inch, it is probably one of the loam classes, such as clay loam, sandy clay loam, etc. This simple test will let you relate your food plot soils to known soil properties.

Loam soil textures are best for cultivation. In fact, the ideal food plot would have a loam to sandy loam topsoil 6 or more inches deep with underlying subsoil having a higher clay content to retain water and nutrients in the lower root zone. Water moves through loams uniformly, aeration is good, and root growth is not hindered. Sandy textures can also be good, but water moves through the soil more quickly, and less water can be held in the pores. Clays have much slower water and air movement but high water and nutrient retention. A problem with clay is that it is easily deformed when wet and therefore can form a barrier to root growth if compacted by equipment traffic.

Having some clay in the soil is important because clay is the most chemically active of the soil particles. Because of their small size, clay particles have a high surface area per unit weight. The surfaces of clay particles also have electrostatic charges that react with many fertilizer elements. In most cases, the amount of clay, along with the organic matter, controls the retention and rate of conversion of nutrients to forms available for use by plants.

In contrast, sand is not very reactive. Silt has low to moderate reactivity and can be an important mineral source. Sand and silt are more important for providing structural stability, water movement and a favorable environment for root growth.

Structure. Different soil structures form when the soil is subjected to wetting and drying cycles or from the activity of roots, worms, nematodes and fungi. If you pick up a chunk of undisturbed soil and break it, it will fall apart into smaller blocks or layers. The shape and size of these blocks defines the soil structure. The soil structure is important because it determines how water and air are distributed through the soil. Structural pores are the bloodstream of the soil and allow water and nutrients to move through the soil.

Structures that may produce problems for food plots include cemented layers in loams and compacted layers in clay that impede the movement of roots, water, air and fertilizer. Examples of structure problems that must be corrected for a productive food plot are compacted clay layers beneath old logging decks and plow pans in

SITE SELECTION BY SOIL

Soil texture affects how fast water moves through the soil and how quickly minerals will be leached out. Many factors will be considered when you choose food plot locations, and soil texture should be among them.

BILL MARCHEL

FROM SAND TO CLAY: *SOIL I.D.*

SAND: Visible individual grains. Will not make a ball when moist.

SANDY LOAM: Makes a ball when moist, but it will not stay together if you toss it up and catch it.

LOAM: Makes a ball when moist that will stay intact if tossed, but it will not ribbon more than 1 inch.

SILT LOAM: Like loam, but when pressed into a thin ribbon it forms pastry flakes. Has a greasy feel.

CLAY LOAM: When moist, will make a ribbon 1 to 2 inches long that barely sustains its own weight.

CLAY: When moist, makes a ribbon 2 to 4 inches long that easily sustains its own weight.

agricultural fields that form from repeated plowing in the spring when soils are moist. These problems can be corrected by deep ripping 2 to 4 feet deep with a subsoiler under dry conditions. If severe structural problems are not corrected, no amount of seed, fertilizer or lime will produce a good food plot.

MINERAL AND ORGANIC COLORS
SHOW YOU THE WATER

Just like the iron in your blood, the iron in the soil changes color depending on how much oxygen is available. Oxygenated arterial blood from your lungs is red, while venal blood from your body is bluer after the cells remove the oxygen. The same thing happens in soil but for different reasons.

When soils are saturated with water for several weeks, the amount of oxygen in the subsoil drops to near zero. Iron compounds control the color of clay and some silt particles. When iron reacts with oxygen, it forms iron oxide and has a red

FOLLOW THE COLOR
The red color in clays, shown above, is a result of iron reacting with oxygen. Water dissolves the iron, and prolonged exposure to water will result in gray-colored clay. Gray clay, as well as black sand, is an indication that a site may be too wet year-round for food plots.

color – just like rust and the iron in your blood. When soil oxygen disappears during saturation, microbial and chemical processes remove oxygen from the iron oxide, and the iron dissolves into the water. When the soils dry out and oxygen is again abundant, the dissolved iron reacts with oxygen to form a red mineral compound. This process results in gray soil colors where the iron oxide was dissolved and redder soil colors where the iron oxide reformed.

In general, clay and silt particles become grayer in color the longer soils remain wet. If you find clay soil that is all gray, it probably stays saturated for months because most of the iron has been dissolved away. Soils that saturate only during the wet season will be mottled with red, gray and yellow colors interspersed.

Topsoil color is more influenced by the amount of organic matter in the soil. Organic material is brown to dark brown under dry conditions but will turn black under long-term saturation. Organic material decomposes fast under warm, moist conditions, slow under cool, dry conditions, and very slow under saturated conditions. Soils with thick layers of black organic material usually are associated with swampy soils or dry, cool soils, like those found in semiarid grasslands. In addition, organic materials can stain soil particles, giving the soil a brown to black color. Sandy soils that are wet will form black and brown coatings on the sand grains as well as fine black organics between grains. So black sand below the surface can be an indicator of wetness just like gray clay is.

Although other factors affect soil color, the strong influence of iron compounds and organics is useful when evaluating most food plot sites. As a general rule, if you have gray clay or black sand in the top 18 inches of the soil, particularly near the surface, the site may be too wet to grow some crops at least part of the year and should be managed accordingly.

RULES OF THUMB

In summary, food plot drainage and potential for plant growth can be assessed by examining the topsoil and upper subsoil texture, structure and color (mottled gray clay, black sand and others). The following drainage/texture classes often create problems and should be avoided as food plot sites if possible:

- *Poorly drained soils that are loam, clay loam or clay: in these soils, roots can't get enough air.*
- *Any soil with heavy clay or compacted layers at less than 18 inches from the surface: roots can't penetrate deep enough.*
- *All excessively drained soils, meaning deep sands, and any soil in a semiarid climate without irrigation: plants have insufficient water.*

The Ideal Conditions. The ideal situation is a well-drained topsoil of at least 6 inches of loamy material and an underlying loam to clay subsoil. This provides a

HARDPAN PROBLEMS

This photo of a tobacco plant provides an extreme example of a hardpan or "plow pan," a compacted layer of soil up to two feet below the surface. Hardpans are caused by heavy equipment, such as logging equipment on log loading decks, and by repeated plowings in agricultural fields, particularly when soils are wet. Roots are seldom able to penetrate a hardpan (as seen in the photo) and the hardpan may cause drainage problems.

To detect a hardpan, use a long, sharp stake or soil-test probe. If the probe can be pushed into the top few inches of soil easily but then hits a hard layer, and it becomes difficult to push the probe any farther, you likely have a hardpan problem. The solution is deep tillage with a subsoiler, moldboard plow or chisel plow to break up the compacted layer. See Chapter 5, the Equipment chapter, for more information.

WWW.FORESTRYIMAGES.ORG

deep, well-aerated root zone for growth along with a water- and nutrient-holding zone to feed the crop between fertilization and rain events. Nevertheless, you can use problem soils, particularly if seasonal differences in soil conditions are considered. For example, poorly drained sands can be productive during the warm/dry season but will be too wet in the cool season. Conversely, well-drained sands may produce adequate forage in the cool/wet season but subject to crop failure in the warm season.

SOIL FERTILITY

Plants require 13 essential elements for growth. These elements are divided into six macronutrients and seven micronutrients, which are listed in the sidebar on this page. Plant growth depends on the amount and form of these elements in the soil. The form of the element controls the availability of the element to the plant. For example, plant roots take up nitrogen only in the ammonium (NH4) or nitrate (NO3) forms. If nitrogen is attached to organic or mineral compounds, it must first be converted to ammonium or nitrate to be available to the plant. Understanding how and why this happens is important when considering fertilizer applications.

There are three soil factors that affect fertility the most: soil acidity, clay reactions and organic decomposition.

13 ESSENTIAL ELEMENTS FOR GROWTH

MACRONUTRIENTS:
Elements needed in the greatest amounts (listed in order of importance).
- Nitrogen (N)
- Phosphorus (P)
- Potassium (K)
- Calcium (Ca)
- Magnesium (Mg)
- Sulfur (S)

MICRONUTRIENTS:
Essential for growth but only needed in very small to trace quantities.
- Iron (Fe)
- Manganese (Mn)
- Copper (Cu)
- Zinc (Zn)
- Boron (B)
- Molybdenum (Mo)
- Chlorine (Cl)

LIMING: CONTROLLING SOIL ACIDITY

Soil pH is a measure of the amount of hydrogen (H+) ions present in the soil that can react with other elements. The term pH means "power of the hydrogen" and is usually referred to as soil acidity. Hydrogen and hydroxide (OH-) are the most common reactive elements in the soil. Liming, which is the application of calcium and magnesium compounds, is used to reduce acidity by adding OH- thereby reducing H+ (they combine to form water).

Effect of pH. Hydrogen has a positive charge, and hydroxide has a negative charge, so these elements react with the other elements to form different compounds. This controls the amount of a plant nutrient that is in a usable form. The higher the pH, the fewer the H+ present and the more OH- present. At pH 7.0 these ions are equal, and the environment is referred to as neutral. As pH decreases, the amount of hydrogen increases by 10 times for each pH unit. In other words, there is 10 times more H+ at a pH of 5.9 than at a pH of 6.9.

POWER OF THE HYDROGEN (pH)

This photo by professional photographer and deer manager Charles Alsheimer shows samples from a brassica plot he planted in New York state. Both plants are the same age, both were planted in the same soil, except that the soil had not been amended with lime in one area. The smaller plant was growing in soil with a pH of 5.4. The larger plant was growing in soil with a pH of 6.7. In acidic soils, more nutrients are bound to free-floating hydrogen atoms and are unavailable to plants as seen in the graphic below.

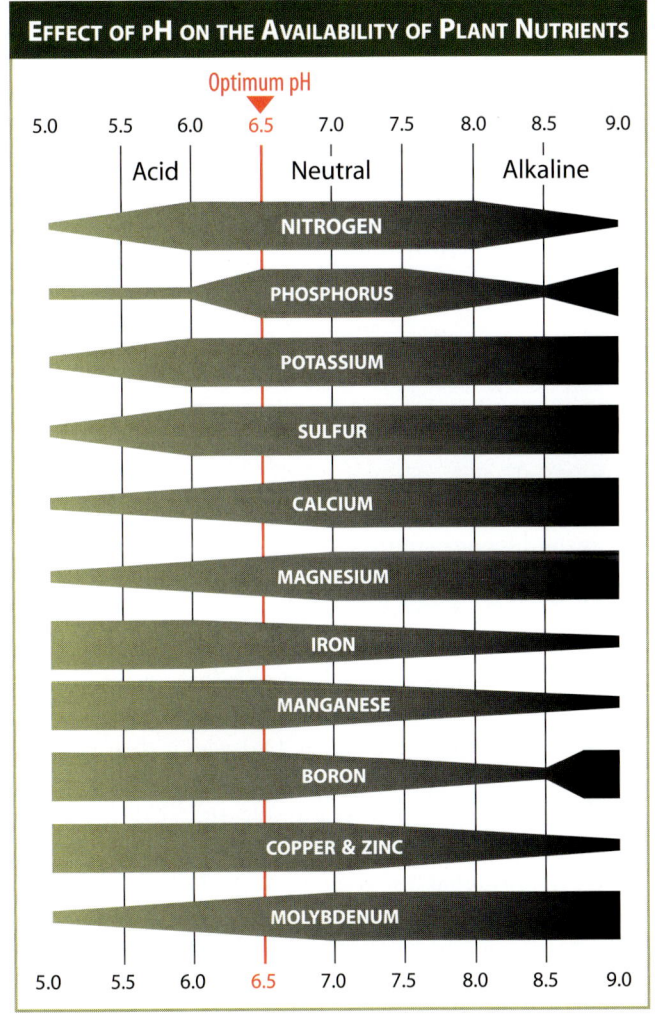

EFFECT OF pH ON THE AVAILABILITY OF PLANT NUTRIENTS

Optimum pH

5.0   5.5   6.0   6.5   7.0   7.5   8.0   8.5   9.0

Acid   Neutral   Alkaline

NITROGEN

PHOSPHORUS

POTASSIUM

SULFUR

CALCIUM

MAGNESIUM

IRON

MANGANESE

BORON

COPPER & ZINC

MOLYBDENUM

5.0   5.5   6.0   6.5   7.0   7.5   8.0   8.5   9.0

So what does this mean for soil fertility? Many of the elements needed by plants are in available forms at slightly acidic to neutral pH (pH of 6.0 to 7.0) but are less available outside of this range. The diagram on page 61 shows how this availability changes across a range of pH levels for critical elements.

Phosphorus (P) is an excellent example. At pH less than 6.0, phosphorus forms a compound with iron and aluminum hydroxides and is not available for plant use. At a pH greater than 7.5, most of the phosphorus will be absorbed by calcium minerals and will similarly be unavailable. Between pH 6.0 and 7.0, these reactions occur to a lesser degree, so there is a large amount of P available in the soil for plant use.

In addition to mineral reactions, the processes by which microorganisms convert decomposed organic matter into available nitrogen can be slowed or stopped at extreme pH conditions.

Liming. Liming is the process of adding a material that will react with the free hydrogen and produce neutral compounds. Lime, or calcium oxide (CaO), is the most effective calcium compound to rapidly neutralize soil acidity but is rarely used for agricultural liming because it is caustic. Instead,

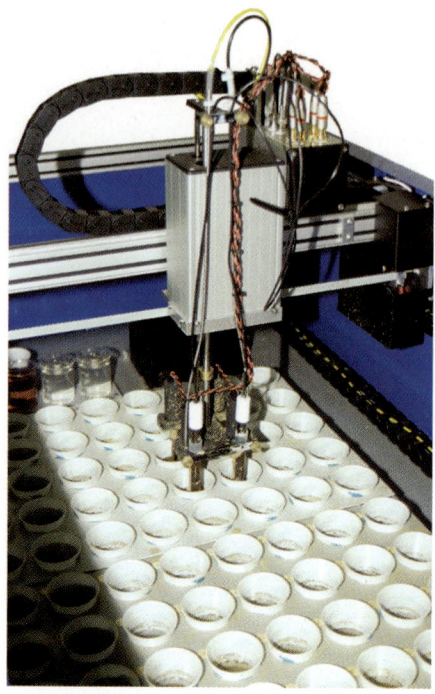

TEST IN PROGRESS
Each of the paper cups in this photo contains soil from an individual sample sent in to a soil lab. A robotic, computer-guided machine moves across the samples, testing the pH of each, injecting liquid calcium carbonate (lime), then measuring the pH again. By measuring the rate of change of the pH, the computer calculates the exact type and amount of lime needed to correct the pH in each sample. This customizes recommendations across a wide variety of soil types.

limestone ($CaCO_3$), a naturally occurring mineral, is ground into small particles used for this purpose. Limestone that contains both calcium and magnesium is called dolomitic limestone and is used to lime soils that are low in magnesium.

Liming works when the mineral dissolves in water. When limestone dissolves, the calcium separates from the carbonate (CO_3) which then reacts with water to form HCO_3 and a free OH^- molecule. This OH^- molecule then reacts with the free H^+ to form another water molecule. As a result, soil acidity is reduced, and free calcium becomes available for plants to use. A similar process happens with slaked lime ($CaOH_2$) or any other material that will dissolve in water, forming free OH^- molecules.

Liming products are selected for their ability to neutralize acid as well as provide plant nutrients such as calcium and magnesium. The rate at which limestone will neutralize soil acidity depends on the fineness of the limestone particles and the level of soil acidity. The smaller the particles, the faster the reactions occur. Unfortunately, the cost of limestone generally increases with fineness. In most states, the grinding process is standardized so that there is a good distribution of coarse and fine particles. In most cases, it may take more than a year for all the limestone to dissolve. Therefore, it generally is not necessary to lime every year.

The amount of lime needed can only be determined by a soil test. A soil testing laboratory will measure the acidity in the soil and then calculate the amount of limestone needed. Remember, too much lime can also be a problem, so only apply the recommended amount, and plow it in to get good distribution through the topsoil. When establishing a food plot, it's best to apply lime, plow it in, and let it settle for a rain or two before applying fertilizer and seed.

Liming is most important in the humid regions of the Midwest, East and South. It is seldom needed in the Great Plains and semi-arid regions.

Clay Effect. As mentioned before, clay is the most reactive soil particle because it has electric charges on its surface that hold opposite-charged molecules. Many important plant nutrient forms have a positive charge, such as ammonium ($NH4+$), calcium ($Ca++$), potassium ($K+$), and magnesium ($Mg++$). Because opposites attract, these nutrients will stick to the clay particles and can be held there until a root hair or water strips them off. Therefore, clay particles act as a storage site for these nutrients and water. This is why soils with clay and/or fine silt particles in the root zone are typically more productive than sandy soils.

The clay effect is not good for all nutrients. Phosphorus occurs in the soil with

TES RANDLE JOLLY

WHY BE AVERAGE WHEN YOU CAN FERTILIZE?
Although many soils contain enough basic nutrients for plant growth and survival, don't be fooled into thinking you never need fertilizer. In most cases, amending the soil with lime and fertilizer allows plants to achieve optimum levels of production and nutritive value, like this lush patch of vetch, a cool-season legume.

a negative charge (H_2PO_4-), and therefore reacts with iron (Fe) and aluminum (Al) oxides that are abundant in clay soils. In general, the more clay in a soil, the more phosphorus will be tied up by the iron and aluminum, especially at a pH less than 5.5. Therefore, when dealing with high clay soils (those that make a good ribbon between your fingers), you may try adding extra phosphorus when you fertilize to improve yield, especially if the pH is less than 6.0. You may want to start off with 25 percent more than recommended to counter the amount lost to iron and aluminum binding. These losses are usually not considered in laboratory recommendations.

Organic Matter. Organic material is an extremely important component of productive soils because the form of nitrogen in the soil is largely controlled by bacteria that require nitrogen. The organic matter provides the carbon source these bacteria need. When you apply fertilizer, much of the nitrogen and phosphorus not captured by plant roots is used by bacteria to make more bacteria. This process creates plant-available nutrients during the growing season.

Natural soils can have hundreds of pounds of nitrogen stored in organic matter that has accumulated over the years but is unavailable to plants. Given fresh nutrient inputs, bacteria convert this material to simpler compounds and in the process produce nitrogen and phosphorus in forms that are available to plants. The result is that nitrogen and phosphorus are captured and then slowly released into the root zone, providing a long-term fertilizer effect. This organic matter cycling reduces the need for a second application of fertilizer midseason to maintain production and reduces the amount of fertilizer required the following year. In addition, organic matter gives the soil better aeration and water-holding ability.

FERTILIZER BASICS: N-P-K

Nitrogen, phosphorus and potassium are the elements required in the greatest amounts by crops and thus form the basis of most fertilizers. Fertilizer formulas are familiar to any gardener who has bought a bag of 10-10-10 at the local hardware store. This formula refers to the percentage of nitrogen (N), phosphate (P_2O_5) and potash (K_2O) in the product. In other words, 100 pounds of 10-10-10 would contain 10 pounds of nitrogen, 10 pounds of phosphate and 10 pounds of potash. If you needed 75 pounds of N per acre for your crop, you would apply 750 pounds of 10-10-10 per acre.

Nitrogen, phosphorus and potassium are not the only nutrients required, but they are the most important. For deer growth, the N and P are essential. However, the K is required for plant growth and to turn the N and P into plant protein. Balance is the key.

Nitrogen is the building block of plant protein. In most soils, carbon is abundant, and nitrogen is scarce. Because protein is composed primarily of carbon and nitrogen, nitrogen is key for a plant to produce the optimal amount of protein. Clovers and other legumes are great food plot forages because they can extract nitrogen from the air as well as from the soil. This is why clovers can produce good quality forage even if you under-fertilize. However, when you fertilize, they do even better. One way to tell if your forage is low on nitrogen is that the foliage will have a lighter green to yellowish green color.

Phosphorus is necessary for growth of both roots and leaves. In addition, it is a primary component of antlers. Without adequate phosphorus your food plots will be stunted and have lower protein production. With ample phosphorus you will get all the growth the other nutrients allow.

Potassium is also essential for plant metabolism and forage production. Potassium is easily washed out of the soil because it is not held as tightly on clay particles as the other nutrients. Therefore, you may need to add potassium annually even though the plant doesn't need as much potassium as it does nitrogen and phosphorus. Therefore, it is important to conduct soil tests each year.

Other macronutrients such as calcium and magnesium typically are provided

Continued on page 68.

FIGHTING FERTILIZER PRICES

Fertilizer prices, especially for nitrogen (N), are closely tied to natural gas prices because natural gas is used in the production of these products. In recent years, marketplace factors, as well as weather factors like hurricanes, have driven up the price of both natural gas and oil, and fertilizer prices have responded. Always remember to apply fertilizer based on a soil test to avoid using more fertilizer than is necessary. Don't skimp, either. By applying less fertilizer than is necessary, the money you have spent on seed and equipment, as well as your time, is wasted on crops that will not perform to their potential.

A REAL WORLD
SOIL TEST AND ANALYSIS

The test results shown below are from an actual soil sample from a forest opening in the southern Appalachian foothills that had never been farmed. Rainfall in the area averages about 50 inches per year and is usually well distributed. The soil is a well-drained Ultisol, or old forest soil, with about 6 inches of brown loam over red-clay to clay-loam subsoil that is about 4 feet thick. The plan was to put in a plot with a basic seed mix of 70 percent wheat and 30 percent clover. This is a good example of a start-from-scratch plot that needs everything. The soil chemist at the lab, Dr. Terrence Fullerton of Agro Services International, was asked to provide a written commentary based on the results. He responded with the following:

"*Sample Description:* The low pH of 4.8 indicates that the soil is very acidic. Wheat and clover grow best at soil pH between 6.0 and 6.8. Lime must therefore be applied to increase the pH. The levels of most of the nutrients are below the optimum range, and this will cause poor plant growth. The levels of minerals critical to animal health, including calcium, magnesium, phosphorus and copper, are also very low. Plants grown on this soil will therefore have poor nutritional value unless proper treatments are used.

Lime: Dolomitic lime is recommended on this soil. In addition to correcting the acidity, it will also provide calcium and magnesium. The entire amount,

Soil Analysis		Interpretation Guide			Fertilizer Suggestions	
Element	lbs./acre	Below	Optimum	Above	Element	lbs./acre
Calcium	323				Calcium	0
Magnesium	52				Magnesium	0
Potassium	75				Potash (K20)	100
Nitrogen	5				Nitrogen	100
Phosphorus	20				Phosphorus	100
Sulfur	49				Sulfur	10
Boron	0.3				Boron	0.7
Copper	2.7				Copper	3
Iron	440				Iron	0
Manganese	5.2				Manganese	10
Zinc	0.9				Zinc	4
Ca/Mg Ratio	3.8				Dolomitic Lime	4,000
Mg/K Ratio	2.7					
pH	4.8					

4,000 lbs./acre, should be applied in a single dose. This should be effective for a few years. The lime should be broadcast evenly over the entire area. If possible, it should be mixed into the soil, as this allows it to react faster and encourages deep root growth. No more lime should be used until soil analysis shows it is needed.

Fertilizers: The fertilizer must contain a balanced amount of each nutrient that is in short supply. Half of the nitrogen should be in slow-release form; this reduces losses by leaching and ensures good, long-term plant growth. For maximum effectiveness, sulfates should be used to provide copper, manganese and zinc.

It may not be possible to obtain a suitable, off-the-shelf fertilizer. It may be necessary to have it custom blended. The exact fertilizer made and its application rate will depend on which raw materials the factory has in stock. A typical formula for this soil will be 13-13-13 plus 1 percent manganese, 0.5 percent zinc, 0.1 percent boron and 0.4 percent copper, applied at a rate of 770 lbs./acre."

Soil samples await testing in a lab.

Because we informed the lab of our goal of providing optimal deer forage, the chemist was able to call our attention to the critical shortage of calcium, magnesium, phosphorus and copper. In most cases, micronutrients are ignored in fertilization, but in this case, copper was necessary, and the rest were added for balance. Copper is an essential nutrient for metabolism and growth in most large herbivores.

Most soil testing labs send you data with a goal of maximizing crop production, because they are usually making recommendations to farmers. If you want to cut back on the amount of fertilizer, you can. You can still get a high quality, nutritious crop, but you'll get less of it. The fertilizer you apply must include all the critical nutrients and be a balanced blend. For example, you could put out only 65 percent of the recommended amount (500 lbs./acre) but the blend must be the same as recommended by the soil test (in this case, 13-13-13). However, it is important to never skimp on the liming requirements. This is critical to allow the fertilizer to be taken up by the plant and not converted to unavailable forms.

by liming. Sulfur is needed in small amounts and is usually not limiting, especially in the East and South where acid rain adds sulfur. If you need sulfur, there are many products that provide sulfur along with other nutrients. Most common is gypsum, which is a combination of calcium and sulfur.

Micronutrients such as iron, manganese, copper, boron and zinc typically only should be added if the soil test indicates that there is a critical shortage. Molybdenum and chlorine are needed in such small amounts that they are rarely limiting.

SOIL TESTING

Soil testing is the key to success. The good news is that it is cheap compared to other aspects of planting food plots. Almost all states have Cooperative Extension programs that will provide basic fertilizer needs from your samples for $4 to $15. You can also get a more detailed evaluation from many of these labs, or from private labs, for about $25 per sample. When you are spending $75 to $250 per acre for lime or fertilizer, you will always save money by knowing exactly what you need to apply.

Planting food plots without conducting a soil test is often a waste of money. You may be able to plant a green plot as an attractant to shoot over by using a popular seed blend and some "off-the-shelf" 10-10-10, but unless you provide a nutrient-balanced feed, you're not optimizing deer nutrition.

Sampling Procedure. You don't need to take a lot of samples if you know how to composite a large area into one sample. Soil testing should be conducted on each food plot because fertility varies based on past history, landscape position and drainage, even on the same piece of property. The procedure is simple – all you need is a bucket and a shovel. See the sidebar on the facing page for a how-to guide.

FERTILIZER APPLICATION

Timing. Soil testing should be done one to three months before planting. It will usually take about two weeks to get the results back and a week to make fertilizer arrangements. Lime should be applied well before planting. If the soil requires a lot of lime – 1 to 4 tons per acre – it is best to apply it at least a month or two before fertilizing and seeding. However, amounts below 1 ton per acre can be applied at the time of planting.

CALIBRATING A FERTILIZER SPREADER

Fertilizer is applied by spreader, typically from a fertilizer company truck, tractor or ATV. Calibration is simple. Fill your spreader with a bag or two of fertilizer, and then, with the spreader running, drive at the speed, gear and RPMs you plan to use during application. Measure the width of application and the distance driven to apply 50 pounds of material. Then calculate the area.

Example: 30-foot-wide band over 300 feet = 9,000 square feet.

One acre equals 43,560 square feet. Divide 43,560 by 9,000 and you find that you applied fertilizer to 0.20 acre. Since you applied 50 pounds, your application rate is 50 pounds per 0.20 acre, or 250 pounds per acre.

If the fertilizer is 34 percent N, as in a 34-0-0 formulation, you have put out 250 pounds x 0.34 = 85 lbs./acre N (a typical application starting out for small grains), and you would only need one pass to apply the fertilizer needed.

1. Start at one end of the plot and walk a zig-zag pattern across the length. The spacing between each sample point should be 30 to 100 feet depending on the size of the plot. You want to have 12 to 15 sample points for each food plot. At each point, stop and push the shovel (or soil probe) straight down to a depth of 8 to 10 inches. Push the shovel forward to form a vertical soil face.

2. Use the shovel to shave a 1-inch slice along the vertical face. This will give you a sample of the whole root zone.

3. Put the slice in the bucket and repeat the process at all the points in the field.

4. Mix soil in the bucket thoroughly, and dump the contents out on a plastic sheet.

5. Use the shovel to cut the sample pile into fourths. If a quarter of the sample is too much to fit in the soil bag, cut a quarter in half and put it in the sample bag.

6. Fill out the data required on the sample bag, and you are done. Be sure the sample number represents something you can use to identify that field. For example, a ridge field could be labeled sample R-1, and a bottom field labeled sample B-1.

7. Send the sample to the lab. Be sure to include the crops that you intend to plant or fertilize. The lab will send you a report with recommendations for your plots.

PHOTOS BY PHIL FRESHLEY

POTASH & PHOSPHATE INSTITUTE

POTASSIUM DEFICIENCY

*Some soils may have ample levels of most nutrients yet lack one or a few critical elements.
This clover, for example, is getting adequate amounts of critical nutrients except one – potassium.
A soil test can pinpoint these deficiencies and guide you in correcting soils before you plant.*

Most commonly, fertilizer is applied to the site immediately before seeding so it will be mixed in during seedbed preparation. In high-production settings, a second application may be surface broadcast mid-rotation to boost production. This is called topdressing, and it usually involves applying nitrogen to grasses or potassium to legumes.

Amount. Fertilizer needs must consider the amount required by the crop minus the amount present in the soil and the amount that will be produced during the growing season by decomposition of organic materials. Most labs have standard amounts of N-P-K for each crop type. Therefore it is essential to tell the lab what you are growing and what time of year. Most small-grain crops will use 75 to 125 lbs./acre each of nitrogen, phosphate and potash for maximum production over a growing season. If your soil and organics have retained 25 lbs./acre of each of these nutrients from previous seasons, your fertilizer needs will be reduced accordingly.

As a general rule, follow the recommendations of the soil-testing lab. The only exception may be where you have organic material content in the soil greater than

3 percent. In this case, you can usually get by with 20 to 40 percent less fertilizer, especially where organic matter exceeds 5 percent. Consult with the soil testing lab if they find an organic matter content over 3 percent. They should be familiar with what happens in your region and climate conditions.

Rate Calculations. The rate of fertilizer application is based on a per-acre basis. One acre contains 43,560 square feet. To determine your fertilizer needs you must:

1. Measure the width and length of the food plot.
   Example: *Plot is 320 feet long and 90 feet wide*

2. Calculate the area: (length x width) divided by 43,560 = acres
   Example: *320 x 90 = 28,800/43,560 = 0.66 acres*

3. Determine the nitrogen needed based on crop uptake and soil test.
   Example: *Winter wheat needs 100 lbs./acre N per year*
   Soil N present = 25 lbs./acre from test results
   Fertilizer N: N required minus N present in soil
   Fertilizer N: 100 - 25 = 75 lbs./acre N

4. Determine the amount of fertilizer per acre based on the formula.
   Example: *Ammonium nitrate is 34-0-0 (34 percent N or 0.34 pounds of N per pound of fertilizer)*
   So: 75 pounds N divided by 0.34 pounds N per pound of material = 220 lbs./acre of fertilizer

5. Determine the amount needed for the food plot based on area.
   Example: *One acre requires 220 pounds 34-0-0; food plot is 0.66 acre. So: 220 pounds of fertilizer x 0.66 = 145 pounds for the plot (or three 50-lb. bags).*

You can conduct this calculation for each nutrient needed. If you are going to apply to many acres, it is often worthwhile to get your local supplier to produce a custom blend that has everything at the right proportions.

A Cautionary Tale from the Author

When you get the optimal fertility on a site, you will grow plants to their full potential. This includes all plants. Last year on one of the properties I help manage we applied everything needed and created a plant production dynamo. We also received 6 or more inches of rain in each month, May through August. You can have too much of a good thing. We grew iron clay peas, rape, corn and other forages and had great responses. We also grew one of the most prolific stands of crabgrass I have ever seen. Deer used these plots regularly, but at least half the fertilizer was squandered on a plant that was useless. The lesson is that fertilization is only one component of producing quality food plots. Weed control can be equally important, so read every chapter of this book.

A PRACTICAL GUIDE TO
APPLYING AGLIME

BY RANS THOMAS

Aglime for food plots comes in two basic forms – bagged lime and bulk lime. Both are ground limestone, however bagged lime comes in two forms: a finely ground powder and pellets.

Pelletized bagged lime is simply finely ground limestone formed into pellets with a soluble adhesive for ease of distribution. With any type of lime, the more finely it is ground, the faster it takes effect in the soil, but the sooner the effect will go away. High-quality pelletized lime is usually finely ground. The fineness is indicated on the bag by how much of the lime will pass through a mesh screen of a certain fineness. Lime that passes through a 60 to 100 mesh-per-inch sieve is of adequate fineness, while lime that passes through a 100 to 200 mesh-per-inch sieve is very finely ground, like most pelletized lime products. Again, the more finely the lime is ground, the faster it affects soil pH, but the sooner the effect wears off.

Bagged, pelletized lime is quick-acting and easy to apply with a gravity-feed spreader. However, it is much more expensive than bulk lime, so it is best for small or remote plots that can't be reached with bulk-lime equipment.

Bagged pelletized lime usually costs $2.50 to $3.50 per 40-lb. bag. Other than price, the disadvantage of using bagged lime is the time and labor it takes to haul, dispense and dispose of several individual bags. At a 1-ton-per-acre application rate, which is common, 50 of the 40-lb. bags will be needed per acre.

Bulk dolomitic aglime has a texture much like moist sand. Bulk lime costs around $25 to $50 per ton, although it may range as low as $11/ton in states where lime quarries are common. It is best to go with bulk lime in food plot preparation for the following reasons:

1. Bulk lime is less expensive. Applied at a rate of 1 ton per acre, bulk lime may cost anywhere from $11 to $50 per acre.
2. Bulk lime that is more coarsely ground has a longer residual effect in the soil, which should reduce the need for lime application to once every three to six years in some cases (follow annual soil testing results to know when to re-apply).
3. Bulk lime application can be much easier and take less time than applying bagged lime using the following "tricks of the trade."

APPLYING BULK AGLIME

Bulk lime and powdered bag lime cannot be applied with a gravity-feed type spreader because it has a minimum 10 percent moisture content, and it will become impacted in the hopper. It is most often applied with a belt-feed spreader. This type

GETTING THE LIME OUT

Pictured at right are four main options for distributing lime on food plots.

1) Spreader truck: truck and driver can be hired from a local farm supply or Co-op outlets, but good road access is a must.

2) Pull-behind, belt-feed spreader: can be borrowed from Co-op outlets and pulled with your tractor or truck.

3) Pull-behind drop spreader: small enough for use with an ATV but, if they have an agitator, will distribute bulk and powdered lime as well as pelletized lime.

4) Broadcast spreader: both pull-behind and PTO-driven models available, but only bagged, pelletized lime can be distributed.

CRAIG HARPER

B+H ENTERPRISES

of spreader consists of a large container mounted on a trailer or truck body with large flotation tires. At the bottom of the container is a chain-link belt that moves the contents out of the back of the spreader and onto two winged distribution pans.

There are three types of belt-feed spreaders: a) a self-contained spreader truck; b) a hydraulically operated, pull-behind spreader; and c) a mechanically operated, pull-behind spreader.

By far, the easiest option is hiring a spreader truck to apply lime for you, but this is only an option for plots with good road access. All hydraulically operated spreaders, including self-contained trucks and pull-behind spreaders, are most useful for large plots. They are difficult to

UNDERSTANDING SOILS AND SOIL FERTILITY

STAGING AREA

Bulk lime can be delivered to your property in a number of ways. You can borrow a trailer like the one above (each bin can be tipped hydraulically to dispense lime into spreaders or truck beds). You can also have the lime dumped at a staging area and distributed with a front-end-loader or other equipment.

calibrate correctly for most of us and are normally set to cast the contents 40 to 50 feet on either side. Because many food plots are often only 1 or 2 acres in size and take on a variety of shapes, you will probably cast some lime outside of the planting area if you use a hydraulic spreader.

A mechanically operated, pull-type spreader is ideal for applying both lime and fertilizer on small food plots. The good news is that many lime and fertilizer dealers keep pull-behind spreaders on their yard and will loan them to you to apply the products you have purchased. This type of spreader has an arm-and-wheel assembly on one side. When you are ready to spread lime, the wheel on the arm is engaged against the large flotation tire of the trailer. As you pull the trailer forward, its wheels turn the mechanical drive wheel, which then drives the chain-link belt and the distribution pans of the spreader. The distance the contents are cast is determined by the speed at which you pull the trailer. Using this spreader, you can lime narrow food plots without overcasting lime. Another advantage is that the gate at the back of the spreader controls the application rate. Once the gate is set, which is a simple procedure, you will be applying the same rate per acre at any speed. The arm-and-wheel assemblies on some trailers can be engaged by a hydraulic cylinder if your tractor has remote hydraulic hook-ups, or the wheel can be engaged manually. Do not put your tractor in reverse while the spreader-wheel is engaged to the trailer tire – on most models this will damage the mechanism, and your lime program may suddenly become much more expensive than you estimated.

There are small versions of pull-behind, belt-feed spreaders made for ATVs that work well, but the smaller hopper means more time spent driving to the lime pile for refilling.

Most pull-types can hold 5 to 6 tons of lime, meaning that at a 1 ton/acre rate you can apply lime to about 5 acres of food plots without dealing with bags. If you want to borrow a spreader, reserve it ahead of time as they are popular with farmers around liming time. Most dealers will load the spreader and calibrate it for the rate that you wish to apply. Simply go to the dealer's location, connect to the spreader with a heavy-duty pickup, and take it to your land, where a tractor (55 hp or greater) will be used to pull the spreader. You can even apply the lime with a four-wheel-drive pickup under dry conditions, but it can be difficult getting started with a full load.

SIDE-DUMP TRAILER

For large acreages, you may have to return to the farm supply for several refills. To avoid this problem, ask your dealer if they can provide a side-dump trailer. These trailers usually consist of four to five large containers that can be filled with several tons of lime each. The containers can be dumped hydraulically. Once the trailer is dropped off, you can dump the lime into the spreader as needed, allowing you to apply lime to a large area without returning to the dealer for refills.

BULK LIME DUMP SITES

Bulk lime can also be brought to your property in a dump truck and piled at a staging area. If you have access to a bucket loader or front-end loader, then a bulk lime dump site may be your best option. Bulk lime can be simply dumped on the

LIME CHECK-LIST

The following is a lime application check-list you may find useful whether using bagged or bulk lime.

1) Pull soil samples from plots in advance of planting and submit them for testing. Allow yourself enough time to get results back and still apply lime at least 60 to 90 days ahead of planting.

2) Cross reference your soil sample pH results with the recommended soil pH level for your plant species to determine the application rate of lime.

3) Determine the individual acreage of each plot and the total acreage.

4) Contact your local seed and fertilizer dealers to locate bulk lime. If your plots are large enough and have good road access, arrange with the dealer to have the lime applied by a spreader truck. Arrange to meet the truck on your property.

5) If you need to spread your own lime, reserve the spreader well in advance and ask that the spreader be pre-calibrated to your desired application rate if the rate is fairly consistent across the plots that will be limed.

6) Spread lime on bare dirt for optimum reaction with the soil. Incorporate the lime by tilling 3 to 4 inches deep after spreading.

7) In larger food plots allow 20 to 30 percent overlap of the outside edge of the spread pattern with a pull-type spreader. Application amounts are weaker in the fringes of the pattern.

8) Return a spreader better than you found it, and you will always be welcome to use it again.

ground, but you may not be able to load the last of it effectively because it will mix in with the soil on the bottom of the pile. If you choose this delivery method, then it may be in your best interest to create a lime dump on your property.

Lime dumps usually consist of a clean, hard bottom with retainer walls of some form on three sides. The most common dump sites have a concrete floor with two side walls and a back wall. Some are dug into a hillside or into the ground. Some have retainer walls made of concrete or piling posts. These sites can help accommodate faster loading, more efficient use of lime, and defer the potential rental cost of a side-dump trailer — but they are only useful when used in conjunction with a bucket loader.

Equipment Needs

By Jim Wills Jr., Ph.D.
and Craig A. Harper, Ph.D.

EQUIPMENT NEEDS

The equipment you will need for planting and managing food plots will vary depending on the size of your food plot program. Small-scale operations can be successful with only a small tractor or ATV, a disk harrow and a hand-held spreader. More extensive programs will benefit from more powerful tractors with a large harrow, no-till drill, cultipacker and a boom sprayer. Indeed, you can establish successful plots with nothing more than a backpack sprayer and a hand-held spreader. However, equipment size and availability are important factors when planning your food plot program.

POWER SOURCES FOR FOOD PLOT IMPLEMENTS: TRACTOR OR ATV?

An important initial decision is whether an ATV or a tractor is required. Will an ATV pull the necessary equipment, or is a tractor necessary? What size tractor is needed? What about four-wheel drive? What location or size food plot dictates the need for use of an ATV? Obviously, the answers to these questions depend on how much you are willing to spend, what types of equipment you have available, the size and accessibility of the area to be planted, and soil conditions.

Although ATVs may pull some larger equipment, their transmissions and drive trains may be exposed to excessive strain and wear. Most ATVs simply are not designed for heavy towing jobs. Ground-engaging equipment such as sub-soilers, plows and disks require significant power for proper operation. Pulling heavy loads at low speeds can really stress ATV drive trains and frames and can cause the engine to overheat if operated for extended periods. Liquid-cooled ATV engines are better

EQUIPMENT TYPE	SIZE/WEIGHT	RECOMMENDED ATV/TRACTOR SIZE
BioLogic Disc	52 inch/347 pounds	300 cc-400 cc
BioLogic Disc	52 inch/462 pounds	500 cc
BioLogic Box Scraper	48 inch/205 pounds	300 cc minimum
Firminator	48 inch/800 pounds	400 cc minimum
Plotmaster 400	48 inch	30 hp tractor/large ATV
Plotmaster 600	72 inch	30-40 hp tractor
Plotmaster 800	96 inch	40-60 hp tractor
Summit Plot-Mule Disk	44 inch/425 pounds	350 cc minimum
Weekend Warrior Disk	52 inch/300 pounds	Large ATV

suited to pulling heavy loads for extended periods. Stick with equipment recommended for ATVs and leave heavier pulling jobs for a tractor or truck. Most ATV
equipment manufacturers suggest a minimum size ATV engine for their specific
product. Manufacturer's recommendations, such as those presented on the facing
page, should be referenced before you select equipment.

ATVs are best suited for food plots in remote locations or small food plots of
a half acre or less. Any food plots larger than 1 acre are best handled with a tractor.
Trucks work fine for towing implements that do not need a three-point hitch for lift-
ing and lowering or a power-take-off (PTO) drive system. However, a truck doesn't
have the maneuverability or traction of a small tractor. Whenever you are using

ECONOMY OF SCALE

You may be wondering if your ATV can tackle the job of serious
food plot management, or if the program you have in mind calls
for a tractor. ATVs are versatile, and they are useful for managing a few, small plots. Small tractors in the 30 to 50 hp range
are the next step up. As features such as four-wheel drive
are added and tractor size increases, so does cost. But a
tractor like the
one above can
accomplish more
work and a wider
range of tasks in
less time.

equipment that requires hard pulling for long periods of time and when working plots in heavy soils, a tractor is a necessity. Tractors are also needed for three-point-hitch implements that need to be raised and lowered or when using implements such as rotovators, mowers and fertilizer spreaders operated with PTO drives. Although there are electrical systems available to lift and lower with ATVs, they are slow and not as durable as hydraulic lifts on tractors.

> ## Do You Need 4WD?
>
> *When shopping for tractors, is it necessary to spend the extra money for front-wheel assist — also known as four-wheel drive? A 2WD tractor is perfect for less-rugged conditions and light-duty work. The 4WD is excellent for hilly and muddy terrain while aiding in demanding tasks such as advanced food plot work and habitat management. In short, if you plan on producing advanced quality food plots and you can afford it, go for the 4WD.*
>
> *—Brian Sheppard*

Small utility tractors in the 30 to 50 hp range are well suited to work food plots in the 1- to 5-acre range. Larger tractors can do the job quicker, but they are more expensive. Four-wheel-drive tractors can handle larger loads than similar-sized two-wheel-drive tractors because of increased traction, but there is some sacrifice in maneuverability. Although a four-wheel-drive tractor costs more than a similar-sized two-wheel-drive tractor, the extra traction can be invaluable in some soil conditions and slopes. In smaller food plots where space for turning is limited, four-wheel-drive tractors in the 20 hp range can be ideal.

POWER	PRICE RANGE	ADVANTAGES	DISADVANTAGES
ATV	Moderate	Useful when planting small plots in remote areas.	Limited pulling ability; May require specialized tillage and planting accessories.
Tractor: 30 to 50 hp	Moderate	Versatile; Works well with small-to-moderate sized food plot programs; Can handle moderately heavy tasks.	Under-sized for larger acreages and really heavy work.
Tractor: 50 to 80 hp	High	The food plot workhorse; Needed for moderate-sized food plot programs; With more power and larger implements, performs tasks much faster than smaller tractors.	Too large for some small plots.
Tractor: 80 to 100 hp	Very High	Needed when considerable acreage is involved; Operates large implements.	Too large for small plots and those with limited access.
Tractor: 100 hp and up	Very High	Needed when large acreage is involved; Operates the largest implements.	Expensive to operate; Too large for moderate-sized plots and those with limited access. Limited adaptability for other uses.

Preparing the Site

Mowers/Drip Torches. Regardless of size, all plots must be properly prepared for tillage and planting. Often the existing vegetation on the plots must be removed before the soil can be tilled. Too much vegetation can even inhibit the effective application of herbicides to "clean up" the area. If your food plot area is overgrown, it's best to use a rotary mower, disk mower or flail mower to remove tall growth and prepare the site for spraying. It also may be important to remove the thatch left on the field, because it will shield the living vegetation from contact with the herbicides. Haying or burning the residue enables fresh growth to be sprayed more effectively, usually one to two weeks after mowing or two to four weeks after burning. Burning fields is easy to do with a drip torch – you can purchase these from forestry supply companies, and some state forestry agencies loan drip torches for use in prescribed burning. Before beginning your burn, you should contact your local forestry officials for advice and weather conditions. Many state forestry agencies require that you call for a permit to conduct a burn. Also before burning, disk a

Drip torches are available from forestry supply dealers.

firebreak completely around the area to be burned. Start burning on the downwind edge of the field. After a burned area of 30 to 50 feet is created, burn the rest of the field by stripping across the field 30 to 50 feet ahead of the fire front. Request on-site assistance from your state forestry agency if you are inexperienced with prescribed fire.

Sprayers. You can spray food plots of less than an acre with a 4- or 5-gallon backpack sprayer. A 4½-foot boom attachment makes spraying small plots with backpack sprayers most effective. Most herbicides are applied at a rate of 20 gallons per acre total mixture, although low volume applications of a more concentrated mixture – as low as 10 gallons per acre – can be effective. Tractor- or ATV-mounted boom sprayers are more effective on plots larger than an acre. Boom sprayers are available in many widths, but boom lengths of 12 to 24 feet are common and practical when spraying 1- to 3-acre fields. Because the boom will extend far past the width of the tractor, be careful to prevent trees, fenceposts and other objects from snagging the boom when turning or following irregular edges around plots. Some more expensive boom sprayers can be equipped with foam or dye markers at each end of the boom to help prevent spray overlap or skips between passes. Calibration of sprayers is essential to ensure proper application rates. Calibration is relatively easy and should be done every time herbicides are applied if you change driving speed, nozzle size or spraying pressure.

HOW TO CALIBRATE A SPRAYER

To calibrate a sprayer, including backpack sprayers, select a driving (or walking) speed that you can easily maintain across the area to be sprayed. Next, select a spraying pressure – this is usually based on the spray nozzle type used for application. Spraying pressures of 20 to 40 pounds per square inch (psi) are ideal for herbicide application. If the sprayer produces a fine mist that drifts easily, the pressure is too high. Most backpack sprayers are capable of generating pressures of 20 to 40 psi , and power sprayers can be adjusted easily within this pressure range.

The next step is to select a nozzle type and size. A 0.2 or 0.3 gallon-per-minute nozzle is usually needed to apply 20 gallons per acre at speeds around 4 mph and spray pressures of about 30 psi. Fan-type nozzles work best for herbicide application. A TeeJet XR8002 or XR8003 is a good nozzle for herbicide application. These nozzles are usually spaced 20 inches apart on a sprayer boom to achieve good broadcast coverage. Backpack sprayers with one nozzle usually spray an effective width of about 20 inches; they are more efficient if a 4½-foot boom with four nozzles is attached.

To select the length of the calibration course, divide 340 by the nozzle spacing in feet. A 20-inch nozzle spacing is 1.67 feet, so 340 divided by 1.67 equals 204 feet. This is the length of the calibration course for 20-inch nozzle spacing. Next, time how long it takes you to walk or drive the sprayer the length of the calibration course. At 4 mph, it will take about 36 seconds to travel 204 feet. Precise travel speed is important. Catch the spray from one nozzle for the same length of time it takes to travel the calibration course, and measure the amount of spray liquid you collect. The number of ounces is equal to the application rate in gallons per acre.

For example: If you collect 22 ounces from a nozzle, the application rate of spray material is 22 gallons per acre. If the calibration rate is more than 25 percent off from the desired rate, change nozzle size to achieve the desired rate. You can increase or decrease travel speed, but this will either slow down your job or result in speeds that can become unsafe or impractical.

SPRAYERS	PRICE RANGE	ADVANTAGES	DISADVANTAGES
Mounted or Pull-behind Sprayer	Low to Moderate	Necessary for plots too large to spray with a backpack sprayer.	Although some are chain-driven or electric, most models require PTO.
Backpack Sprayer	Cheap	Useful and necessary for all food plot programs.	

CARROLL JOHNSON III

MUST-HAVE EQUIPMENT

Even if you own a larger tractor- or ATV-mounted sprayer unit like the one shown above, a backpack sprayer will still have many uses for spot treatments and other applications. If a backpack sprayer is all you have, a boom attachment like the one shown on the left increases your efficiency on larger areas. With any herbicide, always follow label directions closely to achieve maximum effectiveness while using the least amount of herbicide possible.

CRAIG HARPER

EQUIPMENT NEEDS

PHOTOS BY BRIAN SHEPPARD

Deep Impact

When you have soil-compaction problems or heavy thatch to break up, subsoiling equipment can be used for deep tillage. Options include moldboard plows (top, left), sub-soilers (a two-shank model is shown top, right), paratills (bottom, left) and chisel or spring-tooth plows (bottom, right). These implements will not be needed regularly, so if possible, borrow them when needed or buy them used.

Hand Tools For Site Preparation. Rocks, stumps, roots, and tree trunks can damage tillage equipment, resulting in significant repair costs. A dozer or front-end loader is most effective for cleaning a site when creating new plots, but hand tools may suffice when working in smaller plots. In some cases, you may need to cut roots with an axe or saw. Tree trunks or logs may require some chainsaw work to reduce pieces to a manageable size. Rocks may need loosening with a pick or shovel before removal. A small trailer behind an ATV, tractor or truck is handy for hauling larger objects off the plot site.

Preparing Seedbeds

Proper seedbed preparation is critical to the success of most food plot species planted in food plots. Soil conditions vary widely from one location to another and perhaps even between food plots on your land, and a range of equipment may be called for, whether you borrow, rent or buy.

Sub-soilers. If you have heavy soils with underlying hard pans, you may need to sub-soil prior to tillage. Sub-soiling to a depth of 16 to 24 inches will fracture any hard layers that prevent water filtration and root growth (see Chapter 4, Understanding Soils, for more on detecting hardpan problems). Sub-soiling aerates the soil and permits rain water to slowly soak into the lower layers, creating a moisture reservoir during dry periods. In addition, plant roots can penetrate the loose soils easier and find more consistent moisture than near the surface. Deep roots increase drought resistance.

Sub-soilers consist of a strong, narrow steel shank with a standard chisel point mounted on the bottom. The shank is usually mounted to a bar, which attaches to the tractor with a three-point hitch. As many as 12 individual shanks may be mounted on heavy, tubular steel tool bars to increase the width of the sub-soiler. Sub-soilers require 15 to 20 hp per shank to operate 16 to 22 inches deep, depending on soil type. Sandy and loamy soils are less likely to need sub-soiling and require less horsepower to subsoil than clay soils. However, roots or rocks can restrict the sub-soiler shanks and require additional power. If roots are present, work at a slower speed to prevent equipment damage. Sub-soiling in one direction and then repeating at 90 degrees to the original direction will do an excellent job of loosening tight soils. Chisel plows (also called spring-tooth or all-purpose plows) are similar to sub-soilers, but penetrate only 8 to 10 inches deep. They may be used if it is not possible or necessary to till as deeply as a sub-soiler.

Moldboard Plows. Moldboard plows are useful if there is a lot of dead thatch on the site and burning is not possible. If you don't have much thatch remaining, you can skip these implements and move directly to disk harrows or spring-tooth harrows. Because moldboard plows turn over the top 8 to 16 inches of soil, they incorporate the remaining vegetation into the topsoil and help build the organic material in the soil. Typically, moldboard plows should not be used to "disk in" lime and fertilizer because they often turn up a deep layer of infertile, acidic soil that will require additional liming. Moldboard plows are available in single-, double-, or triple-plow models. Approximately 20 to 30 hp is needed per plow.

Disk Harrows Or All-Purpose Harrows. Disk harrows are good choices to break up the soil, incorporate lime and fertilizer and prepare the seedbed. A disk harrow is a common implement on most farms and is suitable for many types of tillage. They are available in a wide range of sizes and widths. Smaller 4- to 6-foot models are ideal for small food plots and can be pulled with a large ATV. Larger harrows require a tractor, and the larger the harrow, the more horsepower required. Larger disk harrows can make short work of planting large fields. On many disk harrows, you can adjust the cutting angles of the blades. The greater the sideways angle of the blades, the more aggressive the cutting action. Round disks work well in many soils, but notched disks are useful where maximum cutting is necessary in heavy soils and when firebreaks are being established. Depending on your soil conditions and the size of your harrow, you may have to make several passes to work the soil into a suitable seedbed, especially if you plan to plant small seed species such as clovers.

When using disk harrows, be sure to raise the harrow when making sharp turns at the ends of the field. This is particularly important when using a three-point-hitch-mounted harrow. Leaving the harrow in the ground when turning can bend or break the disks or the harrow frame, or perhaps cause an accident.

Harrows with adjustable disks can also be useful for covering larger seeds such as small grains, peas or beans that have been top-sown by a seed spreader. Adjust the angle of cut to slight or none and lightly disk the field, but be sure you don't set the disks or the draft too deep.

Spring-tooth harrows consist of five to nine or more heavy, curved, pointed off-set shanks attached to heavy springs and a frame. This type of harrow will cut and loosen soil 4 to 12 inches deep. They are useful where little or no thatch is found and may substitute for moldboard plows or disk harrows.

Rotovators. A rotovator is essentially a large rototiller that operates from the tractor's PTO (*a rotovator is shown on the bottom of the facing page*). Rotovators are generally not necessary for most soils. However, they can be particularly useful when preparing fine seedbeds for small-seeded plants such as clover that need good seed-to-soil contact for germination and seedling development. Except in sandy soils, it

Soil Tillage	Price Range	Advantages	Disadvantages
Hydraulic Disk Harrow (bog disk)	High	Needed for moderate to large acreage; Works soil much faster and more thoroughly than a standard farm disk. Facilitates incorporating lime/fertilizers into root zone very well.	Requires a 50 to 80 hp tractor or larger.
"Farm" Disk (or spring-tooth harrows)	Low	Most popular food plot implement; Useful in many situations, including habitat management applications.	Usually does not perform as well as larger, heavier disks; May not handle existing, dense thatch/vegetation.
Moldboard Plow (bottom plow)	Low	Useful for incorporating dead thatch and existing vegetation into the root zone.	Requires a 30 to 60 hp tractor minimum for best results.
Subsoiler	Low	Needed in some soils to break hardpans, improve drainage and increase soil-water retention.	Requires 30 hp or larger tractor for best results.
Cultipacker	Low to Moderate	Most useful and necessary when planting clovers and other small-seeded plants on a cultivated seedbed; Can be pulled with ATVs or tractors.	
Rotovator	Moderate	Great for preparing fine seedbeds, if needed.	Requires PTO and follow-up with a cultipacker.

CRAIG HARPER

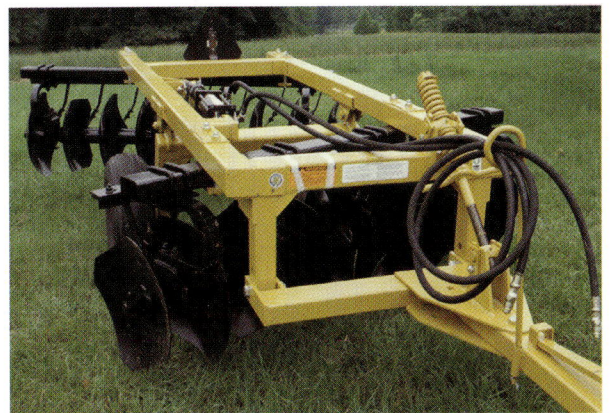

HEAVY DUTY

Offset disk harrows like this one use a single front gang of disks and a single rear gang, "offset" at opposing angles, for serious tillage, such as breaking new ground or plowing firebreaks. Tandem disk harrows, which use two front gangs and two rear gangs forming an "X" shape, are for more general management of food plots.

is always necessary to follow rotovating with one or two passes with a cultipacker before seeding. To determine if you need an additional pass of the cultipacker, walk over the field. If your feet sink more than about 1 inch, make another pass.

Rotovators are most effective when used after plowing or disking, particularly in rocky soils. On unplowed ground, rocks can damage and severely shorten the lifespan of the rotovator. Also, if the plot has not been plowed or disked, and rocks or thatch are present, these materials will tend to rise to the top of the seedbed after rotovating. This can result in much lower germination rates.

LIME AND FERTILIZER SPREADERS

Adjusting soil pH where necessary is critical for optimal plant growth. In many regions, agricultural limestone is used to raise the pH to an acceptable level. It is most economical and efficient to have a local fertilizer dealer apply your lime by truck, particularly when your soil test

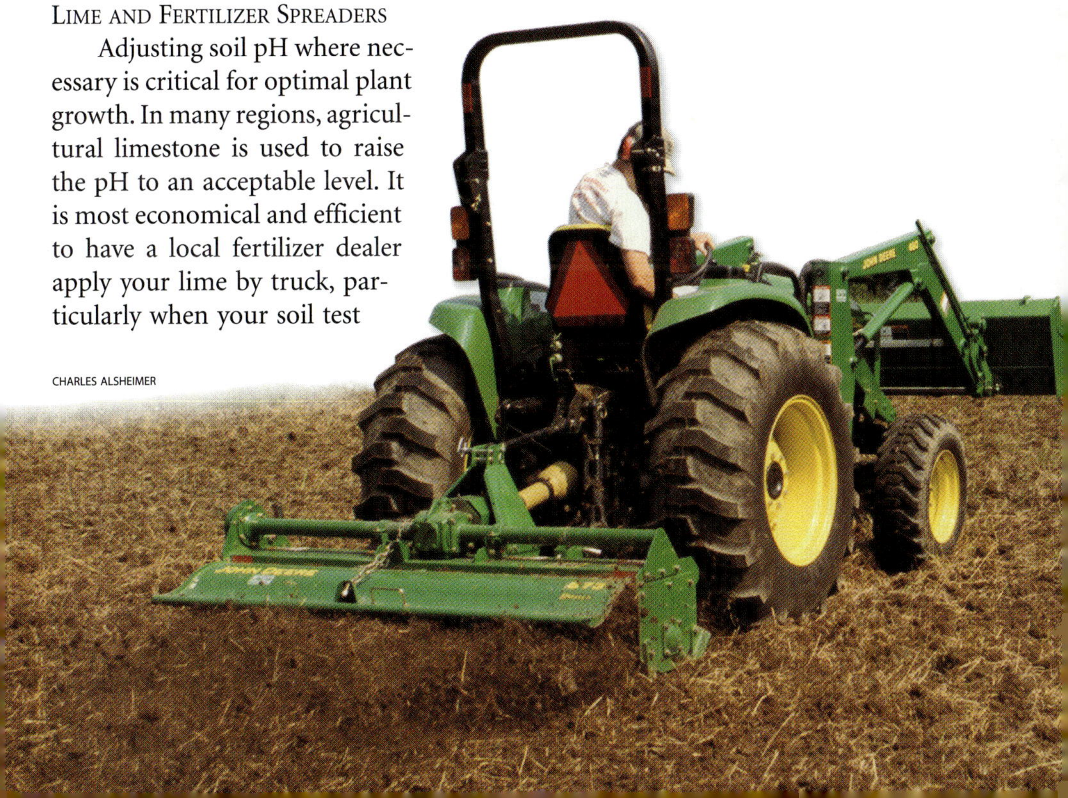

CHARLES ALSHEIMER

EQUIPMENT NEEDS

Smooth Blades: Also known as "finishing" blades, smooth blades have the least aggressive cutting depth but are more economical, more durable and cut more evenly. Best for smoothing tilled soils and cutting light crop stubble while preparing previously planted ground.

Scalloped Blades (*shown here*): Moderately aggressive cutting depth, and the deeper the scallops or notches, the more aggressive the cutting ability. Better than smooth blades for breaking new ground or chopping soil with heavy clods or moderately dense vegetation. Probably the best "all around" disk.

Square Blades (*shown below*): The most aggressive type of disk. These disks are usually installed in an alternating arrangement so that every other disk's cutting point is contacting the soil at any time. This distributes the weight of the harrow across fewer points, allowing deeper penetration. Useful for breaking new ground in tough soils or with heavy structure or trash, such as roots, limbs, stumps or heavy vegetation.

Combination: Rather than buy two sets of harrows, place scalloped blades on the front gang of your harrow and finishing or smooth blades on the rear gang. This allows the front gang to do the cutting while the rear gang smooths the seedbed.

calls for 2 or more tons of lime per acre. However, lime can be spread on smaller plots by using several types of mechanical spreaders or small push-spreaders. Cyclone spreaders are fast and cover acreage quickly but only work well when using pelletized lime, which is more expensive. Drop spreaders spreading pulverized lime are slower but can place material more accurately on the ground and around edges than cyclone spreaders. You can also use both types of spreaders for fertilizer applications prior to seeding or for top-dressing after plots are established. For more on practical application of lime options for spreading, see Chapter 4.

PLANTING THE PLOT

Seed Spreaders. Seeding equipment for food plots varies from hand seeders to large grain drills and planters. For smaller plots, a shoulder-slung hand seeder does an excellent job for top-sowing. These hand seeders also are useful on larger plots when top-sowing clovers and other small seed because they provide a more even distribution than cyclone spreaders. On larger plots, three-point-hitch or pull-behind cyclone spreaders work well, especially when top-sowing larger seed such as cowpeas, wheat, milo and sunflowers. Mixing seed with fertilizer or pelletized lime will increase volume and prevent downward movement of smaller seed in the hopper during spreading operations. Also,

SPREADERS ALL AROUND

Broadcast spreaders for seed, fertilizer and pelletized forms of lime come in many shapes and sizes. Options include PTO-driven "cyclone" spreaders like the one attached to the tractor shown above. There are also smaller, motorized versions that can be attached to ATVs (also seen above) or truck bumpers. The least expensive options include wheel-driven, "push" lawn spreaders and over-the-shoulder or hand-crank spreaders (shown at right).

planning for at least two passes over the plot will help prevent calibration errors and result in a more uniform stand.

Drills and Planters. For larger plots, a grain drill or corn planter can provide several benefits. Drills are also useful on smaller plots, provided there is enough area to operate the equipment. Grain drills are available in sizes from 4 feet up to 24 feet or more. Conventional grain drills require seedbed preparation prior to planting seed. No-till grain drills have an opening coulter – a specially fluted disk blade – that eliminates the necessity of seedbed preparation. Behind the coulter are double disk openers which widen a slot in the soil for the seeding tubes to deposit seed. The opening is then closed with a packer wheel. A good no-till drill is expensive, about $1,200 to $1,500 per foot of width. However, many seed and feed stores and some county NRCS offices rent drills by the day or by the acre.

No-till drills have several advantages over conventional grain drills. Because seedbed preparation is not necessary, no-till drills save time, fuel and wear on

EQUIPMENT NEEDS

Seed Hopper

Seed Tubes

Opener Disks

PRECISION PLANTER

A conventional grain drill like the one above can plant seed in uniform rows and at uniform and pre-set depths, eliminating waste from overseeding, throwing seed out of the plot, and planting too shallow or too deep — problems that can occur with broadcasting. Agitators in the hopper are turned by the rotation of the tires, releasing seeds into the seed tubes at regular intervals. The tubes deposit the seeds in the furrows created by the opener disks. The results of planting with a grain drill are seen below. More elaborate drills include large- and small-seed hoppers, allowing you to drill different sizes of seeds at two different depths at the same time. "No-till" grain drills (right) can cut furrows in unplowed ground, allowing you to drill into remnants of previous crops without disking first. This reduces soil erosion, conserves soil moisture, helps discourage weeds and saves fuel and time.

BRIAN SHEPPARD

Seeding	Price Range	Advantages	Disadvantages
Hand seeder	Cheap	Useful and necessary for all food plot programs.	Slow
No-till Drill	High	Most useful when planting large acreage; speeds up planting time; provides uniform seed distribution and planting depth.	Expensive
Corn planter	Moderate	Very convenient when planting corn and a few other crops; provides uniform seed distribution and planting depth .	Some are difficult to calibrate
Drop spreader	Moderate	Useful for accurate and precise lime spreading.	Not useful for large plots
Cyclone spreader	Low	Very useful and efficient when spreading fertilizers and planting medium-to-large seed (e.g., milo, wheat, sunflowers, cowpeas, etc.).	Most require PTO

machinery. Weed seed already in the soil seedbank between the rows are not disturbed by seedbed preparation and therefore are less likely to germinate. In addition, soil moisture is conserved by not tilling.

Most seed drills will complete the seeding operation in a single pass. Many models come with two hoppers for planting small or larger seeds, which means that mixtures such as wheat and clover can be planted in a single pass.

Conventional or no-till corn planters can be used to plant larger-seeded plants such as corn, soybeans and cowpeas. They consist of separate seeding units for each row mounted on a tool bar frame. Four- to eight-row planters are most common, but single- or double-row units work well for small acreages. No-till planters will have an opening coulter mounted in front of the seed opening disks to cut a slot in the soil. The seeding disks are followed by gauge wheels and packer wheels to control seed depth and cover the seed with soil. Some

S&S EQUIPMENT

This corn planter is a two-row model. Four- to eight-row models are also available, as are no-till models.

planters also have fertilizer boxes to dispense fertilizer beside the seed as they are planted. The planter also may have insecticide and fungicide applicators that dispense these materials as the seeds are planted.

Some corn planters require seeding plates in the seed boxes. These plates are shaped and sized to the variety of seed planted. Some types of planters use air pressure or a vacuum to assist with seed metering. The air drums used in these planters also require sizing to seed type and seed size used, similar to the plate-type planters.

Another type of planting implement is the all-in-one unit, usually designed for use with large ATVs or small tractors. These implements appeared in the 1990s

> ## CALIBRATING A SEED DRILL
>
> Seed drills must be calibrated to verify the seeding rate. To calibrate a drill, measure the operating width of the drill, and select a calibration course length at least 300 feet long. Set the drill's seeding device for the size and type of seed sown. Most drills have a seeding rate chart on the inside of the seed box lid. If the seed is not listed on the chart, select rates for similar size seed. Spread seed evenly over the bottom of the seed box. Detach seed drop tubes from the opening devices at the bottom ends of the tubes and attach plastic bags to the ends of the seed tubes with rubber bands or string. Operate the seed drill along the measured calibration course. Remove the plastic bags and weigh the seed in ounces and convert to lbs./acre.
>
> *Example*: A 7 foot-wide drill pulled along a 300-foot calibration course would cover 2,100 square feet. Because one acre is 43,560 square feet, this would represent 0.048 acres. If 33 ounces of seed was caught in the bags, that converts to 2.06 pounds of seed. To convert seeding rate to lbs./acre: 2.06 pounds divided by 0.048 = 42.9 lbs./acre. Increase or decrease the seed openings on the drill as needed, then calibrate again.

to meet the growing demand for equipment designed for food plots, and a number of companies now manufacture variations of these tools. Usually, these all-in-one implements combine a disk, seeder and cultipacker for one-pass planting, and a variety of other attachments can be added.

Cultipackers. Cultipackers are steel wheels mounted side-by-side on an axle. The wheels have a raised center or rib with each side of the wheel sloping away from the rib in the center. This implement does an excellent job of firming the seedbed without compacting it too much. Various widths of cultipackers are available depending on food plot size. Some larger models have hydraulics to lift the cultipacker, while some smaller models operate with a three-point hitch. ATV models have also been designed with ball-and-socket hitches, but a cultipacker is, by design, a heavy implement – check the manufacturer's specifications for minimum ATV size.

Cultipackers are needed on soft, fine-textured seedbeds prior to seeding clovers and other small seed. Loose soil does not constitute a good seedbed because it does not provide good seed-to-soil contact. Pulling a cultipacker over the seedbed prior to seeding will firm and level the soil and create an ideal seeding surface. After sowing, cultipack the seedbed again to maximize seed-to-soil contact for optimum germination and subsequent growth.

CRAIG HARPER

CULTIPACKERS

You can get cultipackers in all shapes and sizes, from large models for tractors to ATV-sized cultipackers. These tools are valuable for firming soft seedbeds when planting small seeds like clover and for ensuring good seed-to-soil contact after broadcasting any seed type, large or small.

CHARLIE ALSHEIMER

EQUIPMENT NEEDS

CONCLUSIONS

Planting equipment can be expensive. However, it is a worthy long term investment when providing high-quality nutritious forage is a primary objective. Although the initial costs may be high, properly maintained equipment should last decades. To offset costs, good used equipment can often be purchased at local equipment dealers. Alternately, consider buying equipment jointly with neighbors or at least sharing equipment among other landowners, especially those involved in a QDM cooperative.

MANAGE WITH MOWERS

Mowers can be a particularly useful tool in food plot management. They are useful in the battle against food plot weeds as well as for general plot maintenance and improving forage quality. Rotary mowers such as the familiar "Bush Hog" type, sickle-bar mowers and even hay mower/conditioners can work for some uses.

As forage plants mature, their nutritional content tends to decline, and fiber content increases. Mowing can stimulate new, tender growth that is more nutritious and digestible.

Many weeds are annuals, which grow and mature during a few weeks each year. By mowing them before their seeds mature, you can remove the current year's problem as well as help reduce weed problems in subsequent years. Mowing before plowing or disking, even if you've sprayed the field, will also help your equipment run easier across the field, as well as provide a more thorough tillage job. It also helps prevent the plow or disk from becoming clogged with vegetation.

—Phil Anderson

Pull-behind mowers for ATVs can be very useful for light to moderate cutting jobs, although they can't tackle the heaviest brush as well as PTO-driven rotary mowers pulled by a tractor. Here, members of QDMA's Four River Branch in Dixon, Illinois, use a pull-behind mower to maintain their clover demonstration plot.

TIPS FOR USING ATV DISK HARROWS

Harrows attached to tractors with a three-point hitch have the advantage of their weight as well as leverage from the tractor to get good soil penetration. ATV disk harrows attached to a draw bar or ball-and-socket hitch do not have the advantage of leverage from the vehicle and rely on their weight for penetration. This can make it tough to get good tillage on dry, hard-packed soils. In such conditions, try the following:

Wait for Rain: With dry, hard-packed soils, wait until a couple of days after the next heavy rain to do your disking. The disks will be better able to grab and cut the soft, damp soil. However, wait a little longer with heavy clay. Disking very damp clay can cause severe clodding. Never disk very wet soils of any type – this can create a "hardpan" of compacted soil beneath the surface.

Adjust the Angle: Most disk harrow gangs have adjustable cutting angles so that disks can be aligned with the direction of travel for lighter tillage or turned on an angle for greater resistance and aggressiveness. Adjust the gangs for deeper cutting, but be sure your ATV is large enough to handle the greater resistance.

Take it Slow: Many people mistakenly assume that the faster you pull disk harrows, the better they cut. ATV harrows that are attached at only one point, rather than three, have a tendency to begin rocking or "walking" when pulled rapidly. The disks will actually lift off the ground as they rock back and forth, resulting in poor tillage. You will find that in good soil conditions, ATV disk harrows will actually dig in and cut more effectively at low speeds.

Add Weight: As long as your ATV and your disk harrow frame are strong enough, adding extra weight to the harrow will aid penetration. Check with the manufacturer for their recommendations, and watch the weld seams on the harrow frame. If you see cracks developing, remove the weight. Be careful with rocks or cinder blocks, they can scratch and damage your implement. Logs are better but are difficult to put on or take off the implement. Bags of sand are the best option. Long, narrow bags that can be draped across more arms of the frame to evenly distribute the weight work best.

6

Planting Methods

By Craig A. Harper, Ph. D.

six

There are many important steps in establishing a successful food plot. None are more important than ground preparation and planting procedures. The site may be perfect, the timing right, and the seed germination rate high, but if the seedbed isn't prepared correctly or if the seed is planted incorrectly, your food plots will likely fail. This chapter will lead you through successful preparation and planting methods to help avoid failure.

Determining Plot Size

To plant the correct amount of seed and apply the correct amount of lime and fertilizer, you must first determine the size of the plot. Many folks think they can accurately guess acreage, but most are wrong – usually very wrong. Underestimating plot size results in insufficient seeding or fertilizer rates for optimal production, and overestimating plot size can waste seed, fertilizer and money.

Accurately determining the size of a food plot is easy if you have access to a GPS unit. Simply walk around the perimeter of the plot collecting data points and allow the unit to compute the acreage. This is especially helpful when planting irregularly-shaped plots. If you don't have access to a GPS unit, you can determine plot size by multiplying the length times the width in feet and dividing by 43,560 (the number of square feet in an acre). A range finder or tape measure are the most accurate ways to measure, but you can also estimate the distance by pacing.

Successful from the Start

A quality food plot is no accident. It begins with careful attention to soil preparation, the right planting methods for the seeds being planted, and good timing. Some luck may also be involved, usually in the form of good weather, but luck alone cannot produce a lush stand of clover like this one.

CRAIG HARPER

If the plot is irregularly shaped, you may have to block off sections and measure them separately. Methods for calculating the size of roughly circular or triangular plots are shown on this page.

SEEDBED PREPARATION

Once you've chosen the site to be planted and determined plot size, it's time to prepare the seedbed. How you prepare the site can depend on the existing plant cover, soil conditions, equipment availability and the type of forage being planted. This may require some planning before you head to the field.

Preparatory Spraying. If you are planting with a no-till drill or top-sowing without cultivation, spray the site with a broad-spectrum herbicide to kill the existing cover. If you are planting with conventional tillage techniques such as plowing or disking, the site may or may not need to be sprayed depending on the existing cover. Spraying is not necessary if annual grasses or forbs dominate the site. However, if perennial grasses or forbs are present, spray the site prior to plowing/disking. If perennial weeds such as bermudagrass, tall fescue, yellow nutsedge, horsenettle, johnsongrass, curly dock and sericea lespedeza are not eliminated before planting, you are going to run into major competition problems. Timing of spraying is critical. Most perennial weeds should be sprayed when they are young and actively growing. However, read the label on the herbicide container to know exactly when to target your specific weed problem.

Sometimes, specific annual plots can be used to remedy perennial weed problems. The use of Roundup Ready corn or soybeans that are resistant to glyphosate-based herbicides is a good example of annual plots that can help to control perennial weeds from May through September (for much more on weed control, including a photo guide to identifying several of the most common food plot weeds, see Chapter 10).

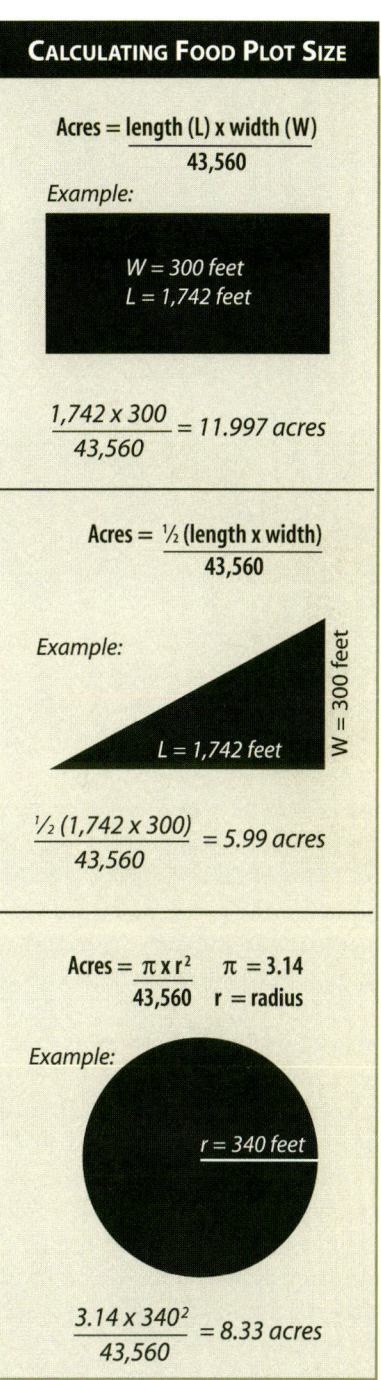

CALCULATING FOOD PLOT SIZE

$$\text{Acres} = \frac{\text{length (L) x width (W)}}{43,560}$$

Example:

W = 300 feet
L = 1,742 feet

$$\frac{1,742 \times 300}{43,560} = 11.997 \ acres$$

$$\text{Acres} = \frac{\frac{1}{2}\,(\text{length x width})}{43,560}$$

Example:

W = 300 feet

L = 1,742 feet

$$\frac{\frac{1}{2}\,(1,742 \times 300)}{43,560} = 5.99 \ acres$$

$$\text{Acres} = \frac{\pi \times r^2}{43,560} \quad \begin{array}{l}\pi = 3.14 \\ r = radius\end{array}$$

Example:

r = 340 feet

$$\frac{3.14 \times 340^2}{43,560} = 8.33 \ acres$$

PREP WORK

Tillage is a critical step in preparing a plot for planting. In general, the smaller the seed, the more finely you should till the soil. However, timing is important – if you till when soils are too wet, particularly clay-based soils, you can cause more clodding and compaction and worsen rather than improve conditions.

Plowing/Disking. Most food plots are planted using conventional tillage techniques with plows and various harrows. Sub-soilers may be necessary to break hardpans and improve moisture drainage and availability, particularly in clay soils. Lime and fertilizer are most effective if plowed or disked into the top 3 to 6 inches of soil. This is especially true for ground that has not been broken or planted in several years. Lime and phosphorus, in particular, leach down into the soil column slowly, so incorporating them into the root zone will improve nutrient availability and plant growth. Ideally, work lime into the plot approximately three to six months before planting and incorporate fertilizers just prior to or during planting.

Most no-till plots are limed and fertilized with broadcast applications prior to planting by using a cyclone spreader or a drop spreader. Some specific crops may require more specialized timing of fertilization. For example, corn may need split nitrogen applications at planting and again when the corn is about 18 inches tall. Be sure to refer to the individual species profiles in Chapter 14 for special requirements by species.

Soil Moisture and Level of Preparation. Proper soil moisture is critical when preparing a seedbed using conventional tillage techniques, especially in clay soils. If the soil is too dry, dirt clods will be large. If the soil is too wet, disks will clog with mud, and large clods will result when the soil dries out. When worked at the proper moisture level, dirt clods fall apart in relatively loose, small particles. Of course, this is less of a concern in loamy soils or sandy soils.

When you are trying to estimate soil moisture, the appearance of the soil surface can be deceiving. Determine soil moisture by digging down to the depth the soil will be worked, and be sure to check soil moisture in a few spots across the field. Dig down 6 to 8 inches with a shovel and squeeze a handful of soil. If the soil sticks together in a ball, it is likely too wet. If it looks and feels moist, yet crumbles, it is perfect. If you don't feel any moisture and the soil is difficult to crumble in your hand, it is probably too dry to prepare a fine seedbed for small-seeded species such as alfalfa, clovers, jointvetch and brassicas.

Larger seeds such as cowpeas, lablab, Austrian winter peas and small grains do not require a fine seedbed. They will germinate well in a relatively coarse seedbed provided they are covered with an inch or so of soil.

If soil moisture is adequate, a previously plowed field should need only one or two passes with a disk harrow prior to planting large seed. Smaller seeds germinate better in a finer seedbed, so additional disking may be necessary. A rotovator is an excellent implement for preparing a seedbed for small-seeded species, although follow-up use of a cultipacker may be necessary. Refer to Chapter 5 for more details on how to use these pieces of planting equipment.

PLANTING METHODS

You can plant food plots either by broadcast spreading seed or using a drill or other planter. However, broadcasting will only work on a seedbed prepared with proper tillage techniques. Seed can be drilled with no-till drills with or without a cultivated seedbed.

Tractor- or ATV-mounted cyclone spreaders are very efficient for planting relatively large plots as well as for spreading fertilizer. Smaller plots can be seeded easily with hand-held broadcast spreaders. Calibrate the seeding rate by marking off a ¹⁄₁₀-acre area (66 feet x 66 feet) and weighing the appropriate amount of seed. This is a critical step in successful planting. Start at a low setting and adjust up as necessary. Your goal is to find the setting at which it takes two passes to apply the correct amount of seed. When broadcast seeding with a hand-held seeder, walk at a slow-to-moderate pace. When using a cyclone seeder, be sure to record the gear, RPM and seeder setting after you determine the correct rate and settings.

SEED SOWER
Small, hand-crank spreaders work well for planting small plots or small-seeded crops.

BIRTH OF A

1 *This series by photographer Bill Marchel of Minnesota shows his steps in creating a new food plot.*

2 *Bill has sprayed the existing vegetation with herbicide and, after the herbicide has taken effect, mowed the plot.*

Most seed drills have the appropriate settings listed for many different seeds on the inside of the seed box lid. However, to be certain of your seeding rate, you may want to calibrate your seed drill just to be sure. The calibration technique for drills is found in Chapter 5.

There are advantages and disadvantages to both conventional tillage and no-till drilling. Conventional tillage incorporates organic material into the soil, recycling valuable nutrients for plant growth. Depending on the existing plant cover and the type of plot planted, you may not need to use herbicides before plowing or disking. However, by disturbing the soil, conventional tillage can stimulate weed production from seeds lying dormant in the soil. Also, exposed soil is subject to erosion, so steep slopes should never be planted with conventional tillage techniques.

Drilling seed requires a conventional or no-till grain drill. New no-till drills are expensive, although, as mentioned in Chapter 5, some government agencies rent no-till drills. Occasionally a good, used conventional drill can be found for a reasonable price. Most drills are also quite large and require large trucks to transport them from site to site. However, there are now some ATV-sized conventional grain drills on the market, and these are easier to get into remote locations and plant smaller acreages.

Prior to drilling with a no-till grain drill, herbicide applications are usually necessary. If you don't spray the existing cover, your germinating seed will have little chance competing with the existing vegetation. This is especially true in regions receiving more than 35 to 40 inches of rain per year. Planting with a no-till drill conserves soil moisture, a major consideration in areas with low rainfall. Even in high rainfall areas, no-till planting virtually eliminates the potential of soil erosion.

FOOD PLOT

3 The plot has now been disked thoroughly, and Bill has used a drag behind his ATV to smooth the seedbed.

4 A few weeks after seed and fertilizer have been broadcast, Bill's plot of oats is doing well.

No-Till Top-Sowing. If access to tillage equipment or no-till drills is a problem, seed can be top-sown after herbicides have been used to kill existing vegetation. This is not the preferred option for planting but can be used to successfully establish food plots. After a two- or three-week wait, small-seeded species can be sown on top of the dying vegetation, allowing rain to carry seed down to the soil. At the same time, the vegetation begins to decay and form a mulch. This method will work with clovers, alfalfa, brassicas, American jointvetch, alyceclover and some other small seeds. It does not work as well with larger seed that requires covering with soil for germination and initial growth.

Frost-seeding is another example of top-sown no-till plantings. Sowing small-seeded cool-season species on the top of frost-heaved ground prior to thawing can be used to establish a food plot in late winter/early spring. A selective herbicide application may be necessary once warm-season weed growth begins.

Seeding Depth. Regardless of planting method, it is important to plant seeds at the correct depth. Planting too deep, particularly with small-seeded plants, is a common cause of plot failure. Grains and other large-seeded plants such as corn, grain sorghum, Austrian winter peas, cowpeas, soybeans, lablab and sunflowers should be drilled or covered by disking approximately 1-inch deep. Cool-season grains germinate better when lightly covered. Small-seeded species such as clovers, alfalfa, brassicas, trefoil and jointvetch should be covered by no more than ¼ inch of soil.

With conventional tillage methods, when planting mixtures in your food plots that consist of both large- and small-seeded species, such as Austrian winter peas and clover, be sure to plant the large seed first. After lightly disking in the large seed, plant the small seed in a second pass, then cultipack.

The correct planting depth can be a problem with some pre-mixed commercial seed blends. With both large and small seed in the same bag, the small seed tends to gravitate to the bottom of the seed box or spreader and is sown before the large seed. To get around this problem, dispense small amounts of seed into the spreader at any one time or stop regularly to stir the hopper contents by hand. With hand-held spreaders, simply shaking the spreader from time to time will keep the small seeds dispersed evenly among the larger seeds.

A distinct advantage to using a seed drill is that you can precisely and accurately place seeds at the appropriate planting depth and planting rate. In addition, with some models of drills, large seed and small seed can be placed into separate seed boxes, allowing both to be sown at a different rate and depth simultaneously.

THE RAIN GAMBLE

It's the right time to plant a food plot, but it's dry and dusty with no rain in the forecast. What do you do? You pack up your truck and head home until rain is in the forecast, then plant just prior to the predicted rain. Clover or other legumes planted on dry ground followed by extended dry weather will result in dead inoculant and poor stands. Also, slight soil moisture followed by lack of rain may cause many seeds to germinate then die as newly formed roots dry out.

If you absolutely have to plant by the calendar and can't wait for rain, drill or broadcast seed and cover at the correct depth (1 inch for large seed and ¼ inch for small seed) as long as you plant above the level of existing moisture in the soil to prevent premature germination. If you can wait for rain, then plant all grasses, grains and brassicas now and hold the clovers until just before the next rain, then top sow. If the first planting has not germinated, cultipack after broadcasting the clover. If you have a no-till drill, which is ideal, drill clover at ¼-inch deep. You also have the option of fall planting of grains or brassicas and holding the clover until late winter (about 4 to 6 weeks before the last average frost date for your area) and broadcasting or drilling into the existing stand at a time when moisture is more consistent and predictable.

Cultipacking. Cultipacking improves the germination rate of top-sown seed, especially small seed that lacks firm seed-to-soil contact after sowing. Using a cultipacker to firm a seedbed is far superior to dragging a piece of chain-link fence or some other object behind a tractor or ATV. These drags may breaks up clods, but they do little to firm the seedbed. In addition, drags can result in seed clumping or "skips."

SMALL PACKAGES

Seeds are survival kits for new plants — they contain energy to push the emerging shoot out of the soil so that leaves can take over energy production. When small seeds such as clover (shown here) are planted too deep, the germinating plant runs out of energy before it reaches the surface. This is why planting depth is critical to small-seeded crops.

Cultipacking is always recommended after sowing small-seeded species. It also may be necessary before planting small seed if the seedbed is fluffy, such as when using a rotovator to prepare the soil. As a general rule, as you learned in Chapter 5, if you leave a boot imprint deeper than an inch, the seedbed needs cultipacking before planting small seeds. Cultipacking also improves germination of large-seeded species and is an important step in successful food plot establishment.

Seed Selection. After determining what to plant, it is important to purchase quality, certified seed with a high germination rate. Each bag of certified seed should have a seed tag attached. If the tag is missing, don't buy the seed. The tag identifies the variety of seed, lot number, seed origin, percentage of pure seed, percentage of inert material, germination rate, test date,

Seed Tag Example	
Variety:	Regal ladino clover
Pure seed:	98.00 %
Inert matter:	1.30 %
Other crop:	0.20 %
Weed seed:	0.50 %
Germination	80.00 %

and the presence of weed seed. If the seed is a legume and it is pre-inoculated, the seed tag identifies the percentage weight of the seed coating. If you order the seed, the salesman or seed representative should be able to provide this information over the phone or e-mail.

Seed germination rates of most food plot seed typically decrease over time. If it has been more than a year since the seed was tested, true germination will probably be lower than that reported on the tag. Quality seed should have a germination rate of at least 80 percent.

Seeding Rates. Seeding rates are normally given on a per-acre basis. It is important to plant at the recommended rate! Recommended seeding rates for various food plot plantings are normally given as broadcast rates. Because of seed desiccation and less precise placement of seed, broadcast rates are higher than those for drilled plantings. If drilling seed, reduce the planting rate by about 40 to 50 percent.

Many food plots are planted with mixtures of various types of seed. When mixing species for a combination planting, the seeding rate for each species must be reduced according to the number of species in the mixture, seed size, composition preferred, and the growth form and desired structure of the resulting stand.

Planting too much seed is a common problem because most people think more is better. However, this is not true when seeding food plots, especially grain plots. When forage plots such as clovers, cowpeas, and chicory are planted too thick, the seedlings are crowded, and plants compete with each other. The plot may still produce abundant forage – only money is wasted. However, when grain plots such as corn and grain sorghum are planted too thick, competition between the plants can dramatically reduce seed production. If the seeding rate of grains such as corn and grain sorghum is questionable, it is always better to sow less seed rather than more. This will allow more seed production per plant. However, it also means more space between plants which may result in a significant weed response.

PLANTING METHODS

INOCULATING *LEGUMES*

Legumes have a symbiotic relationship with various bacteria which attach to their roots and form nodules that extract nitrogen from the air. This is why legumes require less nitrogen fertilizer. Although nitrogen-fixing bacteria are naturally found in the soil, legume seed should be inoculated with the proper bacteria prior to planting to ensure the correct bacteria is in contact with the seed.

You can usually purchase a bag of the inoculant at the same seed store where you purchase the seed. It is important to realize that the inoculant in the bag consists of live bacteria, and there is an expiration date associated with each bag. Store the inoculant in the refrigerator, and never place it in direct sunlight, such as on the dashboard of a truck.

Seed of some varieties of legumes may be pre-inoculated with the proper bacteria prior to bagging. Because pre-inoculated seed is coated to protect the bacteria, it will usually have an off-white or gray color. Sow pre-inoculated seed before the expiration date, as indicated on the seed identification tag. If the inoculant on the pre-inoculated seed has expired, the seed should be re-inoculated before planting.

BACTERIAL ALLIES

Without the presence of certain bacteria, legumes like clover cannot form the root nodules needed to fix nitrogen from the air. The result is clear in the photo above from the Potash and Phosphate Institute. The photo on the right shows the actual nodules visible on arrowleaf clover roots.

Depending on the legume planted, properly inoculated seed may produce up to 100 to 200 pounds of nitrogen per acre. This is significant savings in the cost of fertilizer, especially when mixing legumes with grasses or rotating a legume crop with a grass, such as corn, sorghum, wheat or oats.

Proper fertilization is necessary to optimize the nitrogen-fixation process. Calcium or potassium deficiencies, overgrazing or low pH will limit the process. For example, in acidic soils, rhizobia bacteria can't get the molybdenum (Mo) they need to survive.

Mo is present in most soils in sufficient amounts, but below a pH of about 6.5, this Mo is more difficult to capture. Thus, proper liming is critical. In addition, application of too much nitrogen per acre may reduce nitrogen fixation and will also stimulate competing weeds.

PERFECT MATCH

Many commercial seed blends that contain legumes are pre-inoculated and have a visible seed coating, like the seed shown in this photo. An expiration date for the inoculant coating will be printed on the seed bag and should be checked before planting. When planting non-inoculated seed, you will need to inoculate before planting. The most important step is making sure you buy the right inoculant. The chart at right will help.

COMMON LEGUMES AND THEIR ASSOCIATED INOCULANTS

Legume Group	Inoculant Code	Bacterium
Alfalfa, Sweetclover	A	Sinorhizobium meliloti
Alsike, Ladino white, Red & White Dutch clovers	B	Rhizobium l. b. trifolii
Arrowleaf clover	O	Rhizobium l. b. trifolii
Crimson clover Berseem clover	R	Rhizobium l. b. trifolii
Subterranean clover	WR	Rhizobium l. b. trifolii
Alyceclover American jointvetch Cowpea, Lablab Lespedeza, Partridge pea	EL	Bradyrhizobium spp.
Austrian winter pea Field pea, Flat pea Sweet pea	C	Rhizobium l. b. viceae
Birdsfoot trefoil	K	Mesorhizobium loti
Soybean	S	Bradyrhizobium japonicum
Lupine	H	Rhizobium lupini

6

STEPS FOR *INOCULATION*

1) Purchase the correct inoculant for the type of legume being planted, and store it in the refrigerator prior to planting. Do not expose inoculant to heat or direct sunlight.

2) Inoculants are packaged in a medium of peat, which is black. Moisten the material with just enough water to form a "slurry." One bag of inoculant will inoculate about one bushel of seed, so you would need relatively little inoculant for an acre of clover.

3) Add a commercial sticker to the slurry. If the inoculant does not stick to the seed, the entire process is useless. Commercial stickers are available in a gum arabic powder form or in liquid form. If sticker is unavailable, use a solution of four parts water to one part sugar. Cola/soda should not be used as a sticker because the pH of most soft drinks is very low and the acidic solution may kill the bacteria.

4) Mix the inoculant/sticker slurry with the seed, making sure all seeds are coated with inoculant. This can be done by hand – the bacteria in the inoculant are no more harmful than the bacteria in a handful of soil.

5) Spread the seed out on a tarp or sheet to allow the inoculated seed to dry in the shade for about an hour. Once dry, the seed is ready to sow. Planting on a moist seedbed or just before a rain is important to ensure inoculation success. If the seed is not sown right away, store it in a cool, dry place for no more than a couple of days or re-inoculation will be needed. Never mix the inoculated seed with fertilizers as the salts in fertilizer may kill the bacteria.

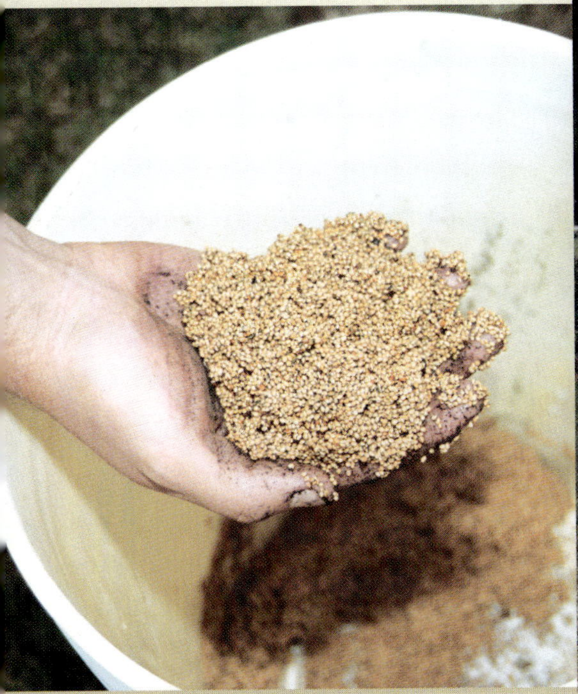

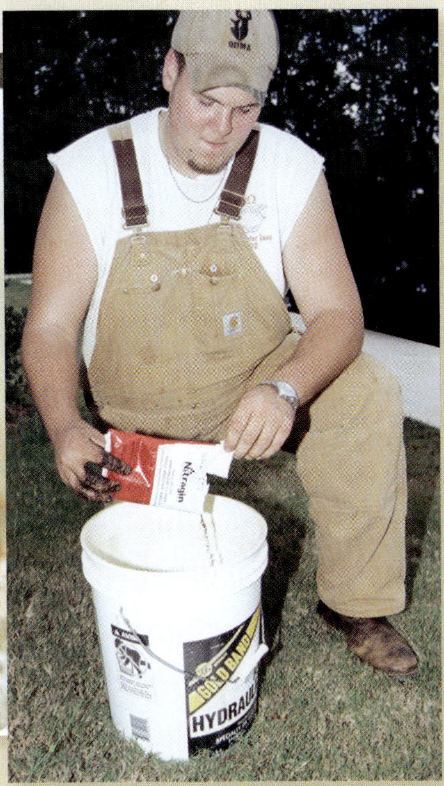

EASY AS 1-2-3

Buy the correct inoculant for the legume being planted, then follow the instructions on the package for mixing the contents with water and a "sticker" to form a "slurry." Seeds are mixed with the slurry until coated and spread in the shade to dry. As soon as the coating has dried, plant the seeds.

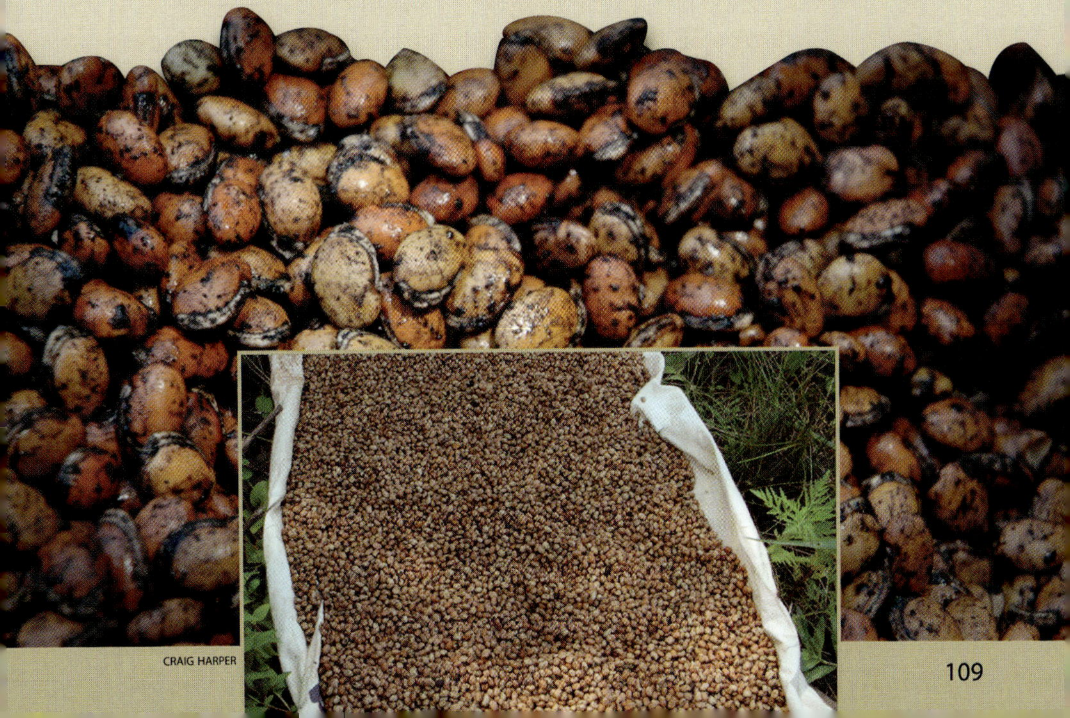

CRAIG HARPER

Selecting
Appropriate Forages

BY KENT KAMMERMEYER
AND KARL V. MILLER, PH.D.

APPROPRIATE FORAGES

Seven

The first and most commonly asked question by hunters who are beginning or seeking to improve a food plot program is "What should I plant?" Confounding the search for an answer is a large and ever-growing field of choices. A recent survey conducted in the Southeast identified 62 different plant species that were commonly planted for deer. Wheat, rye, ladino clover, corn, oats, ryegrass, grain sorghum or milo, soybeans and crimson clover were the most commonly planted species. Wheat, ryegrass, ladino clover, rye and oats were preferred for cool-season plantings, whereas soybeans, peas, alfalfa, reseeding cowpeas and ladino clover were most commonly selected as warm-season plantings.

So, how do you pick a winner? First, understand that no single plant variety or mixture of plantings is suitable for every deer management situation or every planting condition. Therefore, be suspicious of any variety or food plot blend that is promoted to grow anywhere or solve all of your deer nutrition problems.

Chapter 14 will guide you through many plants which you might consider for your food plots. Before you narrow your selection to individual plants or blends, however, you should first consider your conditions and goals. The selection of the appropriate planting in your situation depends on numerous factors such as climate, soil types, available acreage to plant, and deer browsing pressure. However, the most important consideration is the time of year when you want the forages to be available for use.

In broad terms, food plot plantings can be classified as cool-season plantings and warm-season plantings. Cool-season forages are typically planted in the fall or early spring, grow or remain viable through the winter, and mature in the spring or

NUTRITION 365

Select forage plantings based on when they will be available and what needs they fill for whitetails. Cool-season crops can be selected to be attractive during hunting season, to supplement naturally waning nutrition in winter, or both. Warm-season crops should have a mission of boosting nutrition during critical-need times of fawning, antler growth and, in the South, late-summer stress periods.

early summer. These plantings are not killed by frost and continue to provide forage through-out most of the cold months with some species, such as white and red clovers and alfalfa, doubling as warm-season forage. In contrast, warm-season plantings typically are planted in the spring after the last frost and may remain available until the first frost in the fall.

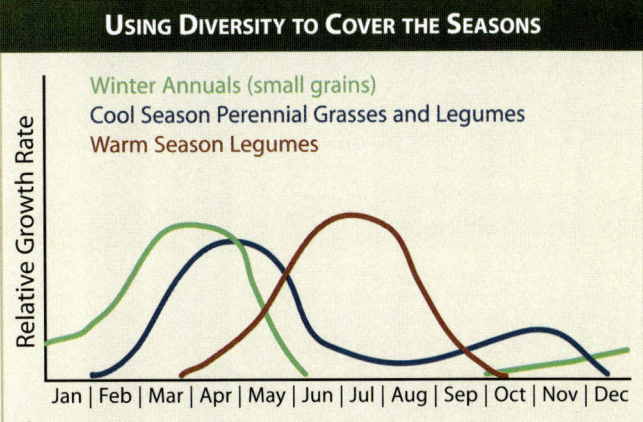

USING DIVERSITY TO COVER THE SEASONS

Winter Annuals (small grains)
Cool Season Perennial Grasses and Legumes
Warm Season Legumes

Relative Growth Rate

Jan | Feb | Mar | Apr | May | Jun | Jul | Aug | Sep | Oct | Nov | Dec

This chart provides a visual understanding of the importance of providing both cool- and warm-season crops as well as annuals and perennials. This diversity ensures strong production across many seasons (Adapted from the Phosphate and Potash Institute).

For both warm-season and cool-season plantings there are a variety of choices available, each of which can target a specific management objective. As a general rule, perennial plantings which re-grow from established root systems for two or more years are better adapted to conditions in the North, and annual plantings, which must germinate from seed every year, are a better fit in the Deep South. There is a lot of gray area in between, and there are numerous exceptions to the rule. For example, wheat can be an excellent annual planting in Michigan, and the perennial white clovers like Osceola can do well on sandy loam soils in Florida. Annuals, especially when planted in the fall, are a better choice to withstand heat, drought, sandy soil and low fertility. Annuals generally put on faster top-growth than perennials, which take time to develop strong root systems before putting on significant top-growth.

APPROPRIATE FORAGES

	Season		Growth Habit	
	Cool	Warm	Annual	Perennial
Clovers				
Alsike	•			•
Arrowleaf	•		•	
Crimson	•		•	
Kura	•			•
Red	•			•
Subterranean	•		•	
White/Ladino	•			•
Other Legumes				
Alfalfa	•			•
Austrian Winter Peas	•		•	
Birdsfoot Trefoil	•			•
Hairy Vetch	•		•	
Lupine	•		•	
Alyceclover		•	•	
American Jointvetch		•	•	
Burgundy Bean		•	•	
Cowpeas		•	•	
Kobe Lespedeza		•	•	
Lablab		•	•	
Soybeans		•	•	
Sweetclover		•	•	
Large/Small Grains				
Oats	•		•	
Wheat	•		•	
Rye	•		•	
Triticale	•		•	
Corn		•	•	
Grain Sorghum		•	•	
Grasses				
Annual Ryegrass	•		•	
Timothy Grass	•			•
Brassicas				
Canola	•		•	
Kale	•		•	
Rape	•		•	
Turnips	•		•	
Others				
Chicory	•			•
Small Burnet	•			•
Buckwheat		•	•	
Sugar Beets		•	•	

Complete descriptions and profiles of each of the species in this list are found in Chapter 14 – Food Plot Species Profiles.

Cool-season annuals typically mature in spring or early summer and then go to seed and die, thus creating fallow ground which may even be available for a follow-up crop of warm-season annuals. Warm-season annuals most often attempt to flower and produce seed in summer and early fall.

However, they will be killed by frost whether they have gone to seed or not.

Perennials, such as white and red clover, trefoil, and alfalfa, tend to tolerate cold, wet, weeds, drought, insects and heavy grazing pressure better than annuals.

RESEEDING ANNUAL

Crimson clover, unlike its red and white clover cousins, is not a perennial. It is a reseeding annual. Like other annuals, it is easier to establish and begins to produce forage faster, but in a given year the duration of its productivity is shorter.

In general, perennial grasses (with the possible exceptions of Timothy and perennial ryegrass) are not good deer forage. However, the perennial legumes such as the white clovers, birdsfoot trefoil, red clover and alfalfa are top deer forage choices alone or in mixtures and double as cool- and warm-season forage, especially in the North.

Although perennials do not require replanting each year, they are not maintenance-free. Perennial legumes will require one or more mowings each year to control weeds, annual topdressing of fertilizer to maintain productivity, and perhaps a selective herbicide treatment if weed problems become severe. Nevertheless, deer managers are usually way ahead of the game if they can plant and manage for perennials on at least half of their food plot acreage.

TARGETING THE COOL SEASON

Cool-season food plots can be used to target two management objectives. In areas where deer seasons are late or extend past the time

APPROPRIATE FORAGES

of the first fall frost, cool-season plots can provide excellent hunting opportunities. The high-quality forage provided is attractive to deer, particularly after cold temperatures have dramatically reduced the availability of natural forages. Additionally, cool-season plots are useful to provide supplemental forage during the nutritionally stressful winter and early spring. The choices of what to plant during the cool season depends on whether the objective is primarily hunting, nutrition, or both.

Cool-Season Hunting Plots. For hunting plots, getting good fall growth in your plots is critical because rapid growth translates to high palatability and attractiveness for deer. Therefore, small grains such as wheat, rye or oats are your best choice. These grains can be mixed with clovers such as crimson or red to provide forage production lasting into the following spring. Arrowleaf and berseem also work well on more southerly ranges. All of the small grains are very easy to grow, but there are some subtle differences among them that can affect which you choose to plant. As a rule, oats have the highest palatability for deer but are the least cold tolerant and will not survive a Michigan winter. Wheat is generally more palatable than rye and very cold tolerant, but it is more susceptible to insects and diseases and requires moderate to high soil fertility. Rye is most tolerant of cold, and it is also more tolerant of poor soils, low fertility and low pH, but it is usually less palatable than oats or wheat. Annual/perennial mixes that contain small grains plus white clovers such as ladino can provide outstanding hunting opportunities for more than one year. The annual grains provide the attraction during the first hunting season. By the second season, the slower starting perennial clovers have become highly productive, providing the attraction in subsequent seasons.

Turkeys, other birds and occasionally deer make use of the seeds of these small grains once the plants mature. Oats are the least desirable because the seed has persistent hulls which make it poor forage for deer and other wildlife. Wheat seed is the most palatable and is highly preferred over both oats and rye.

RYEGRASS: GOOD, BAD OR UGLY?

Annual ryegrass is usually a poor substitute for the small grains like rye, wheat and oats because of its aggressive reseeding. In a mix with clover, annual ryegrass will likely dominate the clover after the first year.

However, annual ryegrass is a moderate fall forage and a good early spring forage that can handle tough situations such as low fertility, shade and damp soils. It is most useful for small, remote hunting plots where proper soil preparation is not possible. However, do not plant annual ryegrass anywhere you would eventually like to plant other cool-season forages, such as clover.

Perennial ryegrass is not as aggressive or competitive as annual ryegrass and has more applications in food plot mixtures, especially in the North (see Chapter 8, the mixtures chapter, for more information).

Cool-Season Plots to Provide Winter Nutrition. In most of the whitetail's range, winter is the most limiting season due to the dormancy of native plants. Dormant plants are low in protein and palatability and high in lignin and cellulose. These forage conditions can cause deer to lose body weight even when forage volume is high. Therefore, cool-season forages which are actively growing in fall and early spring are an important supplemental planting in most of the United States.

BILL MARCHEL

FROSTY FORAGE

Leafy brassicas, including rape, kale, canola and turnips, usually increase in attractiveness for deer after being hit with one or more hard frosts. What had been a field of leafy greens can turn to a patch of stripped stems in winter. This makes brassicas a good choice for filling the winter nutrition gap, particularly in northern climates. For the same reason, deer have more mixed reactions to brassicas in the Deep South. Depending on local conditions, brassicas may be heavily used or not used at all. The photo at left of heavily browsed brassica was taken in the Lower Coastal Plain region of southeast Georgia on land with a moderate herd density and adequate nutrition.

Deer use of food plots usually is very heavy in early spring before native woodlands green-up. Early spring growth is critical for buffering the late-winter stress period. Therefore, cool-season plots designed to provide forage during the late winter and early spring stress period should include some later-maturing species in addition to the small grains. Although the small grains will continue to grow into late winter and early spring, the quality and preference of these plants declines as their lignin content rises in mid- to late spring.

Several annual clovers such as arrowleaf, subterranean and crimson (in the South) or perennial clovers such as ladino and red work well in these situations. Other useful plantings for this time period include chicory and Austrian winter peas. All of these species peak in quality and production in late winter or early spring, and they are highly nutritious and palatable well into midspring or early summer.

Some of the brassicas, such as turnips, rape, kale and canola, can also be used to provide winter nutrition. These species tend to be a little less palatable during the fall. Therefore, deer pressure on these plots tends to be limited until late fall and winter when their availability and improved palatability make them high-quality forages. They are especially valuable in this role in the North.

TARGETING THE WARM SEASON

In parts of the arid Southwest and the Atlantic and Gulf Coastal Plain, late summer can be a serious stress period for deer, especially in drought years. Warm-season plantings can be particularly important in these regions. However, even in the rest of the United States, deer will benefit from warm-season plantings because they are often higher quality than native forages. Effective warm-season plantings supply high-quality forage when native range quality is low. Spring and early summer are overlap periods among cool- and warm-season plantings and high-quality native or naturalized vegetation.

Warm-season plantings target key portions of the deer's annual cycle. Nutritional demands for antler production in males and lactation in females are high during the summer. In addition, weaning fawns require high-quality forages for optimal early growth. Warm-season plantings can also make outstanding bowhunting plots until the first frost, particularly late-planted soybeans or cowpeas.

The best summer plots contain legumes such as alfalfa, alsike clover, alyceclover, sweetclover, red clover, or American jointvetch. Lablab, soybeans and cowpeas are excellent choices. However, in smaller food plots, moderate to heavy grazing pressure on young stands can wipe out a plot almost overnight. If these plantings are used, it may be a good idea to use some type of deer deterrent until the plots become well established (See Chapter 9 for more information on deterrents). If deterrents are not an option, the use of an alternative summer forage such as jointvetch or alyceclover is necessary. These two species are somewhat less preferred and also are able

Lablab is a viny, warm-season, annual legume.

Neck Deep in Protein

Warm-season legumes are excellent sources of protein. This field features a mix of lablab and American jointvetch. The sunflowers have been planted at a light density to provide structure to support the legumes.

to withstand considerable grazing pressure. Red clover is very productive and nutritious in the warm season everywhere except the Deep South. Alsike clover, birdsfoot trefoil and soybeans are good choices for central or more northerly regions.

Late-summer stress periods are often caused by drought and deep, sandy soils. Almost any food plot planted as a summer supplement is subject to drought stress unless it is irrigated. However, alfalfa may be the best plant for deer in arid and drought-prone regions for a combination cool- and warm-season forage. It has a deep root system that withstands droughts, helping the plant maintain very high production and quality. However, alfalfa has its drawbacks. It does not do well in the Deep South, it is expensive, requires high maintenance, high pH and fertility and is subject to weevil damage and weed competition.

Buckwheat, although usually not planted alone because of its relatively short time of availability, does work well in some areas, particularly when combined with another forage such as alyceclover, jointvetch, cowpeas and grain sorghum. Similarly, chicory is a productive, attractive perennial but is a heavy nitrogen user and is also better suited in a mix with perennial clovers at a low rate of about 2 lbs./acre.

Legumes planted during the warm season are excellent protein sources. Other plantings, particularly corn and grain sorghum, can provide carbohydrates and are particularly attractive to deer once the seeds mature. These also qualify as combination winter/summer deer foods and make ideal late summer and fall energy foods. Larger corn fields and bird-resistant grain sorghum, the seeds of which are higher in tannic acid, often provide a source of food well into winter if they are not eaten up early. Corn is a highly preferred planting for deer. It is best incorporated in a deer management system where cooperative farming agreements can be made with farmers so that 10 to 20 percent of the crop is left unharvested. Corn has some disadvantages when planted specifically for deer in small fields. It requires high fertility, herbicides or cultivation to control weeds, and it is quite vulnerable to droughts. Planted in small fields, corn is subject to heavy depredation by crows, squirrels, turkeys, raccoons, possums, beavers and other wildlife.

Grain sorghum almost duplicates the food value of corn without many of the disadvantages. Early maturing or light-seeded varieties, which have a yellow or white seed coating, provide early food for deer in August before hard mast is available. Late-planted or dark-headed varieties of sorghum mature later and resist early browsing. Because the seeds of these varieties contain elevated levels of tannic acid, most birds and animals, especially large migrating flocks of blackbirds, will not eat them. As the mature seed is exposed to weather, it gradually loses its tannins and becomes more palatable to deer, turkeys and other animals. In good acorn years, bird-resistant grain sorghum seed may last until winter before it is consumed by deer.

Grain sorghum is much easier to grow than corn, has far greater drought resistance, and is subject to less depredation and insect damage. However, it still requires a heavy application of nitrogen for proper growth and production.

Whether warm-season plantings or cool-season plantings are most important depends on what other for-

STEVE GULLEDGE

POOR MAN'S CORN

This alias for grain sorghum refers to its food value being almost equal to corn while it is much easier to grow. When the seed heads mature, deer will bite the top off all at once. Sorghum also mixes well with warm-season legumes – note the cowpea vine climbing the sorghum stalk.

ages are available in your area. A general rule of thumb for areas where the winter stress period is severe is 70 percent cool-season and 30 percent warm-season plots. For areas with significant summer stress, this can probably be equalized to an even balance of warm- and cool-season plots.

PALATABILITY, DIGESTIBILITY AND NUTRIENT CONTENT

These three measures of vegetative quality – palatability, digestibility and nutrient content – often go hand in hand. The most palatable species usually are highly digestible and very nutritious. This is where legumes excel. Nitrogen is a key component of protein, and legumes, with the help of special bacteria, "fix" their own nitrogen from the air. Other plants, such as small grains, must get their nitrogen from the soil, and it may be in limited supply. Thus, expensive nitrogen fertilization is required for optimum growth.

Young, tender leaves are full of protein, highly digestible and low in fiber. As leaf growth slows and a plant matures, fiber builds and digestibility is reduced. Protein content also declines along with palatability. For warm-season plantings, all three measures of forage quality peak in spring and gradually decline through summer until quality is at its lowest in the fall. This decline in quality is accelerated by drought, low soil fertility and heat. Conversely, it is slowed by heavy deer browsing.

In contrast, cool-season plantings, which begin or renew their cycle in fall, maintain high nutritional quality through winter until early spring. Quality gradually declines through late spring and summer when the plants flower and produce seed. This is especially true of small grains like oats, wheat and rye when they "bolt," sending up a flower stalk and channeling energy to flower and seed production.

Contrary to popular belief, you may not always want to use the most palatable species you can plant. In plots of less than 3 acres, warm-season species like soybeans, cowpeas and lablab may be wiped out by early grazing pressure within 30 days of planting. The same is true of cool-season plants like Austrian winter peas or blue lupine. To establish these crops successfully in small plots, you may need to plant them in combination with crops that are lower in desirability or protect them with fencing or repellents until they are established, usually 30 to 45 days.

ADAPTABILITY

There is nothing more frustrating or more preventable than planting the wrong plant species on the wrong site. A classic example is alfalfa planted in bottomland with a high water table. This is an area better suited to white clovers or jointvetch. Alfalfa's deep root system is vulnerable to drowning, and you may lose an entire crop when roots are flooded. Another example is planting arrowleaf clover in the fall in the North where it will surely be killed by winter cold. White, red and alsike clovers are a much better choice for cold tolerance in the far North. A third example is planting birdsfoot trefoil in the Deep South where it will wither and die in hot summer temperatures. Summer annuals like alyceclover, cowpeas, lablab and grain sorghum will tolerate those adverse conditions. Planting corn in the arid west without irrigation is certainly a tactical error. Grain sorghum is an obvious choice here.

To continue your search for the answer to "What do I plant?" while avoiding pitfalls like those mentioned above, be sure to study the individual species profiles found in Chapter 14.

8

Selecting the
Right Mixture

By Kent Kammermeyer

eight

Forget Jack and the Beanstalk. There are no magic beans when it comes to planting food plots. In other words, there is no single planting that can fulfill all of the requirements in a food plot program. However, by using a carefully selected combination of plantings, either mixed in the same plot or planted in adjacent plots, you can optimize your food plot production and usefulness. There are myriad commercial food plot mixes available, most of which integrate compatible plantings. But understanding what each of the forages in the mix contributes will help you select the blend that will best fit your unique situation. In addition, if you know what plantings work well together, you can experiment and develop your own specialty blend.

WHY USE MIXTURES?

Every different forage you use in a food plot will have a slightly different time of peak production. For example, if you plant a mixture of small grains such as wheat or oats in combination with annual legumes, the usefulness of your food plot will span much of the fall, winter and spring. The small grains will produce abundant forage in the fall which will carry into the winter. Then in late winter and early spring, production of the legumes really kicks in and your plots will be supplying a

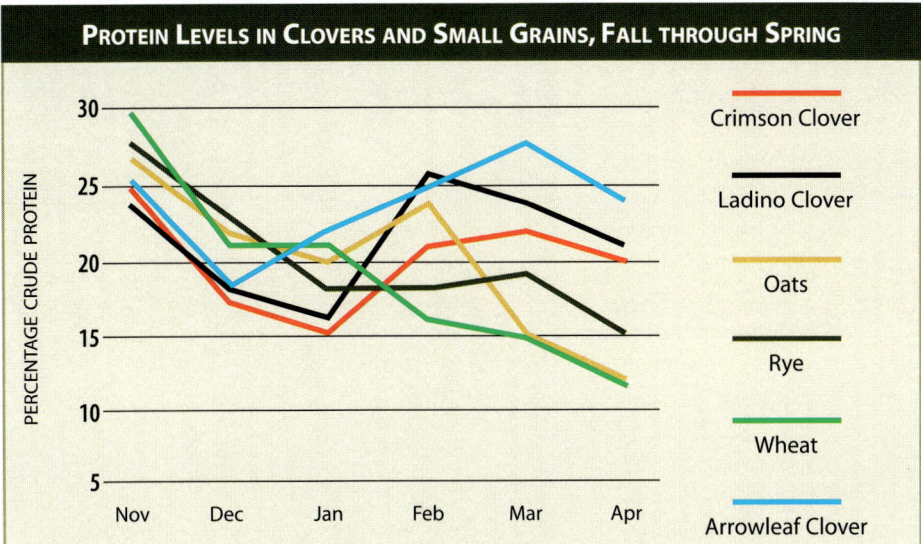

PROTEIN LEVELS IN CLOVERS AND SMALL GRAINS, FALL THROUGH SPRING

PERCENTAGE CRUDE PROTEIN

Crimson Clover

Ladino Clover

Oats

Rye

Wheat

Arrowleaf Clover

In this research, forages were planted separately and fertilized according to soil tests. As a result, protein levels for small grains were high during fall due to nitrogen application but then dropped steadily. In contrast, protein levels in clovers remained high due to their ability to fix their own nitrogen. A light application of nitrogen (about 30 lbs./acre) in a pure legume stand at establishment will improve initial protein levels and early growth. When planting mixtures of legumes and small grains, apply nitrogen fertilizer at establishment according to soil test results for the small grains. Note: Research results vary; many studies have shown clovers with higher protein levels than small grains.

Adapted from Nutrient quality and use of agricultural food plantings by white-tailed deer on the Marion County Wildlife Management Area, Mississippi, 1988, by T. L. David, part of master's research at Mississippi State University.

highly nutritious food source just in time for pregnancy in does and antler growth in bucks. Even among the different annual legumes there will be slight differences in peak production. Crimson clover tends to peak in production about a month earlier in spring than some others, such as arrowleaf clover. However, it flowers, produces seed and dies earlier as well. In contrast, arrowleaf peaks later but will persist into the late spring and early summer. By combining these two species, you can increase the timing of production in your plots by a month or more.

BUCKET OF GRAIN

A bucket like this one can save you from taking a set of scales to the food plot's edge in order to weigh and dispense seed into recommended mixes. The level of measured amounts of grain or other seeds can be marked on the bucket for easy mixing in the field.

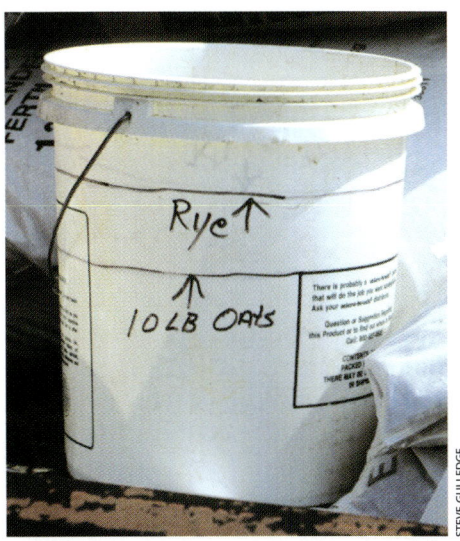

Optimal deer use often coincides with peak protein and production of a plant species. Although wheat and other small grains produce abundant forage in the spring, use of these plantings is concentrated during rapid growth in fall and winter. By spring, small grains begin going to seed. At this time, lignin content increases dramatically in older, larger leaves, and because of this, palatability for deer declines sharply. Here again, including the annual legumes will ensure that there are nutritious and palatable forages available through the spring.

RANS THOMAS

Perfect Match

Small grains and clovers are very compatible, almost to the point of having a symbiotic relationship. This clover/small grain/chicory mix has just been mowed during its first summer after being planted the previous fall. This mowing will rejuvenate and release the clover, allowing it to thrive.

Mixtures can also provide some insurance against a total food plot failure. Some species are more drought resistant, others are better weed competitors, and still others have fewer insect problems. By selecting plantings to include in your mixtures that have tolerances to various problems, you can ensure that at least some of your plantings will be successful.

There are some plantings that do particularly well together – they are almost symbiotic. Because of this, many biologists recommend various clover/small grain mixtures for both cool- and warm-season plantings. Small grains (oats, wheat, rye, etc.) and legumes are very compatible. The legumes provide high-quality forage, fix nitrogen for themselves and even provide excess nitrogen that can enhance the growth of the small grains. The small grains act as a nurse crop to protect the clover seedlings from drought and overgrazing and utilize excess nitrogen which might otherwise be captured by weeds.

Small grains alone are not as palatable or productive as clover/small grain mixes and require higher nitrogen fertilizer rates. The obvious advantage of clover is its high protein (20 to 30 percent) and high calcium content (0.5 to 0.7 percent). However, clover can be more difficult to establish and maintain than small grains. Clovers require inoculation with the proper strain of rhizobium bacteria, soil pH above 6.0, high fertility, and good rainfall for proper stand establishment and production.

Selecting the Appropriate Mixture

The appropriate mix to plant obviously depends on your objectives. Are you planting your food plot primarily as an attractant for hunting? Or is your goal to provide a nutritional supplement? Are you planting summer crops to enhance body and antler growth? Or are you planting cool-season crops to target winter and early spring nutrition to buffer winter stress periods? Are you dealing with the harsh winter conditions of the North, or the hot, droughty conditions of the South? Do you have special considerations such as deep sandy soils?

What follows is a series of mixes for you to consider trying in your food plot program. These recommended mixes should be viewed as a starting point. Experiment with these and other mixes to learn what works best in your area.

Perennial Cool Season Mixes

For the cool season, and beyond into summer, there are both annual and perennial mixes of legumes and small grains. It is obviously an advantage to plant a perennial mixture which comes back year after year without replanting. However, this can be more difficult than it sounds because the number of perennial species suitable for cool-season food plots is somewhat limited, particularly the perennial grasses. This problem is less of an issue in the North than in the South.

Some perennial grasses, such as fescue or orchardgrass, are very competitive and will eventually overtake the clovers. Neither of these species should be planted in a deer food plot. A major objective in cool-season perennial mixtures is to maintain a rich clover component or even allow the stand to revert to pure clover.

A mix of white and red clover with small grains instead of perennial grasses, such as those shown on the right, accomplishes this in many areas. The white is perennial, the red is a weak perennial, and the small grains are annuals. Wheat or rye are the small grains of choice in northern regions. They work equally well in the South, but oats make an excellent substitute for rye there.

The perennial cool season mix can be

SEEDING RATES: DRILL VS. BROADCAST
The seeding rates (lbs./acre) provided in this chapter are <u>broadcast</u> seeding rates. If you are using a grain drill, cut the recommended rates in half.
Also, do not increase the recommended seeding rates – more is not always better! Heavy seeding rates can be counterproductive to optimum growth.

Perennial Cool-Season Mix

North and South:

White clover	5 lbs./acre
Red clover	7 lbs./acre
Wheat	30 lbs./acre
Rye	30 lbs./acre

North:

White clover	3 lbs./acre
Red clover	3 lbs./acre
Alsike clover	3 lbs./acre
Birdsfoot trefoil	3 lbs./acre
Rye	50 lbs./acre

Fall Attraction, North and South:

Chicory	2 lbs./acre
White clover	5 lbs./acre
Red clover	7 lbs./acre
Austrian winter pea	15 lbs./acre
Wheat	25 lbs./acre
Rye	25 lbs./acre

enhanced to provide greater attraction during the hunting season by using a couple of additional forages. Chicory can be added at a low rate to spice up the mix and give it enhanced drought resistance and production during summer and fall. It is a deep-rooted, strong perennial. Austrian winter pea can be added to provide more fall attractiveness. Oats are generally more preferred by deer than wheat or rye, but they may freeze out in northern winters. The end result after the first year is usually a chicory, white and red clover stand with the red clover fading out after the second or third year. The white clover can be maintained almost indefinitely as long as noxious weeds and white grubs can be controlled as needed. The mix may have to be mowed once or twice per summer and fertilized once per year in September. White clover stands, especially the new, persistent varieties, may persist for more than five years with only one or two grub control applications and one or two grass-selective herbicide applications. Typically, however, replanting may be required at three- to five-year intervals.

Perennial grasses may have a place in clover mixes on some far northern deer ranges, particularly where food plots need to double as hay fields. Possible choices include timothy or perennial ryegrass mixed with perennial white or red clovers. The disadvantage, however,

Perennial Cool-Season Grass Mix *North:*	
Timothy	3 lbs./acre
White clover	5 lbs./acre
Perennial ryegrass	20 lbs./acre

is that without careful management, perennial grasses may eventually out-compete the clover and form a pure stand within three to five years. Pure grass makes a very poor deer food plot, particularly compared to a clover mix.

ANNUAL COOL-SEASON MIXES

Annual cool-season mixtures can also be grown in many combinations. Priorities should be given to high-quality legumes and non-competitive grasses with preference given for reseeding varieties. Legumes may include almost any of the clovers, vetches or Austrian winter peas with any small grain, including oats.

In acidic or deep sandy soils in the South, annual clovers such as crimson and arrowleaf or hairy vetch can be substituted for the white and red clovers. The small grains in the Reseeding Attractant, South mix provide production and hunting opportunities during the fall. Crimson clover provides highly nutritious forage in early to midspring, and the arrowleaf pro-

Annual Cool-Season Mix *Reseeding Attractant, South:*	
Crimson clover	10 lbs./acre
Arrowleaf clover	10 lbs./acre
Rye	30 lbs./acre
Wheat	30 lbs./acre
(Or Oats)	(30 lbs./acre)

duction will peak during mid- to late spring. Any of the vetches, such as common, bigflower, or hairy vetch, can be included in the mix as well. However, be sure to seed the vetch at a very low rate (5 lbs./acre), because it can form a dense canopy of vegetation that may shade out some of the other crops in the mix. In some areas, crimson, arrowleaf and vetch will reseed without disking. In other areas, a light disking is required in September.

Brassicas in any combination, including rape, kale, turnips and canola, make a good annual plot in the North when planted in August. Frosts on mature plants in October, November or December cause the sugar content in the leaves to rise, and they become very palatable to deer. Deer even

Annual Cool-Season Mix Brassicas, North:	
Rape	2 lbs./acre
Kale	2 lbs./acre
Turnips	2 lbs./acre

dig them out of the snow in December or January. Be cautious when mixing brassicas with small grains or clovers. With their ability for quick, tall growth, a high rate of brassicas will soon shade out many clover and small-grain seedlings, thus eliminating them from the mix. Clover mixes with brassicas should contain no more than 1 lb./acre of brassica seed.

All four legumes (*shown on the right*) in the Fall Attractant, South mix, especially Austrian winter peas and blue lupine, are fast starters when planted in early fall. Consequently, they are highly palatable and attractive during hunting season. Berseem clover, blue lupine and oats may not survive a cold winter with temperatures dipping below 10 degrees. Austrian winter peas

Annual Cool-Season Mix Fall Attractant, South:	
Crimson clover	10 lbs./acre
Berseem clover	10 lbs./acre
Blue lupine	20 lbs./acre
Austrian winter pea	10 lbs./acre
Oats	30 lbs./acre

and blue lupine may be killed by heavy, early grazing in small plots.

WARM-SEASON MIXES

As with the cool-season mixes, warm-season mixes are best formulated by including legumes and small grains for efficient use of nitrogen as well as weed suppression. However, many warm-season annual food plot mixes may rely exclusively on legumes.

Warm-season plots are designed to provide high-quality nutrients during the periods of antler production, doe lactation and fawn growth. However, depending on when the first frost hits your area, they can provide an added benefit of outstanding hunting opportunities in the early fall.

Grain sorghum mixed with soybeans, cowpeas, lablab or aeschynomene makes an outstanding summer forage plot combined with attraction capabilities into the fall. A tall-growing sorghum helps shade out weed competition and provides a strong stalk for cowpeas, lablab and American jointvetch (aeschynomene) to climb on. If you are

Annual Warm-Season Mix North/South:	
Grain sorghum	7 lbs./acre
Iron & clay cowpeas	15 lbs./acre
Quail Haven soybeans	15 lbs./acre

planting small fields, or if your deer density is relatively high, you likely will have to use some type of deterrent to keep the deer from destroying the young peas or beans. In these situations, aeschynomene becomes the better choice, because it is less apparent to the deer as it begins to grow and is also more tolerant of grazing pressure than the other legumes.

Annual Warm-Season Mix Attractant Mix, South:	
Grain sorghum	5 lbs./acre
Aeschynomene	15 lbs./acre

The grain sorghum won't provide any forage until the seed heads mature, and you can choose when you want deer to be attracted to the sorghum seed. As you learned in Chapter 7, early maturing or light-seeded varieties of grain sorghum provide early food for deer in August. Bird-resistant varieties with elevated levels of tannic acid, such as Novartis KS989, may last until winter before they are consumed by deer. Mixing bird-resistant and non-bird-resistant varieties in the same field can prolong the time that deer will use the field.

Corn can be substituted for grain sorghum in this mixture. However, as we discussed in Chapter 7, corn is more temperamental than grain sorghum. If your conditions make corn a questionable choice, stick with the sorghum.

Mixing aeschynomene and alyceclover, both annual legumes, is an outstanding choice for bottomland food plots where adequate soil moisture is not a problem. Often bottomland soils are either too wet from heavy rainfall or too dry due to sandy soils. This combination will cover both

Annual Warm-Season Mix Attractant Mix, South:	
Aeschynomene	15 lbs./acre
Alyceclover	10 lbs./acre

situations. Aeschynomene grows best in moist soils and can even tolerate very wet conditions. However, production is poor if conditions turn dry. Alternately, alyceclover does not tolerate very moist sites but is quite tolerant of dry soil conditions. So, with either extreme, or with normal growing conditions, you are sure to get a quality food plot.

Both aeschynomene and alyceclover can be a little slow to establish, so the addition of about 15 lbs./acre of buckwheat will provide some forage production while the legumes are coming on. Also, because these crops may be novel to your deer herd, it may take the deer a little while to figure out that they are good to eat. If you don't see much browsing pressure on your plots, don't worry. The deer will figure it out and will soon be making heavy use of these plots.

In the mix at right, alyceclover and red clover are strong summer legumes that provide lots of protein. Alyceclover is sensitive to early grazing pressure so the buckwheat should protect it with fast growth early on. As the buckwheat blooms and goes to seed, the rape is maturing a large, succulent leaf

Annual Warm-Season Mix Attractant Mix, North:	
Rape	2 lbs./acre
Red clover	5 lbs./acre
Alyceclover	15 lbs./acre
Buckwheat	20 lbs./acre

that will provide nutrition after the buckwheat is gone along with the alyceclover and red clover.

Planting Cool-Season and Warm-Season Plots Side by Side

By planting both cool and warm season plots side by side or nearby on your property, you can have the best of both worlds feeding and attracting deer for hunting before frost and after frost. In many areas, warm season plots will last partly or all the way through bow season. By the time gun season opens, the deer switch to cool-season plots. Combine warm-season attractant plots with cool-season attractant plots in any combination based on your location.

Planting Cool-Season Plots Side by Side

There are many mixes or combinations that are not compatible for one reason or another especially if planted in the wrong proportions or at the wrong rates. This is often true of the brassica family, which has the capability to come out of the ground fast and grow tall, thus shading its slower, shorter mix components including clovers, chicory and even small grains. To get the best of both worlds, a better approach would be to plant a clover mix in a separate field or half of a field next to a brassica mix. This takes out the guesswork of shading, seeding rates and plant densities while providing two attractive and nutritious plots for hunting and stress periods. This also makes another strategy for a hunting plot in the fall. The clover, small grain, and chicory mix is growing rapidly in early fall making it very attractive to deer. As soil temperatures cool and growth of the clover mix slows, frosts impact the mature brassica leaves, raising sugar content and making them highly palatable to deer. The deer will quickly learn and switch over from the clover patch to the brassica patch in middle to late fall.

RANS THOMAS

Strip Plot

Brassicas like rape can only be combined with clover/small grain mixes at very light rates, or the brassica will out-compete the clover. One solution is to plant half a plot in brassicas and the other half in clover/small grain. Or, as shown in this photo, alternating strips of each can be planted. This field was planted using a conventional grain drill with the seed hopper separated into two sections. Brassica and small grains were mixed in one side of the hopper (left side of photo) and clover, chicory and small grains in the other side.

8

DON'T *CLEAN THE TABLE*

BY DR. GRANT WOODS AND BRYAN KINKEL

The mothers of food plot farmers must have done a good job. It seems most folks who prepare food plots totally clean their deer herd's table. When a food plot is plowed edge to edge, it is like cleaning the local deer herd's table, not leaving any leftovers to tide them over until the next meal is prepared. If you only have the resources to grow either warm- or cool-season forage at one time, it could be detrimental to your herd to "clean the table." Remember, your guests may leave if asked to skip a meal.

Unfortunately, removing all the forage at once from food plots is all too common. Most food plot farmers probably do this to be efficient. They spray or plow every food plot on the property at the same time. Once this is accomplished, it takes a few weeks to get the food plots limed, fertilized, replanted, and enough plant growth to attract and feed deer again. What and where is the herd eating during this period?

We believe "Yellow Girl" provides a good illustration. Yellow Girl was a doe that lived at one of the Woods & Associates research projects located in the mountains of northern Alabama. Yellow Girl was fitted with a GPS radio collar in the fall of 2000 (the collar was color-coded yellow, hence the name). The 2,000-acre study site is intensively managed for white-tailed deer according to QDM principles. At the time of the study, 5 percent of the property was planted in food plots of winter wheat – no variation, just winter wheat. Yellow Girl, a dominant doe, and her matriarchal group could be located within a quarter mile of one of these plots daily until the wheat began to mature and become more stalk than leaf.

Yellow Girl then relocated the center of her activity over a half mile away to a one-year-old clearcut where early successional plants provided quality forage. It is important to note that before the wheat matured, Yellow Girl did not visit this clearcut. In addition, this new clearcut had been a 20-year-old unthinned pine stand prior to cutting and had not been a source of quality forage anytime during Yellow Girl's life. In this case, the table where Yellow Girl had been dining was cleaned all at once and she was forced to dine elsewhere. This type of forced movement could be a major problem, especially for small property managers.

SMORGASBORD
Mixtures of plant varieties that reach their peak productivity at different times ensure that nutritional needs are covered for longer periods of time.

POOR TABLE FARE

This field of mature rye is almost as unproductive for deer as bare dirt. Planting a variety of warm- and cool-season plots, as well as mixtures of annuals and perennials, will help you avoid periods when the "dinner table" is empty.

The case of Yellow Girl and her matriarchal group makes another important point. They did not leave because the wheat plots were disked under in preparation for spring planting; they left because the single-variety planting had outgrown its usefulness. The food on the table was simply undesirable.

No food plot planted in a single plant species can produce nutritious forage across an entire season. Each plant has a peak stage of digestibility and nutritional content, a stage that for most species is fairly brief. During that period, the plot may be extremely productive and attractive, but afterwards it may be no more nutritionally useful than freshly disked ground.

There are several techniques that can be used to avoid forcing deer in your area to change dining locations.

- *Divide individual food plots into warm/cool or annual/perennial sections.*
- *Create enough plots to plant warm- and cool-season plots in close proximity.*
- *Maintain perennials and overseed with annuals to produce a huge flush of quality forage.*
- *Use a mixture of plant varieties that reach their peak stages at different times throughout the season.*

The advantages of having separate cool- and warm-season plots in close proximity are obvious. There is always food available, even during seasonal plot preparation. The same is true of seed mixtures containing both annuals and perennials – with each having different seasons of peak productivity, a mix produces nutritious forage over a longer period with no "down time."

SELECTING THE RIGHT MIXTURE

COMMERCIAL BLENDS
AND THE WISE CONSUMER

By Lindsay Thomas Jr.

Since the day the first brand-name bag of food plot seed appeared, some skeptics have argued that it is just as good to stick with generic seed and avoid higher prices sometimes associated with commercial blends. However, this is not complete advice. Although "brown bag" seed may be cheaper than the same variety or mix of varieties found in a brand-name blend, there are other factors to consider.

Sometimes, buying and planting a pre-mixed commercial blend is more convenient than buying separate bags of seed and mixing your own blends. This is especially true for small acreages. Also, some commercial blends of legumes come pre-inoculated with the appropriate rhizobium, saving you the trouble of buying and applying inoculant. Further, some proprietary seed varieties may not be easy to find or available at all except in commercial blends. Many seed companies have imported or developed new varieties of crops, and these varieties may be very different from the brown-bag variety at your local seed store.

Obviously, brand-name seed products exhibit a range of quality. There are many companies with a genuine interest in producing a quality product and maintaining a quality reputation. There are also companies more interested in higher profit margins, and they use cheaper, lower-quality seed and spend little on research or testing. Your best defense is to be a wise consumer.

Read the food plot species profiles in Chapter 14 of this book and familiarize yourself with each species and its varieties. Then, read the seed tag before buying any commercial blend. Be very wary of any blend that does not have a seed tag or any other listing of contents by species and percentage. Based on what you have learned in Chapter 14 and other chapters, evaluate the usefulness of any blend for your region, your soils and your food plot goals. Be sure the seed proportions make sense. For example, a small amount of clover thrown into a sack of tall, large-leaved species, such as rape or other brassicas, is not wise use of clover seed – clover will be shaded out in such a mix. Make sure species in a particular blend share common establishment times and recommended growing conditions. If one species is best established in spring for warm-season production and another is best established in the fall for cool-season production, blending these two in the same bag makes no sense – yet there are products like this being sold to uninformed consumers.

Be wary of blends that contain everything but the kitchen sink. For example, a blend of several varieties of one species, such as clover, is common. A blend that incorporates a large array of different species, however, may not be a well-planned blend. Pay attention to whether a particular blend contains annual ryegrass and be sure you want annual ryegrass before you buy – as explained elsewhere in this book, annual ryegrass is an aggressive reseeder and is difficult to get rid of once it is established.

If you have questions about any product, contact the company or visit their Web site. Look for information about testing and research. Some companies conduct extensive testing and research on new varieties and species before introducing them

PASSING THE TEST

This commercial clover blend was among many successful test plots on QDMA's National Headquarters property — clearly this blend was productive and attractive to deer. In some cases in these tests, commercial blends outperformed custom-mixed plots using generic seed. While commercial blends can be advantageous in many instances, the wise consumer should carefully consider the species contained in any blend and make sure they are compatible with the soils, climate and goals of the specific program.

to the marketplace, ensuring that they are attractive, nutritious and suited to specific climates. Some companies research different combinations of varieties, seed percentages and planting densities to create blends that perform exceptionally well when planted on well-prepared soils according to label instructions. Don't be afraid to contact seed companies and ask about their research and testing programs. Although specific results of this testing are often considered to be "trade secrets," any company that actually conducts testing will be more than happy to provide details about where, when and how they research their products. If a company seems evasive or offers vague details about their product testing, this should be a red flag.

Also talk with other hunters about their experiences with particular products. Web chat rooms and bulletin boards, such as the Forum at www.QDMA.com, are great tools for this kind of research. Finally, try your own side-by-side comparisons of products, and stick with those that perform best on your hunting land.

If you opt to use generic or "brown-bag" seed, remember that these products also exhibit a range of quality. Buy only "certified" seed, which has been inspected by the state agriculture department and conforms to standards for minimum germination levels, minimal levels of weed seeds and other criteria. Non-certified or "combine-run" seed has no such regulation – it may be cheaper, but it carries risks, including higher rates of noxious weed seeds.

9

Special
Considerations

BY KENT KAMMERMEYER
AND KARL V. MILLER, PH.D.

SPECIAL CONSIDERATIONS

Every plant that you consider growing has a specific period of optimal production and another period of availability. Production and availability are primarily driven by climate – what works well in northern regions may not do so well in the South, and vice versa. For example, ladino clover in the mid-South reaches maximum production during March through June and then again in the fall months of October and November. However, its period of availability can run from February through November, or later. As you can see, there is a five-month period of high production and a 10-month period of availability for ladino clover in this region. In contrast, the shorter growing season and harsher winter conditions in the North result in a very different timing of optimal production and availability. The same regional variation holds true for many of the forage crops you may consider planting. In addition, there are many species that tend to work better than others in the various regions. Therefore, it's important to refer to the planting zone map in Chapter 14 that is associated with the individual species profiles in that chapter.

There are many examples of regional differences that need to be considered. Let's cover a few here:

- *Planting oats and arrowleaf clover in the North is okay for good fall forage production, but you can count on winter kill where winter low temperatures dip below 10 degrees.*
- *Planting sugar beets in the South would be futile due to hot summers, unfavorable soil types, low pH, weed problems or even lack of use. Beets would also rot quicker in the South.*
- *Birdsfoot trefoil does not do well in the Deep South. Neither does alsike clover.*
- *Despite rumors to the contrary, Osceola ladino clover developed in Florida does well in northern regions.*
- *Arguably, the toughest, easiest-to-grow plant in adverse conditions must be cereal rye. It also grows in the coldest soil temperatures of any food plot species.*

Besides the north-to-south differences in climate, there are numerous special situations that you may face on your particular property. These may have to do with unique soil features, excessively wet or dry soils, limited planting sites that may require growing food plots in partial shade, or growing food plots where the deer herd or natural habitat conditions make it difficult to establish some plantings in the face of browsing pressure.

WHERE THE SAND IS LIKE SUGAR

In many areas, particularly the southern Coastal Plain region, managers are often faced with deep, sandy soils. These soil conditions, when combined with high summer temperatures and periodic droughty conditions, can be a food plot management nightmare. However, there are some considerations that can greatly increase the success of your planting program.

First of all, remember that sandy soils do not hold nutrients well, so more frequent soil testing and fertilizer applications can be critical. Sandy soils also do not hold water well, so selection of plants with high drought tolerance is critical, particularly for summer plantings.

Wildlife biologist Robert Smith of Sea Island, Georgia, has lots of experience with food plot management on deep sandy soils. He provides an initial caution for managers in

RANS THOMAS

IT CAN BE DONE

This food plot of perennial white clover was produced in the Coastal Plain region of the Southeast, which is typified by sandy soils. Though these soils do not hold moisture or fertility well, the right timing, soil preparation and seed selection can lead to success.

this area – "Do not depend on food plots!" He advocates management of native vegetation as a primary habitat management tool, and he uses food plots to supplement these activities. Robert cautions that when you plant food plots, you must expect some failures. Therefore, count on replanting occasionally. He tries to stick with low cost annual species like crimson and arrowleaf clovers combined with rye or wheat for his cool-season plots. He will often mix in Austrian winter peas, Barkant forage turnip and Pasja rape, but he always tries to tailor the mix to the site. For summer crops, he plants mostly annuals such as aeschynomene, alyceclover and cowpeas.

Robert also uses composted, pelletized chicken litter which comes in 1 ton bags from Perdue Agricycle in Seaford, Delaware. He advocates use of leaf litter from local yards to increase the organic matter content of the soil. One other club in his area trucks heat-treated bulk human sewage similar to Milorganite from local wastewater treatment plants, mixes it with lime, and broadcasts it by spreader truck on food plots for combination organic matter, pH adjustment, fertilizer and temporary deer repellency.

Planting method is also an important consideration in sandy soils. No till-drilling is the preferred method, because moisture conservation is the ultimate goal, and because it provides precise placement of seed at the appropriate depth. The top layer of sandy soil dries out quickly following a rain. If planted too shallow, a germinating seed may desiccate quickly and die before the next rain. Planting in partial shade is a viable option because of heat and drought, and when this is done, ryegrass is often added to the mix.

Many food plot managers do not recommend planting perennial clovers in deep, sandy soils, primarily because they can be difficult to establish and difficult to maintain through hot, dry summers. Small-seeded clovers must be planted shallow. In deep sands they may germinate after a rain only to die before the next rain because their roots haven't reached a soil depth with adequate moisture. Nevertheless, perennial clovers can be successfully established in these areas, but you have to watch weather conditions closely. Only plant when soil moisture is high and the

RANS THOMAS

COMBINATION APPROACH

This plot utilized partial shade, it was drilled for precise planting depth, and cereal rye was the choice for the crop, a hardy species more tolerant of tough conditions. All of these factors helped it overcome infertile sandy soil.

forecast calls for a prolonged period of cloudy, rainy weather. Also, plant later in the fall when the weather starts to cool or in February when rain occurs more frequently. Amending the soil with additional organic material can also help hold moisture and ensure establishment. Although it's possible to grow perennial clovers in deep sands, be prepared to replant occasionally because prolonged droughty periods in the hot summer will sometimes eliminate clover stands.

THE FROZEN NORTH

The more northern regions of the whitetail's range also come with some unique problems. Winter is the period of nutritional stress, but unlike in the South, it is impossible to have food plots growing at this time of year. Ed Spinazzola of Michigan, the author of *Ultimate Deer Food Plots* who has been experimenting with food plots for many years, pays close attention to the winter stress period and plans ahead to plant crops that provide late-fall nutrition even with snow cover. Canola and dwarf essex rape planted around the first of August will be tall and fully mature in November when freezes will raise the sugar content in the leaves, making them attractive, high-quality forage. Deer will paw through snow to eat the tender leaves. The same is true for all brassicas, including other rape varieties, kale, turnips and sugar beets. The last two have a bonus of providing tons of extra forage per acre in turnip and beet bulbs. It may take awhile for deer to learn to eat them, but when they do, they will eat them all winter long or until they are gone.

There is one potential problem with this system of using brassicas. In high deer populations or when deer get used to eating them, they will often browse them heavily in the young seedling stage, preventing them from maturing and providing late-season forage. Therefore, protecting the seedlings can become critical – more on protection of young seedlings follows later in this chapter.

Corn is another late-fall and winter forage that is high in carbohydrates. You may have to push stalks over or mow the standing corn to initiate deer grazing. If so, this can help you to extend the grazing pressure and ensure that there is some forage available when deer need it most. Corn is a high-energy food source that is great insurance against excessive winter weight loss until spring greenup. When deer emerge from winter in good shape, spring nutrition can be channeled directly into both body growth and antler production instead of catching up on lost body weight. The high energy provided by corn can also help bucks recover weight lost during the previous rut.

Rocks can be another challenge in some northern regions and mountainous areas, especially New England. In these situations, avoid plowing whenever possible. Rocks beget rocks, and there is almost no end to them as the early settlers found out.

Rock On

In some geographic regions, particularly New England, rocks can be a serious obstacle to preparing well-tilled food plots. Your choices are to painstakingly clear your fields and make them safe for disk harrows or to use herbicides to kill ground cover followed by planting with a no-till drill.

Use a herbicide treatment such as glyphosate followed by no-till drilling to establish food plot stands where rocks are a potential problem.

THE ARID SOUTHWEST

The arid Southwest, where rainfall patterns are highly seasonal and summer rains are sparse, calls for some serious adjustments to planting techniques. The Tecomate Ranch has mastered the technique of banking moisture from fall and winter rains to grow spring crops. Dr. Gary Schwarz, David Morris and Ryan Foster of Tecomate Wildlife Systems have adapted the old phrase "When life gives you lemons, make lemonade." Their version goes: "When it rains, use deep tillage. When it doesn't, use a no-till drill."

In areas where rainfall is limited, it is best to plant spring and fall crops in separate fields to promote optimum plant growth during drought periods. In south Texas, you can usually count on fall and winter rains. This moisture can be saved and used for a spring planting. "Banking moisture" during the off-season is done by tilling deep early so you lose less precipitation to runoff, evaporation and weeds. Fields plowed deep in September and October are then allowed to stay fallow until the following spring planting begins, usually in March. Prior to planting, lightly disk the surface with a finishing disk. Find the moisture depth with a shovel, and set your disks to break the ground just above the damp layer to ensure that little moisture is lost during tillage. Consequently, calibrate your row planter, grain drill or no-till drill to place the seed in the top of the layer of moisture so that it will germinate even without rainfall. Use a conservative seeding rate so that young seedlings do not have to compete with each other for limited moisture. Many people plant too much seed thinking they are going to produce more forage when in reality more seed can reduce yields because of overcrowding and stunting. Sub-tropical legumes such as

MOISTURE CONSERVATION

This lablab growing on the Tecomate Ranch in south Texas, where moisture conservation is critical, has been planted on a wide row spacing of 36 inches. The extra room reduces competition among plants for limited soil moisture.

RANS THOMAS

Hardwood Shade

You can get away with some species planted in the more diffused shade of pines, but hardwood shade is a different matter. After leaf drop in the fall, you can have successful cool-season plots in hardwood stands, like the one shown here.

lablab and burgundy beans are good choices for annual warm-season food plots.

Chemical weed control using selective or pre-emergence herbicides is critical when moisture is limited. Weeds are the number one competitor as they rob soil moisture from valuable food plot plants.

In the Shade

Shade is a universal problem whenever food plots are small, linear or scratched out beneath little holes in a woodland canopy. This is particularly true when you are attempting to plant woodland roads or firebreaks.

Once again, there is no magic bean that will thrive in shade conditions, especially hardwood shade, which is darker and denser than filtered pine shade. There are some plants, however, that are quite tolerant of up to 50 percent shade and even some that will eke out an existence with more shade. The white clovers such as common Durana, white dutch or even ladino will tolerate greater than 50 percent shade. You probably have seen this on shady lawns where white clover and crabgrass will be the only plants growing under oak or maple trees that cast a lot of shade. Subterranean clover, crimson clover, cereal rye, and ryegrass are also more shade tolerant.

A good mixture for shady areas in the South is shown here. In the North, drop the Mt. Barker and crimson from the mix. By the second year, this mix will have all the components of year one except rye.

Shade Tolerant Mix	
South:	
Crimson clover	5 lbs./acre
White clover	6 lbs./acre
Subterranean clover (Mt. Barker var.)	3 lbs./acre
Rye	50 lbs./acre
North:	
White clover	8 lbs./acre
Rye	50 lbs./acre

SPECIAL CONSIDERATIONS

If you're confined to planting small areas such as woods roads where shading is a problem, try to avoid dense forested areas. Choose forested stands where the timber has been recently thinned and there are some openings in the forest canopy. Thinned pine stands usually are preferable to hardwood stands, particularly for summer plantings. Remember, though, that any fertilizer that you apply to these plots will also be used by the adjacent trees and may contribute to making the shading problem worse.

Fall plantings in hardwoods can be quite effective because shading is less of a problem after leaf fall. You may have to mow in the fall after hardwood leaf drop to remove or chop fallen leaves from the plot.

How Wet is Too Wet?

It's unclear if anyone knows the answer to this question. However, white clovers seem to tolerate temporary flooding and saturated ground fairly well. Some improved varieties of white clover, especially Durana,

Wet Soil Mix	
White clover	6 lbs./acre
Crimson clover	10 lbs./acre
Rye	50 lbs./acre

have been seen to survive under standing water for a week, but it's unlikely that longer periods of inundation would be tolerated.

For wet soils, or areas prone to temporary, periodic flooding, a cool-season mix like the one shown here would be an appropriate choice. For warm-season plantings, aeschynomene at 20 lbs./acre would be a prime candidate. In fact, this species can grow quite well in shallow standing water for prolonged periods.

Aquatic Clover?
White clover will survive short periods of flooding and saturated soil, but not repeated or lengthy flooding.

RANS THOMAS

When the Grazing Pressure is On

In some areas, getting food plots established can be a major problem because deer wipe out the planting shortly after the seeds germinate. This often is a signal that you have a deer overpopulation problem, and more intense herd management is necessary. However, deer browsing can also be a problem even when populations are not high. In areas of naturally poor habitat quality, deer are very attracted to high-quality food plots because of the low quality of the native forages.

In addition to increased antlerless harvest, there are a variety of techniques that will help ensure food plot establishment even in the face of deer browsing pressure. Choosing small-seeded species to plant is preferable to larger-seeded plants, particularly when selecting summer plantings. Seedlings from large-seeded plants such as soybeans, cowpeas, lablab or corn are very susceptible to deer browsing, and just a few deer can wipe out a stand almost overnight. Seedlings from smaller-seeded plantings such as American jointvetch (aeschynomene) are much less apparent to deer and can get well established before grazing becomes intense. Some cool-season plantings like Austrian winter peas are equally susceptible, and it may not be worthwhile including them in mixes when high browsing pressure is anticipated. For vulnerable cool-season plantings, time your planting to coincide with peak acorn drop. See the following pages for details on other techniques that can be used to keep deer off food plots temporarily until the plants become well established.

PESTS

Pests include any non-intended foragers on your plots, from woodchucks to white grubs and army worms. Woodchucks typically feed on the edge of a plot and eat in a radius outward from their hole for up to 100 feet or more. They love the same things that deer love, including clovers, peas, beans, annual small grains and other legumes. Beavers can do the same when your plots are located near streams. They can be particularly destructive in fields of corn or grain sorghum. Rats, mice, moles and voles commonly become abundant on the edges of food plots. Skunks use food plots and dig cone-shaped holes when white grubs are present in large numbers. These grubs are June beetle and Japanese beetle larvae that feed on live and dead roots of plants. They target the high-quality plants like clover and thereby create an opening for invasion of plant pests like crabgrass or foxtail grass. Chemical control options are available for grubs and need to be employed when grub densities are excessive. The conical-shaped holes resulting from skunk digging in early spring are the tip-off that you need to start a grub control treatment. See your local agricultural extension agent for chemical grub control options.

There are three species of army worms (common, yellow-striped and fall) found in the eastern United States that can damage food plots. The full-grown larva of the common army worm is about 2 inches long, dark gray with yellow and green stripes. The moth is grayish brown with a white spot on each fore wing. There are usually two generations in a year, the larvae hatching from eggs in late spring and again in late summer. The army worm only periodically builds up outbreak populations. Mild winters followed by slightly drier than normal spring and sum-

DAVID KEITH, UNIVERSITY OF NEBRASKA-LINCOLN ENTOMOLOGY

ARMY WORMS

Army worms occasionally become problematic in food plots, especially following mild winters and dry springs. They can be controlled with insecticides if the infestation is caught in early stages.

mer conditions appear to contribute to outbreaks. Armyworms are sometimes serious pests, especially in the second generation of the summer and into early fall. They can be controlled by Sevin insecticide if applied early in the infestation.

PROTECTING *YOUNG LEGUMES*

By Rans Thomas and Lindsay Thomas Jr.

In previous chapters, the importance of planting warm-season annual legumes like soybeans, cowpeas and lablab for high-protein spring and summer forages has been established. An important step in growing these crops is protecting them during early stages of growth. Warm-season annual legumes are among plant species that follow a germination pattern in which the first two leaves of the plant grow above ground (see the illustration below, provided by the Potash and Phosphate Institute). If this young growth is browsed, the plant dies. With small grains, grasses and some other groups of plants, the first two leaves remain protected below ground – these plants can survive early browsing and rebound.

Although overbrowsing problems are often due to high deer densities, even light browsing on very young warm-season annuals can wipe out portions of a potential food plot. To grow these crops successfully, you will often need to protect them long enough for the plants to become established and capable of withstanding browse pressure. Two main options are available: repellents and fencing.

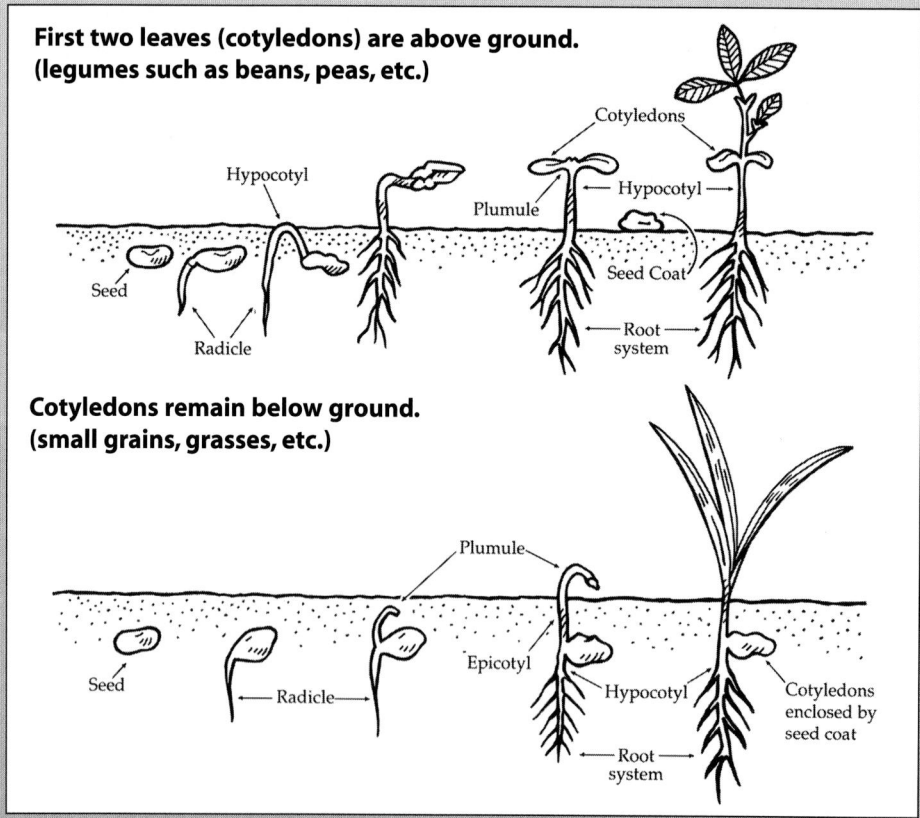

First two leaves (cotyledons) are above ground.
(legumes such as beans, peas, etc.)

Cotyledons

Hypocotyl

Plumule

Hypocotyl

Seed Coat

Seed

Radicle

Root system

Cotyledons remain below ground.
(small grains, grasses, etc.)

Plumule

Epicotyl

Seed

Radicle

Hypocotyl

Cotyledons enclosed by seed coat

Root system

RANS THOMAS

SCALPED!

The upper inset photo shows what a healthy, protected young lablab plant looks like. The other two photos are from a field of lablab that was browsed heavily too early, leaving skeletons of dead lablab plants — those leafy plants that remain outside the browse exclosure are coffeeweed, which, untouched by deer, will now take over this field. Though high deer density was a factor in this particular field, even light browsing of young warm-season annuals can eliminate large portions of plots.

REPELLENTS

Commercial products are available to deer managers to assist in temporarily repelling deer from food plots, although their effectiveness may vary with deer density and weather.

PlotSaver is a system that involves a ribbon "fence" that is staked around the perimeter of a plot. The ribbon is sprayed with a liquid repellent, which is supplied in the PlotSaver kit.

Another type of repellent is slow-release, organic fertilizer produced from treated human sewage. Several brand name products are produced by wastewater treatment plants around the country and are usually available at home and garden centers. The fertilizer is broadcast on crops at a rate of about 250 lbs./acre. At an analysis of 6-2-0, organic fertilizers supplement but do not replace complete fertilizers. One brand, Milorganite, was tested by University of Georgia researchers and found to reduce deer browsing of soybeans at an application rate of 240 lbs./acre. During this study, the researchers found that a one-time application of Milorganite provided sufficient repellency to allow the soybeans to become established.

Both PlotSaver and Milorganite were tested at QDMA's National Headquarters in the summer of 2005. Both approaches reduced early browsing of warm-season mixes compared to plots that were not protected at all. The effect of the Milorganite wore off more quickly than the PlotSaver.

SPECIAL CONSIDERATIONS

REVERSIBLE FENCES

Fencing food plots is a more expensive option than repellents, but it is a one-time cost since the fenced field can be used again and again. Fences are also nearly foolproof at keeping deer out regardless of deer density or weather conditions. "Reversible" fences are designed so that deer can easily be admitted to the plot once the crop is established.

Some fence systems are designed to drop the top 2 or 3 feet of fence to allow deer to jump over. This is effective for mature deer, but fawns may not be able to get into the food plot to feed and stay with their does. The best method is to lift the bottom 3 feet from the ground, allowing deer to go under the fence. The bottom segment will be independent of the permanent upper section of the fence, and by using metal clips or wire to attach or detach the fence, you can lower or lift it as needed. Some fences use a hinge system to lift the bottom segments. However you design a fence, be sure the fence opens completely all the way to the corner posts and does not taper downward at the corners. If deer are forced out quickly by a predator, they usually run for the corners and can get caught in the bottom segment if it tapers down to the corner post.

BACK OFF
This photo was taken at QDMA National Headquarters in summer 2005. This doe is pausing at a PlotSaver ribbon surrounding a warm-season mix. She turned and left after the photo was taken. PlotSaver, as well as the organic fertilizer Milorganite, reduced browsing in protected plots compared to adjacent "control" plots with no protection.

Although this design is highly effective, it is a costly venture at between $3.50 and $4.50/ linear foot to erect metal deer fencing. Some hunters and landowners may also consider the fencing option to be visually unappealing.

OPEN AND SHUT
Reversible fences are designed to keep deer out until a crop can sustain browsing, and then the lower half of the fence is raised.

RANS THOMAS

JUST UNDER THE WIRE

A hinge system (upper left inset) allows the lower half of a reversible fence to be lifted easily, or the lower panel can simply be attached with a wire loop (right inset). Raising the bottom of a fence is better than lowering the top, because fawns can access the plot along with their mothers. These fences can also be a good place to find shed antlers.

Managing Weeds
In Forage Plantings
By W. Carroll Johnson III, Ph.D.

MANAGING WEEDS

Dr. Marshall McGlamery, a retired weed scientist at the University of Illinois, once described a weed as "a plant whose virtues are unknown, but whose vices are." In other words, a weed is simply any plant growing where we don't want it. Weeds can become major problems in food plot programs when our management techniques match the requirements of the weed species. Weeds are adapters and survivors, and this fact can make them expensive to manage and control. However, a little forethought can help prevent a weed issue in your food plots.

Any plant can be a weed depending on the conditions. Some grow in the warm season, while others grow in the cool season. Some are annuals and become re-established from seeds each year, while others are perennials that re-establish from roots, tubers, rhizomes or stolons. Control methods often depend on these specific characteristics. Therefore, accurate identification of your problem weeds is critical to managing your particular weed problem.

Weeds compete with the desirable plants in your food plots for water, light and nutrients. Although the presence of a few weeds can be an aesthetic loss, having a few weeds in your plots is not always bad. Some weeds can actually be beneficial and add a measure of habitat diversity for some species of wildlife. However, some other species, such as sicklepod (or "coffeeweed"), johnsongrass, crabgrass and others have few redeeming qualities and should be controlled whenever possible. Depending on the type of weed and the food plot crop planted, there is a level of weed infestation or critical density where measurable losses begin. Weed numbers fewer than this are somewhat inconsequential and typically do not justify control measures. Conversely, when weed numbers reach critical density, control is justified. The critical density justifying control is specific to each weed species, to each crop grown, and to each specific set of growing conditions.

Little is known about the critical density of weeds in small acreage crops such as food plots for deer. In most cases, common sense is the best measure. In other words, use your knowledge and experience to help determine if a weed or a mixture of weeds is causing an intolerable reduction in forage growth and yield. This threshold will vary because some managers hate to see any weeds in their plots and will do whatever it takes to eradicate them. Others see a few weeds as an annoyance but nothing to be overly concerned about.

For many food plot managers, weed management is synonymous with chemical weed control using herbicides. However, use of an integrated weed management program, fine-tuned with common sense, can save a lot of time, effort and

FIGHTING WEEDS WITH DISK HARROWS

Most people think weed problems require herbicides. Actually, you can do a number of things to prevent and control weeds before resorting to herbicides. These things include careful site selection, crop selection and tillage practices. If a seedbed can be thoroughly tilled at least twice at two-week intervals before planting, many weed seedlings can be controlled.

money. Integrated weed management is simply the use of a combination of cultural, mechanical and chemical weed-control practices to prevent losses caused by weeds. Although there are a variety of herbicides available for food plot management, weed management should first emphasize cultural and mechanical controls followed by herbicides as a last resort.

CULTURAL WEED CONTROL

Cultural weed control is the use of crop production practices that provide weed-control benefits. Usually, the strategy is to maximize the competitive ability of the crop, especially in the early seedling stage. Production practices such as site selection, along with site preparation and planting techniques, can help ensure a rapidly growing and uniform forage crop with minimal weed competition.

SITE SELECTION

If you are going to the trouble and expense of establishing a food plot, be sure to choose a site where the forage will thrive. A good site for a food plot from an agronomic perspective will be well drained, open to light for the majority of the day, free of large rocks and timber debris, and have a crumbly, tillable soil. A site of this type will have the potential to grow healthy forage plants that will compete with weeds. If the site is of marginal quality, forage growth will be poor, and weeds may become an unending nightmare.

Prior history of the potential food plot site is also an important consideration. Old, fallow agricultural fields can be ideal areas to plant food plots. However, be aware that there is often a smorgasbord of weed seeds left over from the former agricultural days waiting in the soil. This "seed bank" can respond with an explosion of weeds as soon as the soil is disturbed.

> ## DON'T BE A WEED SEEDER
>
> In his talks on food plot management, researcher and consultant Dr. Grant Woods mentions a simple tip for reducing your weed battles — keep clean equipment. After mowing or disking weedy or overgrown areas, be sure to clean thatch and debris off your tractor and implements before taking them to an established food plot where weed control is already underway. This thatch is likely full of weed seeds that will fall or blow off your equipment as you work.

SITE PREPARATION

Site preparation sets the stage for a successful food plot. Your choice of site preparation technique can also have important weed management implications. Any type of site preparation that disturbs the soil will stimulate the seed bank, and in many cases, the more severe the disturbance, the more severe the potential weed problem. Weed seed dormancy is often broken by a combination of tillage practices that brings deeply buried seed to the upper layers of the soil profile where light triggers seed germination. This must happen in the presence of adequate soil moisture for seeds to absorb water and within appropriate temperature and oxygen regimes. In addition, many types of weeds require a scarification, or scratching, of the seed coat for germination. Reduced soil disturbance is one of the reasons why planting with a no-till drill, particularly after an area has been treated with a broad-spectrum herbicide, can be an effective weed-management technique.

Although soil disturbance can stimulate weed seed germination, it can also be used to control weeds. This type of site preparation weed control, commonly referred to as stale seedbeds, involves preparing seedbeds several weeks before actual planting. Between the initial seedbed preparation and planting are opportunities to till the soil repeatedly. Each tilling will stimulate weed seed germination and control weeds that have germinated following the previous tillage. Weed seeds usually germinate and emerge from the top 3 inches of soil. Repeated shallow tillage will stimulate and control weed seedlings before planting, thereby reducing the amount of viable weed seeds in the germination zone. A good rule of thumb is to thoroughly till the seedbed at least twice at two-week intervals before planting. Sequential tillage should be in perpendicular passes for maximum effectiveness. The tillage implement of choice for site preparation and stale seedbed weed control is a disk harrow. Tractor-pulled disk harrows have enough weight to till the soil 3- to 6-inches deep without requiring an excessive amount of horsepower.

Forage Species Selection

Choosing the correct forage for your area is a critical step in cultural weed control. If the forage is not adapted to your region, it will not grow very well, and weeds will be a problem due to a lack of competitive ability by the forage crop. Genetically improved forage varieties are excellent competitors with weeds compared to non-improved selections. They are often selected for seedling vigor, rapid vegetative growth, and multiple pest resistance, in addition to desirable forage quality characteristics. These attributes also enhance the competitive ability of the forage with weeds. Pay the extra price for these improved varieties. They are worth it.

Other Agronomic Practices

When soil nutrients and pH are at optimum levels,

RANS THOMAS

Fighting Weeds with Bullets

When deer population densities are too high for the available nutrition, overbrowsing is a problem on both food plots and native forage. The iron and clay peas that once stood in this field might have outcompeted the coffeeweed, nutgrass and other weeds that now dominate, except the peas were browsed to death. The weeds then took advantage of the situation, producing millions of seeds that will ensure continued problems in this food plot. By preventing overbrowsing through population and habitat management, you also make weed management easier.

forages can grow rapidly, giving them the capability to successfully compete with weeds. Soil fertility problems will surely result in poor forage growth, which exacerbate weed management efforts. Do not guess on soil fertility. Use soil-testing services to determine the soil fertility status of your food plot site.

Quality of forage seeds is an often-overlooked component of cultural weed control. Poor-quality seed may be old, improperly handled or stored inappropriately. Regardless of the reason, poor-quality seed will result in unevenly distributed or sparsely established forage seedlings that provide an open door for weed establishment.

Always use the recommended seeding rates when establishing forages. While it is tempting to reduce seeding rates to save money, this will make weed management much more difficult. Forage plants that are widely spaced due to a low seeding rate are poor competitors with weeds. Conversely, many hunters plant too much seed (often double rates per acre) and skimp on fertilizer. This is an unwise practice causing tiny seedlings to compete with each other, slowing growth and wasting money.

MECHANICAL WEED CONTROL

Tillage and mowing are types of mechanical weed control that are practical weed-management techniques in deer forage plots. Shallow tillage will cut or uproot annual weeds, which will not re-grow if the weeds are small. If forages such as corn, sorghum, soybean or peas are planted in rows, cultivation between rows is effective.

Weed seed production can be prevented by timely tillage between annual plantings or reestablishment of perennial forages. If a forage plot is harrowed to prevent weed seed production, thoroughly till the site and repeat as needed. Many times, large weeds will be partially controlled if harrowed only once and may still produce seed. Given the effort and investment necessary to establish quality deer forages, the expense of additional tillage is insignificant considering the potential returns.

Mowing using sharp blades to cleanly cut broadleaf weeds is an effective form of control if the weeds are significantly taller than the forage. This technique is particularly effective for controlling broadleaf weeds in clover mixtures. However, mowing will only temporarily control grasses. The growing point of a grass plant is close to the soil surface, below the point of cutting, so grasses will simply re-grow from below the point of cutting. Mowing is also only temporarily effective in controlling perennial broadleaf weeds, which often re-grow when mowed.

Although mowing can be used to help control weeds, it can also exacerbate problems with some perennial weeds. Timing is critical. Mowing too early allows some weeds to produce suckers, increasing the number of flowers and seeds produced, while mowing too late may unintentionally help disperse the viable seed. For example, most thistles are perennials and produce only one flowering stalk under normal growing conditions. However, if thistle is mowed prior to, or when flowering, it usually will produce numerous new flowering stalks from the crown which produce more flowers and more wind-blown seed.

PREVENTING WEED SEED PRODUCTION

Controlling weed problems in food plots is not a quick-fix. In fact, the best weed control option is to use preventative measures such as planting practices that help prevent a problem from developing. Once a weed problem develops, the long-term success of managing weeds depends on depleting the numbers of weed seeds in the upper soil layers and preventing further weed seed production.

THE NUMBERS GAME

Annual weeds are propagated by seeds, with the number and size of seeds varying according to species. For example, pigweeds are among the smallest weed seeds. They are black, shiny and about the size of a grain of table salt. In contrast, annual morningglory seeds are dark brown, shaped like an orange slice, and about the size of a BB shot. One pigweed plant can produce more than 200,000 seeds, whereas morningglories produce much fewer seeds. What does this mean? If we assume that a food plot has an infestation of morningglory at a density of one plant per 10 square feet, and each plant produces about 500 viable seeds, there would be more than 2 million seeds produced per acre! That means the potential exists to produce 2 million morningglory seedlings the following year, not counting seeds already in

156

Continued on page 162.

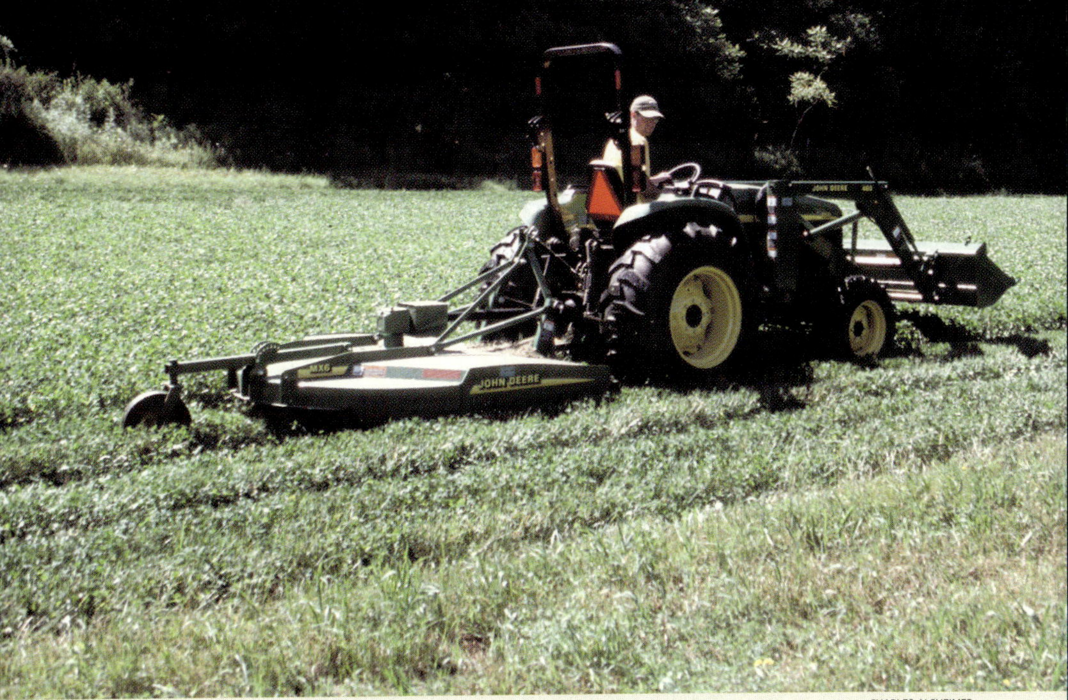

CHARLES ALSHEIMER

FIGHTING WEEDS WITH MOWERS AND CULTIVATORS

Mowing clover (above) to a height of 3 to 6 inches in the summer is a good way to control tall, broadleaf weeds while also rejuvenating the clover. Cultivation (below) works for controlling weeds in row crops like corn, soybeans, peas and sorghum.

TES RANDLE JOLLY

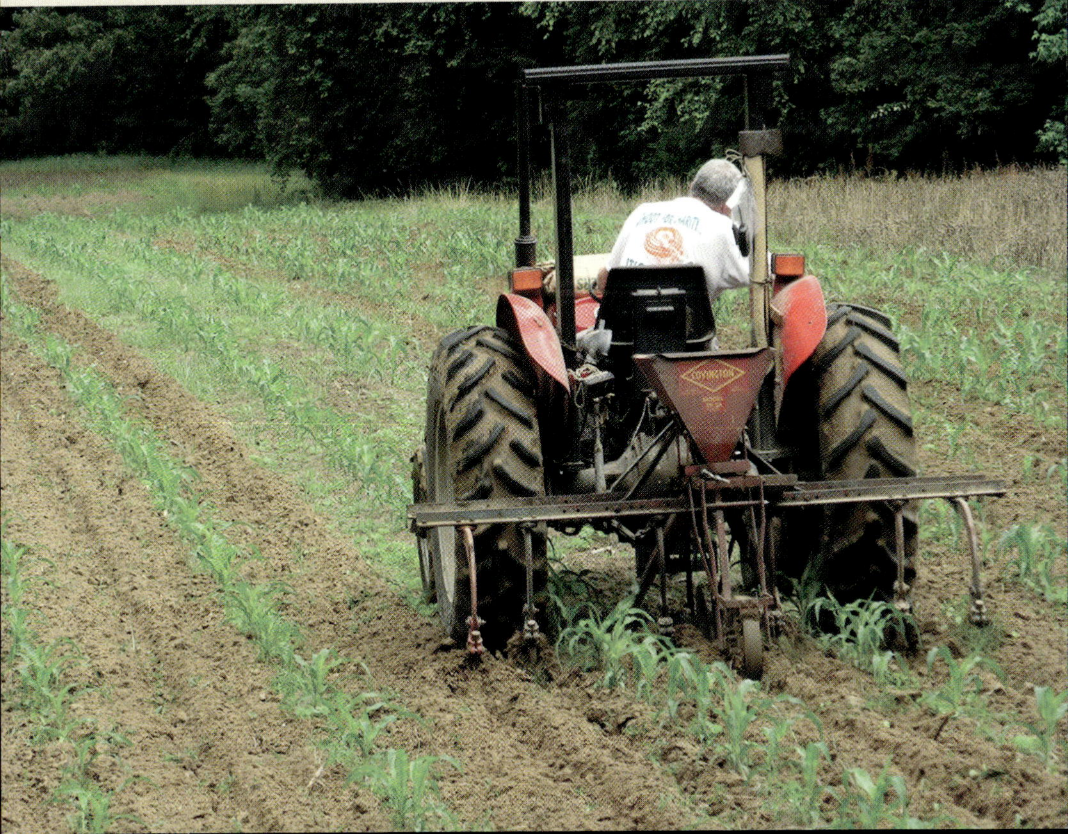

16

of the MOST
NOTORIOUS
Food Plot Weeds
in North America

YELLOW NUTSEDGE
Cyperus esculentus
Sometimes called yellow nutgrass but it is in the sedge family. This non-native species spreads through tuber growth as well as seeds.
ROBERT H. MOHLENBROCK, USDA–NRCS PLANTS DATABASE

HORSENETTLE
Solanum carolinense
This warm-season perennial weed often can become a problem in perennial clover plots.
TED BODNER, SOUTHERN WEED SCIENCE SOCIETY, WWW.FORESTRYIMAGES.ORG

SICKLEPOD
Senna obtusifolia
Also known as coffeeweed, sicklepod is an annual legume and is therefore difficult to treat in warm-season legume crops like soybeans.
TED BODNER, SOUTHERN WEED SCIENCE SOCIETY, WWW.FORESTRYIMAGES.ORG

QUACKGRASS
Elytrigia repens
Quackgrass is a non-native invasive in the North and West. It does not tolerate long, hot summers in the Southeast.
DR. LYNN CLARK AND ANNA GARDNER, IOWA STATE UNIVERSITY, WWW.FORESTRYIMAGES.ORG

COCKLEBUR
Xanthium spp.
Both spiny and rough cocklebur are problematic annual weeds, particularly in warm season plantings.

GARLIC MUSTARD
Alliaria petiolata
A non-native, invasive biennial herb that invades both fields and forest openings of the North. Crushed leaves give off a garlic odor.

BERMUDAGRASS
Cynodon dactylon
An introduced, perennial, mat-forming, warm-season grass native to Africa. Difficult to control without repeated herbicide applications.

FOXTAIL
Setaria spp.
The foxtail grasses are summer annuals that can become problem weeds, particularly in perennial clover plots.

MANAGING WEEDS

MORNINGGLORY
Ipomoea spp.
Several species of these climbing or trailing vines can become problems in food plots.

BILLY CRAFT, WWW.FORESTRYIMAGES.ORG

CURLY DOCK
Rumex crispus
This introduced species is a perennial weed with a large tap root and is capable of producing 40,000 or more seeds in one year.

STEPHEN SOLHEIM, WISCONSIN STATE HERBARIUM

COMMON MULLEIN
Verbascum thapsus
Mullein is a biennial. During the first year it grows as a low-growing rosette. The flower stalk appears in the second year, after which the plant dies.

TED BODNER, SOUTHERN WEED SCIENCE SOCIETY, WWW.FORESTRYIMAGES.ORG

LAMBSQUARTERS
Chenopodium album
One of the most common summer annual weeds.

CHRIS EVANS, UNIVERSITY OF GEORGIA, WWW.FORESTRYIMAGES.ORG

PIGWEED
Amaranthus spp.
Dozens of species of pigweeds are found across North America.

ROBERT H. MOHLENBROCK, USDA-NRCS PLANTS DATABASE

VELVETLEAF
Abutilon theophrasti
Non-native annual herb.
Inset photo shows flower and seed pods.

CHARLES T. BRYSON, USDA-ARS, FORESTRYIMAGES.ORG
INSET: STEPHEN SOLHEIM, WISCONSIN STATE HERBARIUM

JOHNSONGRASS
Sorghum halepense
A Mediterranean native brought in as a pasture grass, now considered one of the most noxious weeds in the world.

CHARLES T. BRYSON, USDA-ARS, FORESTRYIMAGES.ORG

THISTLE
Cirsium spp.
(Canada thistle is shown here).
Several species are problematic, particularly the North.

NORMAN E. REES, USDA-ARS

161

MANAGING WEEDS

Continued from page 156.

the soil from preceding years. The calculations are even more impressive when you consider that pigweed can produce 400 times the number of seeds as morningglories. Therefore, it's obvious that one of the keys to weed management is to deplete the numbers of seeds in the soil and to prevent future weed seed production.

If effective weed control is continued for several years, eventually the amount of weed seed in the soil will be reduced, and weed management becomes easier. However, this change is not permanent. For example, a study in Colorado clearly demonstrates the importance of sustained, uninterrupted weed control. In this study, weeds were intensively controlled in a corn field for five years. As a result, they reported a seven-fold reduction in the number of pigweed seeds and a 10-fold reduction in the number of other weed seeds. However, once the weed management was stopped, it took only two years for the number of weed seeds to recover to within 50 percent of the original density.

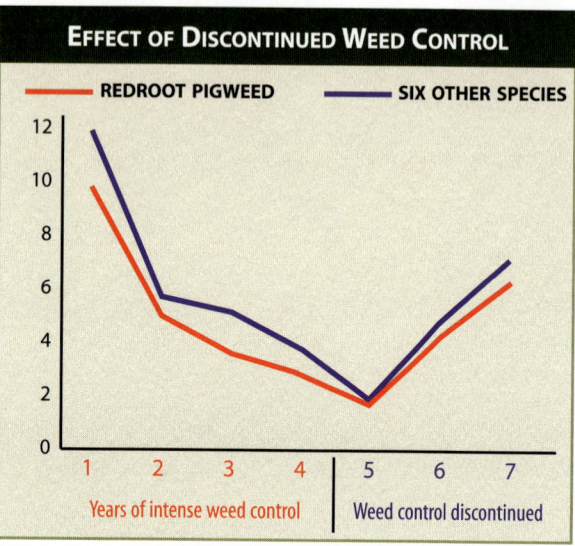

Adapted from *Weed Science,* "Weed seed decline in irrigated soil after six years of continuous corn and herbicides," 1984, by E. E. Schweizer and R. L. Zimdahl.

EFFECT OF WEED SEED BURIAL AND SOIL TYPE ON SEED GERMINATION RATES

Numbers to the right of species names are percentages of seed that remained viable after lengthy burial times.

Weed Species	Years buried in silt clay loam soil				Years buried in very fine sandy loam soil			
	0	6	12	17	0	6	12	17
Redroot pigweed	66	3	7	0	66	9	7	1
Common mullein	98	92	85	72	98	90	90	95
Common dock	76	87	83	77	76	94	73	61
Ivyleaf Morningglory	69	7	8	7	69	6	6	3
Velvetleaf	15	70	25	25	15	60	29	35
Common lamsquarters	28	48	42	28	28	14	16	7
Yellow foxtail	94	7	2	0	94	56	9	0
Large crabgrass	12	15	1	0	12	1	0	0

Adapted from *Weed Science,* "Seed longevity of 41 weed species buried 17 years in eastern and western Nebraska," 1996, by O. C. Burnside, R. G. Wilson, S. Weisberg, and K. G. Hubbard.

How long it takes for intense weed management to reduce the seed bank depends on how long weed seeds remain viable in the soil. This varies among species and among soil types. A 17-year research trial conducted at the University of Nebraska compared the germination rates of various weed species after they had been buried in two different soil types. The germination rates of some species such as foxtail, crabgrass, pigweed and morningglory declined significantly over the 17-year period. However, it's amazing that the germination rate of common mullein, curly dock, velvetleaf and common lambsquarters seed remained consistently high even after burial for 17 years. The important conclusion is that many types of weed seeds can remain dormant for long periods and germinate when stimulated. Therefore, efforts to deplete numbers of weed seeds in the soil must be sustained for several years before benefits can be seen. It is also critical to prevent new seed production every year. Skipping weed control for only one or two years can put you right back where you started.

LOCAL HELP

If you don't have spraying equipment, in some areas you can contract with a farm supply or co-op service to hire a sprayer truck like this one.

RANS THOMAS

CHEMICAL WEED CONTROL

Herbicides are certainly the most useful tool for managing weed problems, but it is critical to understand the capabilities and selectivity of any herbicide you use. Be sure to always read the label that comes packaged with the herbicide. The label will provide details on the types of plants controlled, application rates, application timing, and safety issues. If you don't have a copy of the label, you can obtain them from the manufacturer's Web site or at *http://www.cdms.net*. These sites are regularly updated with information on most pesticides, including herbicides. Always remember, it is your responsibility to follow all guidelines on the label because the label is the official legal reference on correct use of herbicides.

NON-SELECTIVE OR KILL-ALL HERBICIDES

Many actively growing weeds can be killed before planting food plots with herbicides such as glyphosate (Roundup® and generics). This broad-spectrum herbicide is particularly useful for controlling perennial weeds such as johnsongrass, common bermudagrass, bigroot morningglory and horsenettle. It also effectively controls many annual weeds. Glyphosate enters plants through the foliage only, so it will only control emerged weeds that are actively growing. It has no significant effect on seed in the soil or non-emerged seedlings. The ability of glyphosate to control actively growing annual and perennial weeds makes it ideal for site preparation and stale seedbed weed control. Glyphosate concentrate (41 percent), mixed with water to make a 1 or 2 percent solution (for example, 0.8 to 1.6 quarts of Roundup concentrate mixed in 20 gallons of water) and applied before planting food plots, boosts overall weed control. The lower concentration (1 percent solution) is sufficient for many annual weeds, while the higher concentration is needed for most perennial weeds. After spraying, do not till or mow the food plot for at least seven days to allow ample time for glyphosate to enter the weeds and translocate throughout the plant.

For effective control of troublesome perennial weeds such as johnsongrass, it is best to spray glyphosate in summer or autumn but before a killing frost. Perennial weeds readily translocate glyphosate to underground vegetative structures – roots, rhizomes, stolons and tubers – during the autumn, just prior to dormancy. This ensures herbicidal activity on the entire plant.

GLYPHOSATE-RESISTANT CROPS

One major innovation in modern agriculture has been the recent development of crop varieties that have been genetically engineered to have resistance to direct applications of glyphosate. Currently, there are significant plantings of glyphosate-resistant soybeans, cotton and corn across the United States, and this technology is being extended to include other crops. Glyphosate can be applied directly to glyphosate-resistant crops, offering simple, broad-spectrum weed control without crop injury. This technology can also be used for weed management in food plots.

BRIAN SHEPPARD

ROUNDUP READY

The photo on the left shows corn that is about to be engulfed by coffeeweed. With Roundup Ready corn, a grower can spray glyphosate over the field, as shown below, killing the weeds without harming the corn. This method has a number of advantages over methods used to control weeds in conventional corn.

Choosing a glyphosate-resistant crop cultivar will allow managers to conveniently control weeds using glyphosate. A useful variation is to plant glyphosate-resistant crops in rotation between plantings of other forage species. This will provide control of troublesome weeds that may be difficult to manage in some forage plantings. But remember, glyphosate will severely injure or kill conventional crop varieties, so make sure that you are using glyphosate-resistant crops by checking the label on the original seed bag. Also remember that any seed residues from these crops that volunteer in the field the next season cannot be killed with glyphosate.

BILL LEA

THE ROOT OF THE PROBLEM

The extensive fibrous root systems of grasses, like this fescue, make them intense competitors for nutrients and water.

GRASS CONTROL

Grasses are often the most common and troublesome weeds in food plots. Grasses are prolific seed producers. For example, crabgrass can produce 3,700 seeds per plant; barnyardgrass can produce 7,100 seeds per plant, and foxtail 4,000 seeds per plant. Grasses also have an extensive fibrous root system that makes them intense competitors for nutrients and water.

The simplest method to control grasses in broadleaf forage plantings is to use a postemergence herbicide that exclusively controls grasses. Sethoxydim (sold under the trade names Arrest®, Poast®, Poast Plus® and Sethoxydim G-Pro®) was the first selective postemergence grass herbicide registered. Initially, this broad group of herbicides was only registered for use on major agronomic crops such as soybean, cotton, peanuts and alfalfa. Later, specific products with the same active ingredient were registered for other uses such as agronomic crops, vegetable crops, tree fruit

EXAMPLES OF HERBICIDES CONTAINING SETHOXYDIM

Brand Name	Manufacturer	Concentration	Rate	Crop oil?
Poast	Micro-Flo	1.5 lb. ai/gal.	0.5 - 2.5 pt./acre	Required
Poast Plus	Micro-Flo	1.0 lb. ai/gal.	0.75 - 3.75 pt./acre	Required
Arrest	Whitetail Institute	1.0 lb. ai/gal.	0.8 - 1.4 fl.oz./1,000 ft^2	No
Sethoxydim G-Pro	Gro-Pro	1.0 lb. ai/gal.	0.75 - 3.75 pt./acre	Required

Note: Refer to the individual herbicide labels for detailed instructions on weeds controlled, rates, adjuvant requirements, and crop restrictions. This information can be found at http://www.cdms.net.

MANAGING WEEDS

Texas panicum, like all grasses, is difficult to identify at this 2- to 3-leaf stage of growth. However, this is the ideal stage of growth for control using post-emergence grass herbicides.

Large crabgrass can be easily controlled with sethoxydim at this stage of growth. However, sethoxydim efficacy is quickly reduced as large crabgrass grows beyond this stage.

Goosegrass is not as sensitive to sethoxydim as other annual grasses. Thus, sethoxydim needs to be applied before goosegrass reaches this stage of growth.

PHOTOS BY CARROLL JOHNSON III

and nut crops, turf, ornamentals, and wildlife forage plantings. Sethoxydim is commonly used due to the availability of small-unit packaging well suited for use in wildlife forage plantings, particularly alfalfa and clover. Clethodim (sold as Select®, Prism® and Arrow®) is registered for grass control in many broadleaf crops and alfalfa, but not clover. Remember, it is your responsibility to follow the instructions on the label, including the list of crops on which the specific herbicide can be used.

Sethoxydim controls annual and perennial grasses after they emerge. It does not control non-emerged grasses, nor will it prevent future grass emergence from seed. All of the grass-specific herbicides are more effective on smaller, younger grasses. A small grass has two to four leaves, which is the ideal stage for optimum herbicide effectiveness. An example is seedling Texas panicum in the two- to three-leaf stage of growth (see photo, top left). Texas panicum at this stage of growth is consistently controlled by sethoxydim. Large crabgrass at the 5- to 6-leaf stage of growth and larger (center left) is difficult to consistently control with sethoxydim. Goosegrass (bottom left) at any stage of growth can be difficult to control with sethoxydim. If the grasses are beginning to produce seed, don't bother spraying any postemergence grass herbicide – you'll just be wasting time and money.

Mowing can supplement herbicides for control of grasses, but it must be done at the right time. As a general rule, spray first and then mow about two weeks later. Mowing forces grasses to produce numerous new shoots from the base of the plant. Because each shoot has its own growing point, grasses that have been mowed are more difficult to control with herbicides. Sethoxydim is a systemic herbicide, which means it is translocated throughout the plant. Waiting two weeks before mowing will allow the herbicide to move through the plant, improving control.

Grass-specific herbicides have little effect on broadleaf plants and sedges, although there are a few exceptions. If they are applied at registered rates, postemergence grass herbicides will not injure clover, alfalfa, brassica species and other broadleaf forages. They also will not control broadleaf weeds such as pigweeds, lambsquarters, morningglories or sedges. These herbicides will, however, injure or kill grass forages like corn, grain sorghum, rye, wheat, oats and ryegrass. So, if you are planting a mixture of forages that includes any of these grasses, you cannot use a grass-specific herbicide.

Despite their beneficial attributes, postemergence grass herbicides are not foolproof. Large annual grasses cannot be controlled consistently, and perennial grasses will require two or more applications for satisfactory control. Their performance is also dependent on optimum weather conditions. If weather conditions are excessively hot (greater than 95 degrees), cool (less than 50 degrees), or droughty (plants are visibly wilting from moisture stress) herbicide performance will be disappointing.

STEVE GULLEDGE

SPRAYER CALIBRATION

With any herbicide, applying the exact amount of chemical is critical to success, so your sprayer unit must be calibrated – whether it is a backpack sprayer, an ATV-mounted model or a large, tractor-mounted boom sprayer. The Equipment chapter (Chapter 5) contains instructions for sprayer calibration.

Postemergence grass herbicides usually require a spray tank additive for optimum performance. The best choice is crop oil concentrate, a mixture of paraffin- or vegetable-based oil plus a surfactant that forms an emulsion when mixed with water. The oil helps the herbicide penetrate the leaf surface, and the surfactant helps the spray droplet spread across the leaf surface. The correct selection and use of a crop oil concentrate is crucial for optimum performance from postemergence grass killers, so follow the instructions on the herbicide label.

The postemergence grass killers are quickly absorbed by the grass foliage, and wash-off by rainfall is not likely. However, symptoms of injury to the grasses take about seven to 10 days to develop, and the first symptoms are very subtle. Often, first-time users of these herbicides fear that the herbicide is not working. Be patient – these grass killers begin to affect the growth of grasses at the growing point where the youngest leaves are beginning to unroll. At about seven to 10 days after treat-

167

MANAGING WEEDS

ment, an unrolled leaf can be easily pulled from the plant, exposing brown decaying tissue at the base. The entire weed will soon develop a yellow-purple cast, and then all visible foliage will appear wilted and brown. This process takes longer in larger grasses, or in droughty conditions. Re-growth of larger annual grasses or perennial grasses will likely occur, making a second application necessary in about two or three weeks.

Grasses are not the only weed problem that you may encounter in your food plots. However, the various grass-specific herbicides are effective, versatile and simple. Therefore, they can be an excellent investment if grasses are a problem in plots planted in clover, alfalfa or any other broadleaf forage crop.

BROADLEAF WEED CONTROL

Broadleaf weeds can be more difficult to control with herbicides than grasses. There are few herbicides that will control broadleaf weeds without injuring the broadleaf forage. This problem is compounded when food plot mixes are used. Therefore, it is important to know what forage species are in your seed mix and only use herbicides on those listed on the herbicide label.

Pendimethalin (Prowl®) and pronamide (Kerb®) are registered for preemergence weed control in certain forage legumes. These herbicides are applied immediately after seeding the forage but before weed emergence. Neither herbicide will control weeds after they emerge. Both provide residual control of annual grasses and some broadleaf weeds. Neither herbicide is marketed for small-acreage plantings nor are they packaged in small units.

Imazethapyr (Slay® and Pursuit®) controls many broadleaf weeds, some grasses, and suppresses perennial nutsedges in clover and alfalfa. Many forage spe-

PRE-EMERGENT WEED CONTROL

In some cases when weed management practices are not already in place, weeds can completely overtake a food plot before planted seed can begin to grow. This is especially true with warm-season plantings, like the lablab shown here – nutgrasses and coffeeweed are surrounding the lablab and will likely conquer it. While cultural and mechanical weed-control techniques should be used wherever possible to avoid these problems, an option among chemical treatments is to prevent weed problems with pre-emergence spraying. The trick, however, is to identify problem weed species before planting so you can match the pre-emergent herbicide needed with a planting that is labeled for that particular herbicide. When the appropriate pre-emergent herbicide is used for an identified weed problem, later maintenance is relatively easy.

RANS THOMAS

cies tolerate imazethapyr when applied at the registered rate and stage of forage growth. However, imazethapyr will severely injure brassica species (rape, canola and turnip), chicory, ryegrass, grain sorghum and sunflower. Therefore, don't use imazethapyr on commercial seed blends that contain these species. Imazethapyr also remains active in the soil, and this soil activity can influence future forage plantings. Some species require a very long time between spraying and planting, whereas others such as peanuts, peas and soybeans can be planted immediately (see table on this page).

There is an extensive list of weed species that are controlled by imazethapyr. Legume crops (soybeans, peanuts, peas, alfalfa and clover) generally have acceptable tolerance to imazethapyr, making it an excellent choice for weed control in legume-based food plots. However, it likely will do little to control weeds that are in the legume family – sicklepod being a notable example – so correct weed identification is important. Contact your local Cooperative Extension Service office if you need weed identification assistance.

REPLANTING AFTER IMAZETHAPYR	
Imazethapyr remains active in the soil and can influence future plantings. Below are the recommended waiting times between spraying and planting for several forage species.	
FORAGE SPECIES	**MINIMUM WAIT**
Brassica	40 months
Ryegrass	40 months
Chicory	40 months
Forbs	40 months
Grain sorghum	18 months
Sunflower	18 months
Oats	18 months
Rye	4 to 18 months*
Barley	4 to 9 months*
Corn	8 to months
Wheat	4 months
Clover	4 months
Alfalfa	4 months
Pea/bean	Anytime to 4 months**
Peanut	Anytime
Soybean	Anytime

*Varies according to geographic location. Refer to the label for specific statements.
**Varies according to type of pea or bean.

Clover and alfalfa need to be at or beyond the second trifoliate stage of seedling growth (about 2 to 3 inches tall) before application. Earlier applications will stunt these crops and reduce stand vigor. Imazethapyr should be applied to seedling weeds when they are less than 3 inches tall for consistent results. Refer to the imazethapyr product labels for detailed information on the optimum weed size for each species.

The soil residual properties of imazethapyr also control many weed species before they emerge. Imazethapyr can be applied from 3 to 6 fl.ozs./acre, with a maximum rate of 6 fl.ozs./acre per year. An effective strategy in legume forages where weed pressure is heavy is to split applications using 3 fl.ozs./acre in the spring and 3 fl.ozs./acre in the fall.

Although forage legumes have excellent tolerance to imazethapyr, they can be injured if the herbicide is applied at excessive rates. Therefore, avoid the temptation to apply extra imazethapyr to boost broadleaf weed control. An accurately calibrated and properly operated sprayer will ensure the correct rate is applied. Use an ATV or tractor-mounted sprayer to apply imazethapyr because they are capable of applying herbicides precisely and uniformly. A backpack sprayer is not a good choice for applying imazethapyr. See Chapter 5 for information on sprayer calibration.

Assuming that an appropriate surfactant or crop oil concentrate has been used, imazethapyr will be adequately absorbed by the weed foliage within one hour after

MANAGING WEEDS

application. Nevertheless, avoid spraying when rainfall is imminent or during a drought. Imazethapyr symptoms take about seven to 14 days to appear. Symptoms include stunting and yellowing of foliage, followed by plant death.

Another herbicide that controls broadleaf weeds in clover and alfalfa is 2,4-DB (Butyrac 200®). This herbicide mimics plant growth hormones, causing susceptible plants to have grossly distorted growth habit before death. 2,4-DB is chemically related to the more familiar 2,4-D, but forage legume response differs between the two herbicides. This distinction is important because 2,4-DB can be used on legume forages such as clover and alfalfa, while 2,4-D will severely injure or kill forage legumes.

The rate of 2,4-DB on seedling clover and alfalfa is 1 to 3 qts./acre. It is more effective on small weeds than large weeds. It also has no significant soil residual properties, so it will not carry-over to future forage plantings. Although legumes and grasses are tolerant of 2-4-DB, chicory, brassica species and other forbs are sensitive to 2,4-DB. Therefore, use 2,4-DB only on pure stands of clover or alfalfa or those mixed with grasses. Many of the commercial blends of forage seeds contain species sensitive to 2,4-DB.

USING A WICK-BAR IN FORAGE PLANTINGS

The most universally accepted herbicide with wide familiarity among the general public is glyphosate. Glyphosate is nonselective – it kills most plants indiscriminately. However, glyphosate can be applied selectively by ensuring minimal contact

to desirable species. This can be done by applying glyphosate with a wiper-apparatus, commonly called a wick-bar or rope-wick applicator. A wick-bar is a non-pressurized device that wipes a concentrated solution of glyphosate on individual tall weeds. Its most basic form is a PVC pipe filled with a glyphosate and water solution that saturates a series of overlapping wicks that run the length of the PVC pipe. The wicks are set in the PVC pipe with o-rings and compression-fittings to control flow of herbicide and prevent dripping. Normally, the wick-bar is mounted on a tractor or ATV. The design is very simple, and you can make your own wick-bar applicators and

CARROLL JOHNSON III

RANS THOMAS

WIPE ON

Wick-bar applicators like these are used to wipe glyphosate onto taller weeds while passing over food plot crops. This method targets specific plants and uses herbicide conservatively. Plants must be "wiped" in one direction and then wiped with a return pass in the other direction. Wick-bars can be mounted on tractors or ATVs, but you must be careful that herbicide is not wiped off the target plants onto the underside of the vehicle, where it may be wiped on the wrong plants.

CHARLES ALSHEIMER

MANAGING WEEDS

mounting hardware. There are suppliers of kits to mount height-adjustable wick-bar applicators on the front of an ATV. The wick-bar was developed to control johnsongrass in cotton. However, it is also effective on tall annual broadleaf weeds such as ragweed, cocklebur and pigweed. The key is to wipe the weeds twice in opposite directions at a slow ground speed of about 2 mph.

Because glyphosate is absorbed by the plant foliage and translocated throughout the plant, it is the herbicide of choice for wick applicators. If an adequate amount of foliage is covered by a concentrated glyphosate solution, the entire weed is usually killed. However, the performance of glyphosate depends on conditions at the time of treatment. Control may be poor if weeds are under drought or heat stress.

The wick-bar is only effective when weeds are taller than the crop. This means that the weed would have to be present for several weeks or months before treatment. In other words, the weed would have been competing with the forage crop for several weeks or months. Therefore, a wick-bar is a tool for salvage weed control or food plot rescue, not the primary means to manage weeds.

When using a wick-bar, the vehicle needs to have ample clearance over the forage, and the wick-bar should be mounted on the front of the vehicle. As the weeds are wiped, they will be pushed down as the vehicle passes over, depositing some of the herbicide from the treated weeds onto the bottom of the vehicle. Unless the vehicle clears the forage plants, the forage may acquire glyphosate from the bottom of the vehicle, causing crop injury.

It is also useful to have manually or hydraulically controlled height adjustments for the wick-bar. Variations in weed and crop height, along with changes in topography, make on-the-fly height adjust-

BE MINDFUL OF INVASIVES

The vast majority of problematic weeds in food plots are non-native invasives that were introduced to this country either accidentally or – as in the case of species like johnsongrass – intentionally. Several of the worst weed species that are highlighted in this chapter are non-native. Though some weeds have benefits for wildlife, most invasive weeds have no value of any kind. Believe it or not, many invasive plants, shrubs and trees are bought and sold every day at garden and home centers in your hometown. Help avoid spreading these species by learning about them. One of the best places to start learning is online at www.invasive.org, or contact you local County Extension office.

HERBICIDES IN REVIEW

Type:	Generic:	Brand Names:
Non-Selective (Kill-All)	glyphosate	Roundup, Glyflo
Grass-Selective (kills grasses)	sethoxydim	Arrest, Poast, Poast Plus, Sethoxydim G-Pro
Broadleaf-Selective, Pre-emergence	pendimethalin	Prowl
	pronamide	Kerb
Broadleaf-Selective, Post-emergence	imazethapyr	Slay, Pursuit
	2, 4-DB	Butyrac 200

ments desirable. Weeds should be at least 6 inches taller than the forage, and the wick-bar height needs to be set at least 2 inches taller than the forage.

Refer to the instructions on the herbicide label for applying glyphosate through a wick-bar. According to the label, Roundup Ultra Max® in the wick-bar needs to be mixed at a 33 percent solution: one part Roundup Ultra Max® concentrate and two parts water. Although this high concentration may lead you to think that this is an expensive treatment, in practice it is not because there is little herbicide wasted when it is precisely applied to the weed.

SUMMARY

Remember, the principles of effective weed management in food plots are an integration of cultural practices (site selection, site preparation, stale seedbed weed control, uniform forage stand, preventing weed seed production), mechanical weed control (mowing, tillage, hand-weeding), and judicious use of herbicides. Depending on only one component of the system for weed control will not work. Integrating all three components will give managers of forage plots a chance to successfully manage weeds.

WEED IDENTIFICATION WEB LINKS AND REFERENCES

www.weedscience.msstate.edu/swss
Web site for the Southern Weed Science Society, where you can purchase the "Interactive Encyclopedia of North American Weeds," a comprehensive DVD-ROM prepared by Thundersnow Interactive Inc.

www.QDMA.com
Web site of the Quality Deer Management Association, where you can purchase "Forest Plants of the Southeast and their Wildlife Uses," by James H. Miller and Karl V. Miller.

www.wssa.net
Web site for the Weed Science Society of America (WSSA). This link accesses technical data bases on weed identification, terminology, herbicides, and links to other weed resources.

www.btny.purdue.edu/extension/weeds/notillid/notillweedid1.html
Weed identification site for Purdue University (Indiana).

www.weeds.iastate.edu/weed-id/weedid.htm
Weed identification site for Iowa State University.

http://muextension.missouri.edu/explore/manuals/m00169.htm
Weed management guide for forages prepared by the University of Missouri.

www.oardc.ohio-state.edu/weedid
Weed identification site for Ohio State University.

www.rce.rutgers.edu/weeds
Weed identification site for Rutgers University (New Jersey).

www.ppws.vt.edu/weedindex.htm
Weed identification site for Virginia Tech University.

www.uwyo.edu/CES/PUBS/B1126.pdf
Print-on-demand publication by the University of Wyoming on weed control in alfalfa.

11

Monitoring
Food Plots
BY LINDSAY THOMAS JR.

MONITORING FOOD PLOTS

eleven

Every food plot you grow will teach you something that will make your next food plot better, but to get the most out of this education you have to pay attention in class. Your food plot education will save you time and money over the long haul by increasing your efficiency and success, so it is time well invested. Yet, very few food plot growers take the time to monitor their plots, ask the right questions, or even remember what and how they planted last season. Even if you live far from the land you manage, you can monitor and learn from your experience.

KEEP RECORDS

You've got the ATV on the trailer along with a set of disk harrows, a broadcast spreader, a chainsaw, gas cans and other tools. The pickup is sagging with the weight of fertilizer, lime and seed. You're ready for a weekend of food plot planting. But don't forget two vital pieces of equipment – a notebook and a pencil. This equipment will be the key to your food plot improvement program.

Start your record keeping by naming every plot you intend to plant, including subsections of plots that will contain different crops. Avoid using simple numbers or letters to designate plots – these are easy to forget. Rather, choose names that reflect

the shape, location or history of the plot. Chances are you already refer to your plots with names like the 12-point Plot, the Rye Patch or the Cul-de-Sac. Divide your notebook into sections, one for each named plot. Supply each section with loose-leaf notebook pages as well as a hole-punched pocket folder to hold items like receipts, soil-test results and photographs.

Once your notebook is prepared, record as much information as you can about each plot. At a minimum, this information should include planting dates, seed varieties or blends, seeding rates and planting methods. Make notes about soil conditions at the time of planting. Record the amounts and types of fertilizer and lime applied to specific plots. You may even want to keep track of rainfall, the date of the first or last frost, and other weather factors. Imagine any information that you might need when you are troubleshooting a struggling crop, or trying to reproduce a successful one. The sample food plot record sheet on the next page is one example of a format that includes spaces for most everything you would need to record over the history of a food plot.

As your monitoring efforts continue, keep recording what you observe as well as steps you take to correct problems or improve production. Even hunting observations and harvest records for individual food plots can help, and tracking the hours spent hunting individual plots will help you avoid over-pressuring some areas and neglecting others.

MONITORING FOOD PLOTS

PLANT LIKE A SCIENTIST

Some people buy several types of seeds and commercial blends and then mix them all into a broadcast spreader, or the hopper on their grain drill. Certain mixes contain blends of compatible species that can be grown together, such as small grains and clovers. However, avoid planting everything but the kitchen sink in one plot. Many plants don't do well together because of varying planting depths due to differing seed size, different planting densities, and competition among different crops. It is also difficult to learn from a "kitchen sink" approach. If you've never grown lablab, jointvetch or buckwheat, how will you tell them apart in your mixed plot? These examples may be easy to sort once you know what they look like – but when it comes to mixing varieties of clovers in the same plot, even the experts can be stumped. If a species included in this mega-mix never appears, how will you learn the cause of its failure? Was it because the pH of the soil was too high or too low for that species? Did another plant in the mix out-compete the missing species, or was it not adapted to your climate?

Until your food plot knowledge is well advanced, it's best to plant something different in each plot – either a single species or a commercial or recommended blend of a few species that grow well together. Better yet, you might want to carve one or more of your food plots into sections and plant "microplots." This is where the crop scientist in each of us can really come out. With multiple sections in a single plot, each with its own experimental planting and monitoring effort, you can truly learn what crops do best in your soils, what crops are most preferred by deer, when that preference is highest, and what crops are easiest to grow or require more maintenance.

WHAT'S A MICROPLOT?

Microplots are not flower-box sized squares in a checkerboard food plot. You still need room to customize each microplot to the crop you plan to grow. This means room to prepare the soil correctly and apply lime and fertilizer at rates that may differ. Planting methods may also differ from those used in the next microplot. One microplot of small-seeded crops like clover might be planted with a hand spreader and then cultipacked, and the next microplot of large-seeded plants might be disked after seeding. Also, if you plant a highly preferred crop in a small plot, deer could wipe out the planting overnight – especially if you are planting warm-season legumes like cowpeas or lablab. Obviously, some of us are blessed with more open ground for food plots than others, but in most cases a test plot should be a minimum of ¼ acre. A 1-acre food plot, therefore, could be divided into four microplots.

Arrange your microplots in a way that suits the open ground. If you have a long, narrow plot with room to turn the tractor at the ends, make your microplots into long, narrow strips that parallel each other. This also gives deer an equal chance of encountering everything you plant. If one test plot is close to dense cover and another is more exposed, deer naturally will be biased toward the one closer to cover. Take factors like this into account when planning your experiments.

Remember to record what you planted where. The age-old gardener's method of tacking the seed packet to a stake will work fine for marking microplots. Or, you

FOOD PLOT RECORD

Plot_____ Acres_____ Year_____

Date of Soil Test/ Results	
Lime lbs./acre: appl. date:	
Fertilizer analysis: lbs./acre: appl. date:	
Tillage Record	
Species or Blend Planted	
Planting Rate/Depth	
Planting Method	
Weed Control Efforts	

Additional Comments:
(Weed issues, rainfall observations, plot quality)

MONITORING FOOD PLOTS

can map your plots on paper using a hand-drawn outline of your microplots. You can also make notes on a topo map or photocopy of an aerial photograph. Some tech-savvy food plotters even use hand-held GPS units and import waypoints into GIS software for the ultimate food plot map.

The next time you are at the seed store, standing before the racks of different food plot products trying to decide which one to try, pick several. Use the knowledge you have gained from this book about the species and blends most likely to be suited to your climate and soils, read the seed tags closely, and select several likely candidates. Plant them in microplots next to each other and find out for yourself which one you and the deer like best.

MONOCULTURES: WHERE'S THE FUN?

In contrast to the kitchen-sink food plotter, some people fill the bed of a pickup with sacks of a single type of seed, such as wheat or rye, and then plant every food plot in this one crop. The many advantages to offering a diversity of food plot crops have been covered elsewhere in this book, except one – the fun of it. The food plot addict in most of us can't withstand the opportunity to try a new blend, a new seed variety, or a new planting technique, just to see what kind of success it brings. The satisfaction of working with dirt, improving habitat and witnessing deer using the plots you have created will be enhanced by diversity.

FOOD PLOT SCIENTIST AT WORK

Planting different food plot crops side by side is a good way to meet deer nutritional needs over a broad window of time, but it's also a good way to compare the performance of different seed varieties and commercial products. Be sure to place a browse exclosure on every "microplot" and carefully record and mark what is planted in each strip.

CHARLES ALSHEIMER

After planting your plots, be sure to record what you observe. Ask more complex questions than simply "Which plants do the deer like most?" For example, deer may prefer a plant only during a certain time of year or during a certain stage in the plant's maturity. Without long-term monitoring, you won't learn these things. Other questions may include:

- *Which plantings seem to be the most or least drought tolerant?*

- *Which plantings hold up best to heavy deer grazing pressure?*

- *How well did my weed control method work?*

- *Did my planting method result in an adequate stand?*

There are unlimited questions to ask of your food plots, and many of the answers will be found in your notebook – if you keep good records!

Just because deer don't use a particular crop the first year you plant it does not necessarily mean that crop is a poor choice for your

H. W. WILLIAMS AERIAL PHOTOGRAPHY

EQUAL OPPORTUNITY PLOTS

When designing experimental plots for testing one crop against another, remember that proximity to cover will influence browse pressure. A plot close to cover or travel zones is likely to get more use than a plot far removed from these areas, regardless of what is planted. In this subdivided field, each plot adjoins wooded cover.

food plots. Sometimes, deer have to learn that an unfamiliar plant is valuable. For example, buckwheat, turnips and lupine are usually preferred plants, but they are not common agricultural crops in certain regions. When planted for deer, these crops may go untouched for a time, perhaps a year or more, before deer lock in on the desirable food source. Therefore, when trying crops that have never been grown in the area but are highly rated, give them time to prove themselves before writing them off. Also, remember that factors such as native food sources, deer density and weather can influence browse levels on food plots.

BROWSE EXCLOSURES

Often, food plot farmers complain about crop failure because nothing seemed to grow in the field they planted, especially in small plots. The plants germinated fine but never grew more than an inch or two in height. While it appeared that the

MONITORING FOOD PLOTS

crop failed to thrive and produce impressive amounts of forage, often the culprit is heavy browsing by deer. This is where a browse exclosure, also called a utilization cage, is important. A browse exclosure is a simple, wire exclosure that prevents deer from feeding in a small portion of a plot. The crop can grow inside this cage without browse pressure, providing a visual gauge of pressure outside the exclosure. This simple piece of "equipment" is crucial to much of your food plot education and will speed your journey up the learning curve.

You should place at least one browse exclosure on every food plot or microplot you plant (place them randomly before the plot germinates). Browse exclosures also provide an unbrowsed section of the plot where you can observe overall plant health. They will also help you gauge competition among plant species and assess which plants seem to disappear first in response to deer browsing. For example, in a clover/ rape mix planted at QDMA's National Headquarters in Georgia, browse exclosures contained only healthy, leafy rape that had shaded out all the clover. Outside the cages, however, deer had browsed back the rape, and clovers were thriving.

Too much browse pressure is obviously a bad thing. If the crop inside the cage is lush, tall and thriving, while outside the cage there is only crop stubble, weeds and deer droppings, you probably have too many deer for your current habitat conditions. To solve this problem, you should increase food plot acreage, take steps to improve native habitat, or buy more bullets. Most likely, a combination of all three is needed, but site-specific recommendations should come from a local, experienced wildlife biologist.

If the crop appears the same outside as inside the cage, and you see little indication of deer browsing the crop, continue monitoring. Any number of factors could

CONTINUING EDUCATION
A browse exclosure can teach you more than just how much deer are eating. You can also witness how browsing affects plant growth and maturity. Outside this exclosure, the crimson clover has been maintained at a short, leafy growth stage by browsing. Inside the exclosure, the clover has matured into much taller stems, produced flowers and will soon go to seed.

- Select 4-foot-high welded wire fencing with 2x4-inch panels.

- Wearing gloves and using wire shears, cut the fence into 10-foot long sections. Each 10-foot long section will form one browse exclosure. When cutting through the horizontal wires, make the cut close to the next vertical wire, leaving tag ends of horizontal wires projecting.

- Roll the section until the ends connect to form a cylinder. Bend the tag-end wires of one end around the vertical end wire of the opposite end, forming loops that attach the ends of the rolled cage together.

- Drive sturdy stakes of rebar or wood into the ground on opposite sides of the cage and secure the cage to the stakes with wire ties. Or, "weave" the stakes through at least three panels near the bottom of the cage by bending the panel wires slightly, then drive the stake into the ground. The cage should be secure enough to withstand wind as well as animals pushing against it.

be at play. As long as the crop is healthy and thriving, you have done your best to produce a quality food plot. Now, wait for a change in the weather or native forage conditions to lure deer to your plots. However, if this continues very long, you may want to consider switching species or mixes next year.

WEATHER MONITORING

Rainfall plays a major role in seed germination and forage production. Tracking rainfall may help you pinpoint the cause of less-than-desirable production or complete failure.

The best way to track rainfall is with a rain gauge located somewhere on the property. The local meteorologist can tell you how much rain they received at the television studio, but your plots may have received a very different amount, particularly during summer. Plastic rain gauges are inexpensive. You may want to put more than one on your property, particularly when plots are separated by large distances. Check your gauges regularly and, of course, record rainfall in your notebook. To minimize your own presence around food plots, place your rain gauge at a site that is removed from your plots and also convenient to visit.

Another resource becoming available across the country is automated weather monitoring stations. Internet users can log onto websites linked directly to weather equipment via satellite and get real-time information about the weather at that site — no meteorologist necessary. These are often established by state universi-

MONITORING FOOD PLOTS

ties or government agencies, and the networks usually include dozens of monitoring sites scattered around individual states. No matter where you live, you may be able to view conditions at a monitoring station near your food plots. These sites provide a lot of valuable information including soil temperatures at different depths, wind direction and speed, rainfall levels, air temperature, sunlight intensity, barometric pressure, and more.

Because these automated sites are hosted by different entities in each state, there is no easy way to find the one in your state. At the time of this printing, the website of the High Plains Regional Climate Center, a unit of the University of Nebraska at Lincoln, was hosting a list of links for automated weather monitoring networks across the country (list found at *http://hprcc.unl.edu/aws/ links.htm*). A general Internet search for "automated weather monitoring"

HIGH-TECH METEOROLOGY

Although rainfall is an uncontrollable factor in food plot success, seeing how your plots respond to differing levels of rainfall will guide future decisions – including timing of planting, site selection and crop selection. If you live far from your hunting property and cannot check a rain gauge regularly, automated weather monitoring stations found on the Web can help.

or "automated weather stations," plus your state's name, will also likely lead you to your state's network.

FOLLOW-UP SOIL TESTING

Most food plot growers are aware of the importance of soil testing prior to planting a food plot. However, these adjustments are not permanent – soil acidity will climb again, and elements will be depleted from soil, some at faster rates than others. Yet most food plot growers only apply an initial dose of lime and fertilizer, brush the dirt off their hands and consider their work done – no more spreading lime or fertilizer!

All of us wish quality food plots were this easy, but they aren't. It's often a good idea to conduct follow-up soil tests to stay in touch with your soil's fertility while a plot is in its productive stages. This is particularly important when managing perennial food plots such as alfalfa and perennial clovers. Periodic soil tests allow you to learn how long your soil amendments are impacting soil pH and fertility. It also allows you to address nutrient problems in the middle of production by top-dressing if necessary.

In the initial stages of your program, it is a good idea to conduct follow-up soil tests about every six months until you have achieved the fertility your crops need.

CHARLES ALSHEIMER

KEEP IN TOUCH

Most food plot growers know about soil testing and fertilizing before planting a plot. Fewer use soil testing to check up on an existing crop. This is an important monitoring step because the effects of fertilizer and lime are temporary, and top-dressing with the right fertilizer in midproduction may extend the productive life of a food plot.

After that, annual soil testing is a good routine to follow. As always, keep records of your soil test results.

TESTING YOUR CROPS FOR NUTRIENTS AND PROTEIN LEVELS

You can really go to the next level by having plant samples tested for protein and nutrient levels and digestibility. This is a common practice for testing pasture forages and hay, and the testing can usually be done at the same lab that tests your soil samples. Prices vary by lab but are generally more expensive than soil tests. The information you get from plant tissue sampling can verify that your soil-amendment efforts are paying off by showing you where the nutrients went — into the plants, and ultimately into the deer. This information can also add another level of troubleshooting. Testing can help identify gaps in nutrient levels which will aid future soil amendments. It can also verify a suspected weakness in certain nutrients that resulted in a visible symptom, such as poor color or poor growth.

Plant sampling can be done as often as you like. Most people only use plant sampling to help identify the cause of an observed problem. However, you can sample more frequently just to satisfy your curiosity. For example, monthly sampling can show you how the nutritional level and digestibility of your forages change as the plants grow and mature. It can also show you the nutritional boost you received in response to a top-dressing of fertilizer.

TIPS FOR COLLECTING PLANT SAMPLES

• For routine sampling, collect samples from a healthy, clean portion of the plot, not from areas that have been damaged by machinery, browsing, insects or weather.

• Follow the instructions of the kit to know which part of the plant and how many plants to sample. This will vary based on specific crop types.

• If you are testing plants with a suspected nutrient deficiency, try to submit two samples: one of normal plants and one of plants that appear to be having problems.

• When you are troubleshooting a food plot, it's a good idea to submit a corresponding soil sample collected at the same site where you collected plant samples. Send the plant and soil samples in separate containers, but attach them or mark them in a way that identifies them as corresponding samples so that the lab can consider the results of both.

MONITORING FOOD PLOTS

In addition to protein levels, fiber, total digestible nutrients, and digestible energy, the laboratory will send you a report that lists levels of major elements, including nitrogen, phosphorus and potassium, as well as a long list of micronutrients, such as magnesium, sulfur, calcium, manganese, and iron. Most labs report these nutrients in terms of a sufficiency range – whether present in levels that are too low, about right for optimum production, or at levels that are too high. When you request a plant analysis kit from the lab, ask for a guide to interpreting the results. Many labs have brochures or handouts that help you interpret the results and determine actions to take.

A plant analysis kit will contain instructions on how to collect and submit samples. Follow them carefully. If you are conducting routine testing on healthy crops, follow the instructions on when to collect samples, usually a specific stage of plant maturity. For testing crops that are struggling for undetermined reasons, collect samples immediately so you can try to solve the problem before you lose the stand.

INFRARED CAMERAS AS A FOOD PLOT TOOL

Another tool for monitoring food plot success is an infrared-triggered camera. Browse exclosures can give you a visual account of how much of the food plot deer are consuming. A trail camera can tell you which deer are using it and when.

HUNTING SHEDS IN COOL-SEASON FOOD PLOTS

One challenge of producing quality food plots is carefully monitoring and maintaining your plots while keeping your presence around these plots at a minimum. Too much human activity around a plot will impact when and how often deer use the plots, reducing both nutritional benefits and hunting success. Obviously, just before and during hunting season is the time to be conscious of human activity around plots. In the winter months after hunting season, this is less of a concern, and that works out well for shed hunting. Cool-season food plots can be a very good place to locate freshly dropped sheds. In fact, folks who make a hobby of shed hunting place food plots at the top of their list of prime areas to search. The sheds in this photograph were found in just a couple of hours of walking winter food plots on a south Texas property. Use infrared-triggered game cameras to tell you when most of your bucks have shed their antlers. Then, quickly but thoroughly search your food plots. Collecting sheds each year can verify that your QDM efforts are working by providing evidence of bucks that survived hunting season. And these sheds will look a lot better on display at your hunting camp than embedded in a flattened tractor or ATV tire later in the year!

Place a camera on the edge of the plot so that its field of focus is on a productive portion of the plot. If you are planting a tall crop such as corn or sorghum that will eventually obscure deer movement, leave an unplanted strip in front of the camera or mow a strip in front of the camera to detect deer as they enter the plot. Place the camera as soon as the food plot is planted, even though it may be some time before the crop is attracting deer. This way, you will have baseline information on random deer usage of the area before the crop is productive and attractive. Although these set-ups may not produce as many photographs as a baited camera site, that's okay — the important aspect will be the trends in use over time, not in total numbers of photographs.

For this purpose, a digital trail camera is best, because you will not have to visit the site as often to replace film, minimizing human scent. Make sure you set the camera to record the date of the photograph. Begin a log that records the number of images taken per week or per day. Ultimately, you will be able to plot a chart that shows deer usage of the crop. You will probably see something like a bell-shaped curve showing use starting at a low level, gradually increasing toward the peak, then falling off again. With this information you can begin asking questions that will help you understand your plot's productivity and how it might be improved. For example, at what level of plant maturity did deer usage peak? Your camera has not only recorded the dates that deer passed through the monitored portion of the plot, it has recorded a visual snapshot of what the crop looked like at that moment.

TONY NIENAS

FOOD PLOT SPY

Your infrared-triggered camera can reveal which stage of growth in a particular plot is most attractive to deer by tracking fluctuations in deer use over time. Of course, you also get a visual record of individual deer that use your plots.

KEEP YOUR EAR TO THE GROUND

The more you experiment with your food plots, the more you can refine your techniques and crop selections to local conditions. Many maintenance techniques are specific to certain crops and are covered in other chapters of this book, such as mowing perennial clovers in summer to control weeds and reinvigorate the food plot. However, no book can replace on-the-ground observation and record keeping for identifying successful techniques, pitfalls and winning crop combinations on your land. Besides, learning from your food plots is both fun and rewarding.

12

Hunting Food Plots

BY LINDSAY THOMAS JR.

HUNTING FOOD PLOTS

In recent years, food plots have exploded across the American landscape. Few blocks of Eastern woodlands are not sprinkled with small and large openings, planted powerline rights-of-way, planted logging decks and other green patches. Most share a common feature: they are watched over by a deer stand of some kind. In many cases these are large, permanent structures such as elevated, enclosed box stands, or "condo" stands.

Food plots make great deer stands for many reasons. They are often found along a road or trail network, and this ease of access makes them ideal stand sites for guests, youth hunters, parent/child hunting teams, senior hunters or any hunter on a tight schedule. Food plots can help hunters achieve their desired doe harvest, especially when extra help must be invited in for the purpose. When plots are being heavily used by deer and the rut is on, they can be a likely place to glimpse mature bucks. But there is no doubt that many clubs and landowners are relying too much on their food plots as stand sites. There are some who argue that food plots are contributing to the erosion of hunting skills among modern deer hunters.

As a food plot manager, you must carefully consider how and when you hunt your plots. Too much hunting pressure ultimately inhibits use of a plot by deer – both overall use and daylight use. Sightings and harvest success decline, and the effectiveness of the food plot as a nutritional delivery system is reduced. With forethought given to your hunting strategies and food plot management decisions, you can avoid this situation.

THE FLEXIBLE HUNTER

Understanding soil fertility and planting techniques is critical to a quality food plot effort, but these skills cannot replace the ability to scout natural food sources, investigate deer travel patterns, interpret buck sign, select productive stand sites in woodlands, and hunt with stealth. Food plots are not always the most attractive food source or most productive area for sightings on a given property.

Use of food plots by deer fluctuates based on factors such as the growth and stage of maturity of the crop. Other factors such as nearby alternative food sources are extremely important. Hard mast, especially oak and beech, is a good example – when certain species of oaks are dropping their fruits, deer may ignore other food sources, including food plots. The hunter who loyally sticks to his food plot stand at a time like this is likely to see few deer. This is when the hunter needs hunting and woodsmanship skills to know when to transition to "Plan B."

TOO CLOSE TO THE ACTION

Many food plot deer stands, like the one shown here, are located right on top of the food plot with little thought or effort given to concealment of the stand. Even light use of such a stand – especially on a small plot like this one – will quickly reduce daylight sightings of deer.

The 2004 hunting season provided examples across several states of low hunting success due to over-dependence on food plots for stand sites. In Georgia, for example, with fall food plots planted and ready, many hunters eagerly awaited opening day of gun season in late October. Two major factors were at play when the day finally arrived: warmer than normal temperatures and a heavy crop of acorns in the woods. Hunters on food plots saw far fewer deer than those who hunted in woodland sites, even during the rut – which came and went quietly in the warm, wet weather. For several weeks, the warm weather remained, and many food plots grew tall, untouched by deer. Without a cold snap, deer had little need to feed heavily, and there was still a lot of natural forage available due to the lack of frost and plentiful acorns. Then, in mid-December, the cold weather finally arrived, and with acorns depleted, whitetails began to mow the offerings of food plot planters. By then, however, many food plot hunters had given up on the season.

Hunters must also avoid being predictable by hunting the same food plot continuously throughout a season. There is ample evidence that hunting over food plots reduces use of the plots. One excellent example is a case study of two hunting clubs in Alabama conducted by Westervelt Wildlife Services. The two properties, 1,004 and 1,378 acres respectively, are adjoining and share a creek as a dividing boundary. Biologist Kevin McKinstry with Westervelt reported in the October 2003 issue of QDMA's *Quality Whitetails* magazine that between 1999 and 2002, both clubs had successfully implemented a QDM program, including elevated doe harvests and buck restrictions that protected bucks under 3½ years of age. Over the four years, the percentage of 3½-year-old and older bucks in the buck harvest climbed, and the observed adult sex ratio went from nearly four does for every buck to a one-to-one sighting ratio in 2002. However, the data from the two clubs revealed one very important difference. While one club's sighting rate had remained steady at about one deer seen per hour hunted throughout the four years, the other club's sighting rate declined to 0.3 deer per hour in 2002. In this club in 2002, on average, a hunter

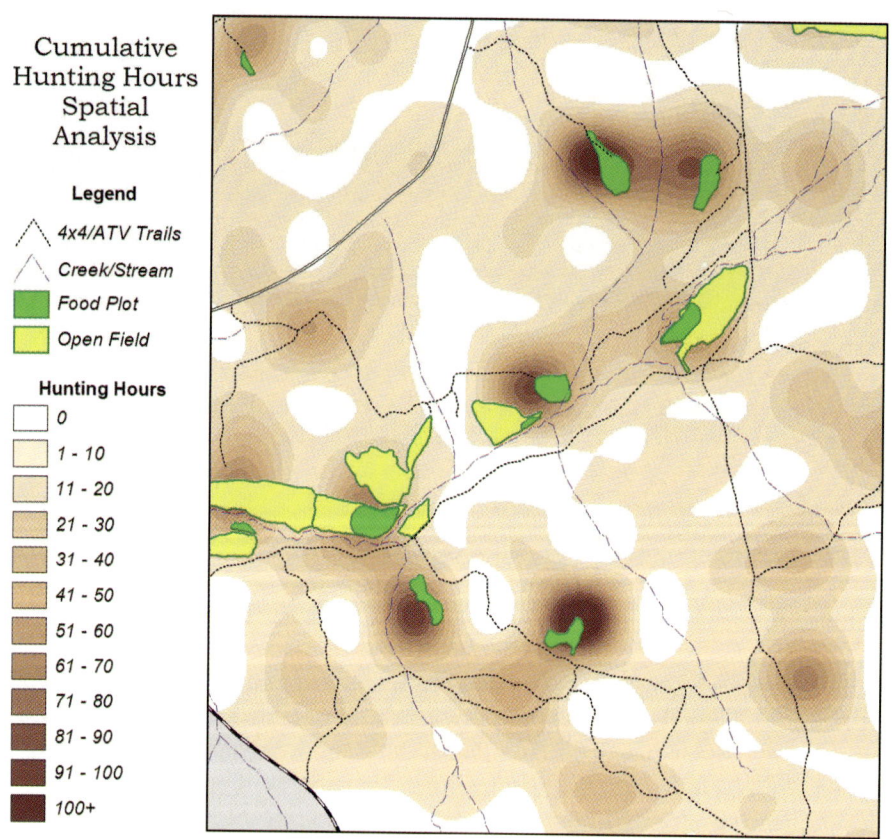

Cumulative Hunting Hours Spatial Analysis

Legend

- 4x4/ATV Trails
- Creek/Stream
- Food Plot
- Open Field

Hunting Hours

- 0
- 1 - 10
- 11 - 20
- 21 - 30
- 31 - 40
- 41 - 50
- 51 - 60
- 61 - 70
- 71 - 80
- 81 - 90
- 91 - 100
- 100+

MAPPING OVER-PRESSURED PLOTS

This GIS map was created for an actual hunting property by Woods & Associates Inc., a consulting firm led by deer researcher Dr. Grant Woods. It depicts hours of hunting pressure by location over a six-year period. Most of the food plots are the focus of intense hunting pressure while the majority of the property is hunted seldom or not at all. Interestingly, before this map was created, hunters on this property reported they were hunting all areas of the property evenly. Woods & Associates has noted that white areas on maps like this one often produce unexpectedly high success, especially for mature bucks, once these areas are identified and hunted.

On Alert

In situations where food plots are heavily hunted, harvest data often shows that mature bucks are seldom seen, much less killed, in food plots. By keeping pressure light, designing food plots that appeal to a deer's need for secrecy, and hunting plots only when conditions are right, hunter satisfaction and success will remain high.

had to put in more than three hours in the stand to see one deer. A closer look found the problem. The hunters in the club with the declining sighting rate spent 77 percent of their stand time sitting over their food plots. On the other club where sighting rates had remained steady, the scenario was reversed. Hunters spent 73 percent of their time hunting on clearcuts, roads and woodland stand sites and only 23 percent of their time hunting food plots. Further, Kevin noted that none of the 4½-year-old and older bucks killed on the study area were taken over food plots.

Techniques to Reduce Pressure

Here are several techniques you can use to avoid over-pressured food plots.

Create separate "nutrition" plots and "hunting" plots. Nutrition or "feeding" plots, like sanctuaries, are never hunted. They are free-use zones for deer year-round. As such, they should be created with maximum nutrition in mind. Choose large, easily accessible openings for these plots, so that all necessary equipment, from lime-spreading trucks to tillage and mowing equipment, can be brought in for high-level crop management. Establish cool-season perennials that can be managed for multiple seasons of production, and plant warm-season annuals – together these provide nutritious, abundant forage at times of high nutritional need.

Create "hunting" plots that are suited to their job so that success requires fewer hours of stand time and less pressure. Hunting plots should be designed to encourage deer use during daylight, so select openings that are smaller, more remote and less visible. Hunting plots should blend into the surroundings with irregular borders

TES RANDLE JOLLY

ARCHER'S PLOT

Large, open food plots not designed with hunting in mind will likely require more hours of hunting effort per kill for bowhunters. Smaller plots, like the narrow strip shown at right, may be used more often by deer during daylight hours. All hunters, but especially bowhunters, will be able to harvest deer in the plot more effectively.

CHARLES ALSHEIMER

or long, linear shapes in which deer always feel close to cover. Choose crops that are productive and attractive in the fall and that grow quickly even with a minimum of seedbed preparation. Annuals often meet this demand better than perennials, but mixes that include both will fit the bill nicely. Ideally, if you have enough acreage, view any given stand site on a small or large food plot as "disposable" – use it during the right wind and weather conditions, make the harvest, then, like any successful predator, move on to another site. Plan several sites to cover your needs for the coming season.

RANS THOMAS

Be stealthy. Once you've gone to the trouble of planning hunting as well as nutrition plots, don't build a "shooting house" in the middle of your hunting plots. Use small ground blinds and climbing or lock-on stands that are less intrusive, and place them away from the edge of the plot with ample concealment. Always choose stand locations that are downwind from the plots based on prevailing winds for your area. If the wind is wrong on a particular day, don't hunt that stand. Plan your access route so that you can enter and exit the site quietly and without crossing known deer travel routes or bedding areas. In the afternoon, deer often enter food plots as darkness is falling and shooting hours end — by hunting away from the edge of the plot and planning a concealed access route, you can leave the stand without disturbing these deer.

Can't Miss It

Even though this box blind is partially concealed, its fixed location allows hunters to easily be patterned unless the stand is seldom hunted or pressure is rotated. Neither is likely since the convenience and comfort of this stand will attract repeated use. Climbers and other portable stands allow you to be flexible and unpredictable in your hunting habits.

Hunt around, not on top of, food plots. When planning the locations of new plots, take hunting into account. Position food plots near bedding areas or thickets, natural or manmade funnel points or established game trails, so likely approach patterns can be predicted. Instead of hunting over the plot itself, hunt the edges of nearby bedding areas or thickets where trails or other access zones lead to the plot. Deer, particularly bucks, may not enter plots in the afternoon until darkness is falling, but just before dark they move into nearby access zones. When you hunt these zones, your scent and presence are not associated with the plot itself. Deer may seek new routes to a plot to go around a pressured area, and you can move your stand site in response. To make deer access routes even more huntable, some hunters strategically place the windrows of stumps and debris created when new ground is cleared for food plots. The windrows act as barriers, limiting access points into the food plot and making approach trails more predictable.

HUNTING FOOD PLOTS

Don't invite predator/prey encounters. QDMA member Jeff Sturgis of Michigan was named the 2004 QDMA Deer Manager of the Year for his efforts at improving and managing his small property. In an article he wrote on small-acreage success in *Quality Whitetails,* Jeff explained that he had established a network of open trails for his own access to hunting sites. However, he never plants these trails in attractive crops for deer – he doesn't want to invite deer to encounter him or his scent on these access trails. For small property managers, attraction is critical, but plan ahead so that attraction features like food plots and sanctuaries are separated from hunter-access routes.

Hunt your plots only when conditions are right. Even though you've designed and planted a plot for hunting purposes, you should hunt it sparingly. Be selective about conditions. Hunt when your food plot is at peak production and desirability for deer, when other food sources are not competing with your plot in attractiveness, and when the wind direction is right. Also, consider how weather is likely to affect deer feeding patterns. Hunt during cold snaps when deer feed more heavily, and avoid periods when above average temperatures reduce deer activity. A falling barometer associated with the approach of a weather front usually corresponds to increased feeding activity. Activity usually drops significantly for the first 24 hours after the passing of a significant cold front – the typical windy, clear day with "bluebird" skies and high barometric pressure – but climbs again on the second and third day when winds calm and temperatures drop. Stack as many of these timing advantages as you can in your favor and your patience will likely be rewarded.

ROGER KINGSLEY

GOOD SHOT!

Being proficient with your weapon and taking only low-risk shots that kill quickly will reduce time spent blood trailing.

Minimize human presence in the plot even after the shot. Be proficient with your weapon of choice, and wait for the right shot. This results in quicker kills and less likelihood of prolonged blood-trailing efforts, particularly by groups of people. Plan how you will get the deer out and where you will field-dress it. Do not field-dress it in or near the plot. Recover the deer and get out of the area as quickly as possible.

Monitor food plots cautiously. Chapter 11 emphasizes the importance of monitoring your food plots, but even while monitoring you should keep a low profile. Don't check a food plot regularly by walking through it and looking at tracks or browse pressure, or driving by regularly in a pickup or ATV. This goes for nutrition plots as well as hunting plots. Those of us who have grown up in farm families know that when farmers aren't planting, maintaining or harvesting a crop, they are riding by in a pickup looking at it. It's a natural urge to watch your crops responding to your care and see how they are coming along. Resist this urge prior to and during hunting season. In fact, you should keep all ATV traffic to a minimum between September and January, especially on smaller properties.

But maintenance and monitoring are necessary for successful food plots. Check them only when necessary. Place your rain gauge back at camp, not at the edge of the plot. Place your browse exclosures where they can be viewed from a distance with binoculars. When you must go in to an active, productive plot to monitor, top-dress, overseed, mow or conduct other maintenance, do so at mid-day rather than at times of peak deer activity, such as dawn and dusk.

When trying out a new blend, a crop that you've never planted before or a crop that requires high maintenance, use a feeding plot. For hunting plots, plant something that has worked well before and requires little maintenance. This will reduce your desire to "check" a hunting plot.

FOOD PLOT SHAPE AND LAYOUT

There are many shapes and designs for food plots that can enhance hunting success, and the topography and habitat types in your area will dictate what works for you. The general goal with a hunting plot is to offer an area large enough to produce sufficient forage to be attractive to deer, secluded enough to appeal to a deer's need for nearby cover, with concealed hunter access and a stand site that is downwind and hidden.

HUB-AND-SPOKE

The narrow lanes of this hunting-plot design attract daylight use by deer yet provide significant acreage of forage. Permanent hunting sites like this must be designed and installed with prevailing wind directions in mind.

HUNTING FOOD PLOTS

One example of a popular and effective design for a food plot features a central stand site with narrow lanes or "senderos" radiating outward from the stand, preferably through heavy cover suitable for deer bedding areas. This arrangement is also known as a hub-and-spoke design (*shown on page 197*). The number of lanes is up to the designer, but more lanes equals more area for the hunter to monitor. It's best to design a hub-and-spoke with fewer lanes and short angles of separation so you can monitor the lanes without constantly turning your head. It's also unwise to make the lanes longer than you, or a guest, can make an accurate shot.

The specific shapes of hunting plots will depend much on your existing landscape and your ability to alter it. However, these general guidelines are almost universally applicable when planning a hunting food plot:

TES RANDLE JOLLY

Skinny Plots, Fat Deer

In large fields, deer browsing is usually concentrated on edges that border escape cover. Narrow plots like this one are all edge and are likely to produce more daylight sightings of deer if they are hunted wisely.

• Design hunting plots that are shaped to offer concealment to deer – something that large, rectangular plots do not offer. This may reduce the area of the plot that will be visible to the hunter, but it will likely increase a deer's sense of safety in the plot. Make sure these irregular shapes do not create a problem for your equipment – working a set of disk harrows in and out of small nooks and crannies will be tedious and perhaps impossible.

• Use the landscape to your advantage. For example, place your plot at the bottom of a wooded slope and your stand further up the slope, with a narrow open lane for viewing. Anything you can do to remove the hunter from the plot – while still allowing them to effectively view most of the plot and shoot accurately – will be a positive step.

• Help blend open plots with surrounding cover by eliminating hard edges. "Edge feathering" has become a catch-phrase in food plot circles, and it refers to feathering the edge of taller natural cover by thinning or planting taller crops along the edges of plots. Good choices include Egyptian wheat and corn. This creates a buffer zone of cover between the woods and the open plots. Deer may feel safer emerging into this zone of cover first, but they may be visible to the hunter before they emerge into the open plot.

• Create narrow fingers of planted crops that radiate from the more open plot into heavier cover. These fingers or funnel routes might even be an unplanted, cleared path. Wary deer emerge onto these fingers that offer more concealment and gradually travel or feed their way into the more open, hunted areas. For such paths to be effective at funneling wary deer into food plots, they should be located far from the stand site. It is okay if the hunter cannot see deer on these paths – that is part of the safety effect. Many times, a desire to see every corner of the plot leads hunters to place stands in exposed locations.

H.W. WILLIAMS AERIAL PHOTOGRAPHY

STAY MOBILE

This large network of narrow, linear food plots in a stand of dense plantation pines is a combination of utility rights-of-way and lanes not planted in trees. The landowners initially built a permanent "shooting house" at one end of the main powerline (indicated by "S"), but after three seasons of pressure, success evaporated. The solution was to use a portable climber or tripod to hunt a different junction or lane each time, avoiding predictable hunting patterns. A network of narrow plots lends itself well to this wise hunting strategy.

• Create a staging area or "foyer" attached to, or just off the edge of, a larger plot. This foyer is planted in a food plot crop, but it is small – you will be limited to a small tractor, ATV equipment or manual tools for plot preparation. The foyer should be placed on a side of the larger plot that is most likely to be the entry point for deer. Planned right, this foyer will become the main entry point into the larger food plot. Where mature deer might not filter into larger, open plots until dusk, they may enter the more concealed foyer much earlier. Wait until conditions are right and deer are using the larger plot regularly. Hunt the foyer, make a kill, then give the site a rest of at least one week.

Browse pressure in the foyer may become intense if it becomes the main entry point for deer using the plot. Thus, the crop in this area may not remain productive or attractive for long. You can also create two or three foyers off the same large plot to divert traffic, which also allows you multiple focal points for shifting hunting pressure.

HUNTING FOOD PLOTS

• Break large, open plots into smaller sections by planting fruit-tree hedgerows. These linear orchards will not only help deer feel less exposed, they add attractiveness with mast. Hedgerows can also act as travel lanes for access to the food plot. Use a wide variety of fruit plantings for these hedgerows, including pears, crabapples and persimmons. Be sure to protect seedling fruit trees from deer browsing with plastic tree shelters or wire cages, and allow a buffer zone between the plot and individual trees to avoid disking tree roots.

H.W. WILLIAMS AERIAL PHOTOGRAPHY

FRAGMENTING OPEN GROUND

Large, open fields can be converted to plots that offer improved hunting opportunities by subdiving with fallow ground or planted hedgerows of mast-bearing trees and shrubs. The fallow strips visible in the field above will grow up into early successional cover that will allow deer to feel safer using these fields during daylight. The fallow ground will also provide good fawning cover and natural forages.

The two fields on the lower left have each been split in half for an effective hunting set-up. One half of each field is planted in a cool-season perennial, the other half in an attractive warm-season crop. The strip down the middle of each field is planted in corn. Deer become accustomed to feeding in these fields during the warm season when there is no hunting pressure, and they easily switch over to the cool-season side during hunting season. The standing corn, while also a source of attraction and nutrition, serves as a visual break and cover for deer.

CONCLUSION

Even the most craftily designed food plot can be rendered ineffective by too much hunting pressure. Use your hunting instincts with food plots just as you would with any other deer stand location. Many hunters have a magic location that they save for the perfect conditions or the peak of the rut, and they hunt this stand with the utmost caution and stealth. Food plots that will be hunted should be treated the same way. With the right mix of hunting plots, nutrition plots and a game plan for managing pressure, your food plots will provide hunting opportunities and habitat benefits year in and year out.

THE ETHICS OF HUNTING FOOD PLOTS

The non-hunting public and even many hunters believe that shooting deer over piles of bait is unethical and outside the boundaries of fair chase. Food plots are often dragged into this debate by those who claim that shooting deer in food plots is no different than shooting them over corn poured from a sack. In states where hunting over bait is illegal, hunters who wish to make it legal often argue that "Shooting deer in food plots is legal, so why can't we shoot them over a bait pile when the two are essentially the same?" On the other end of the ethical spectrum, some purist hunters believe that hunting over planted food plots and hunting over bait should both be illegal.

There are some fundamental differences between food plots and bait piles. Obviously, a hunter is in complete control of the amount of food in a bait pile, the timing of the supply, the size of the site being baited and its location. If an automatic, time-controlled feeder is being used, the availability of bait and use of the site by deer can be manipulated with greater precision. Bait, unlike a food plot or supplemental feed, has one purpose – to attract a deer into the hunter's sights as quickly and with as little effort as possible. Once this is achieved, there is no reason to continue supplying bait.

With a food plot being an agricultural crop, many factors beyond the hunter's control determine whether or not a crop is ultimately useful to deer. Hunters cannot control rainfall, temperature, insect pests, disease and other factors. Also, food plots are available to deer whether a hunter shows up or not, and they likely are available long before or long after the hunting season.

However, by examining hunter intent we see the greatest distinction between food plots and baiting. Food plots usually are planted as part of a broad management plan and concern for the quality of the deer population. Are you reading this book because you want a quick, easy kill on opening morning of hunting season? Probably not. Managers like you often provide crops year-round, even when the plots cannot be hunted. Indeed, they often plant plots that are strictly nutrition plots which will never be hunted. Further, this type of land manager is probably also involved in forest management, prescribed burning, tree planting and other practices that improve deer habitat. Their enjoyment of hunting has as much to do with giving to the deer herd as taking from it. For these hunters, there is an enormous difference between food plots and bait piles.

13

Creating
Leopold Landscapes

By Craig Dougherty, Ph.D.

thirteen

I like to read on airplanes. I read for escape – to make the time pass quickly. For this therapy, I prefer the company of old friends. Books authored by the likes of Burrows, Thoreau, Muir, Leopold and Black Elk spirit me off the plane and home to my mountaintop in southwestern New York. I prefer books about wildlife and wild places and how to do right by the land; books that inspire me to become a better steward of the land tomorrow than I was today.

Of my "old friends," Aldo Leopold is the one I turn to most. Part philosopher, part naturalist and part wildlife manager, Leopold has taught me how to make sense out of my passion for the land and my need to interact with it. He writes that men and land should exist in a state of harmony, a condition where both men and the land will end up better by reason of their partnership. He blends lofty phrases like "harmony with the land" and "ecological conscience" with pragmatic advice such as the importance of harvesting does to keep deer numbers in check and plantings for wildlife. His writings are a virtual prescription for Quality Deer Management (QDM) and are as relevant today as when he wrote them more than a half century ago.

Leopold's writings have guided my son Neil and me as we converted our 500-acre Steuben County property from an uninteresting expanse of woods with so-so deer hunting to a mixture of food plots, woodlots, brushy cover, wooded expanses and wet areas. Our property has a healthy population of ruffed grouse and wood-cock and is home to dozens of songbird species and birds of prey as well. It is a stop-over place for migratory birds and holds an assortment of waterfowl and shorebirds. The occasional bear passes through leaving fresh tracks in the mud. We have created a ragged patchwork quilt of wildlife habitat. I call it our Leopold Landscape.

Like so many other landowners today, we focus most of our energy on the white-tailed deer. We practice QDM on our property, and for the past 15 years we have worked to improve the quality of our deer herd and deer hunting. We harvest does to keep deer numbers in check and let young bucks mature. We plant wildlife food plots and create escape cover and browse. We work year-round creating wildlife habitat. Over time, the age structure of our buck population has increased, and the number of does per buck has decreased. Our deer have grown healthier as evidenced by weight and antler development. We have had more than our share of hunting success and would be lying if we said that our success wasn't, in part, measured by an official Pope & Young tape measure. It is, and we make no apologies for it. We love hunting big whitetails as much as the next guy, and this, ostensibly, is why

KINDRED SPIRITS

The cabin at Craig and Neil Dougherty's New York farm, known as "Kindred Spirits," has witnessed many campfire gatherings and heard many hunt stories retold. From this porch, Craig and Neil have watched as their work has transformed a run-down farm into a "Leopold Landscape."

we purchased the property.

But with time we began to notice other signs of success. Softer, less easy-to-read signs, like when at least once or twice each spring Neil and I, sitting by our traditional end-of-the-day campfire, make eye contact and knowingly nod. Tonight's the night. It's show time – the woodcock are flying and the grouse are drumming. It's one thing to catch the woodcock silhouetted against the fading sunset. It's another to do it at the exact instant a grouse starts drumming in a nearby thicket. This is the show we look for every spring – a show worthy of a standing ovation yields a smile of satisfaction and an evening of good thoughts. To us it's a sign that things are as they should be. Our habitat work has been paid in full and then some! Leopold writes, "When land does well for its owner and the owner does well by his land, we have conservation."

Visitors to our campfire are thrilled by the sight and sound of the spring woodcock and grouse. They understand the significance of what they have just witnessed, but they don't seem to be able to feel it as we do. They didn't sweat over the saw and axe; they didn't dig the worming bog. And, because they didn't touch the land, they are mere spectators at the event. They are denied the impossible-to-describe feeling

of completeness and inner satisfaction that comes from knowing that you have done something right by your land and it is responding in kind.

I have learned that the stiff joints and muscles which come from running a bushhog for six hours are merely a reminder that something good has happened, not a sign of old age or failing health. I love to gaze out upon a 3-acre food plot and the dozen or so deer it feeds each night. The feeling is both comforting and exhilarating. I feel an inner peace and satisfaction and a sense of accomplishment which can never be delivered by measuring deer antlers. I am experiencing first-hand the love, respect and admiration for the land that Leopold writes about in his famous essay "The Land Ethic." Neil feels the same way, and so does my hunting partner, Steve, who was so overtaken with land stewardship that he bought two old, grown-over farms of his own to work on with his dad and son. And there are hundreds of thousands more of us out there, including almost the entire membership of the Quality Deer Management Association.

I came to Leopold later than most. After years of searching I had finally found a way to make sense of my attraction to the land, my passion to do more for the land, and my need to receive more in return. For me, Leopold connects the dots between hunting, spirituality and stewardship. The more I did, the more Leopold made sense.

Through most of his professional career, Aldo Leopold worked to reverse a number of destructive land management trends. Leopold pleaded with private landowners to "do right" by the land and the wildlife who inhabit it by retaining and/or restoring the small farm landscapes. These landscapes resembled ragged patchwork quilts of fields and woodlands and grown-over places dedicated to providing farm families with their basic wants and needs. Stone walls were good for wildlife as were unkempt hedgerows and undrained wet areas. These farmsteads were home to plentiful wildlife and the opposite of the large-scale, efficient agribusiness operations so popular with the "progressive" teachings of the times. He recognized that eliminating these landscapes would lead to a loss of wildlife, an outcome that would benefit neither the land nor the landowner.

Leopold believed that private landowners could do right by the land if they would only adopt a few, easily implemented practices. He argued for a moratorium on the elimination of hedgerows between and around fields. Leopold also believed field edges, corners and end-of-field turnarounds should be left to wildlife. Draining wetlands to create cropland was an enormous waste of waterfowl and winter pheasant habitat. Streams should be allowed to meander and be skirted with nest-building brush while ponds benefited both man and beast alike.

Leopold was also one of the earliest biologists to address deer overpopula-

DOING RIGHT BY THE LAND

Most deer managers have the primary mission of improving the quality of their deer and the quality of their deer hunting. But by planting a diversity of food plots, by creating edge and bedding cover, by planting wildlife trees, by improving habitat in many ways, deer managers find that they have also created habitats for a host of other game and non-game species.

tion issues. While others called for unlimited deer to hunt, Leopold cautioned that burgeoning deer numbers would damage the land and wildlife. Woodlands cannot regenerate when overbrowsed by deer.

Unfortunately, much of Leopold's message fell on deaf ears. Failing family farm economics trumped Leopold's wildlife conservation message. Leopold's argument of leaving something for wildlife was a tough one to swallow when there were mouths to feed, especially with the professional agriculture community touting large-scale agribusiness practices as the salvation of the farming industry.

Leopold, like many other early conservationists, seemed to overestimate the importance of conscience and underestimate the importance of economics. In fact, it could be argued that even today, Leopold, while often quoted, is seldom followed, especially when it comes to the conflict between large-scale farming and timber production and wildlife habitat. Economy-of-scale business models make money, and money is the engine driving America. Sure, we want to follow Leopold and be better stewards of the land. But, when it really comes down to it, it's usually all about big money and big business.

LEOPOLD LANDSCAPES

Fast-forward 50 years. Enter the deer hunter, the backbone of a multi-billion dollar hunting industry. White-tailed deer hunting is big business, and white-tailed deer hunters are willing to spend big bucks to hunt big bucks. It is nothing for a gung-ho hunter to hunt deer in three or four states. Hunting outfitters and deer managers in states like Iowa, Illinois and Texas recognize the value that quality whitetail hunting affords, and they view deer hunting as a business. When deer herds are managed for quality instead of quantity, land stewardship, wildlife habitat and conservation take on new meanings.

But many hunters prefer to stay home and "grow their own." Hundreds of thousands of deer hunters are creating quality deer hunting on lands they lease or own by following the teachings and philosophy of the Quality Deer Management Association. Wildlife habitat creation, combined with managing deer numbers, age structure and sex ratios, is prescription for thousands of enthusiastic quality deer managers. All of a sudden, Leopold has become not only relevant but real. Leopold Landscapes are being created wherever deer and deer hunters are found.

When we acquired our property 16 years ago, it was a mere ghost of the farm it had been at the turn of the twentieth century. It had grown up into 350 acres of mixed hardwood forest and another 150 acres of thick pole timber trying to become hardwood forest. There were no open spaces left, and the wooded areas showed serious signs of over-utilization by deer. The property hadn't seen a plow or mower in 50 years or more . . . a far cry from the farm landscape it had been 100 years earlier.

The solution could have come right out of Leopold: create more food and cover by clearing, planting, cutting and creating spaces where different habitat types intersect. Open up 10 or so miles of log trails and plant with wildlife forage mixes. Clear old log landings and grownup fields to create 30 acres of food plots. Release 100 or so old apple and pear trees. Thin timber stands, and harvest mature timber to encourage acorn production and regeneration. Clear-cut 15 to 20 acres of hardwoods for cover and browse. Sounds simple, but it took time, work, and outlays of cash for equipment, seed, lime and fertilizer.

It also took motivation; but boy were we motivated! At first we were motivated by visions of big bucks and hunting like we read about in magazines but have never experienced. We spent 15 years creating a Leopold

QUALITY FOOD PLOTS

Neil and Craig Dougherty inspect one of many food plots they have created on their property over 15 years of management. Their interests began with deer hunting, but planting food plots intensified their connection to the land and fueled a desire to go further in their land stewardship.

Landscape in order to have quality deer hunting for our friends and ourselves. Our primary mission, plain and simple, was to create a great place to hunt deer, see deer, and harvest some high-quality animals.

Becoming good land stewards and intensifying our connection with the land came later. It was an unexpected outcome of the work we did creating quality deer hunting. Over time, developing a land ethic became more and more important to us. We liked the feeling we got when we did right by our land, and we wanted more. Without our knowing it, the means had become the end.

Are there others like us? We've had so many hunters ask to visit our property that we started a tour and seminar program. Over the years, we have hosted thousands of visitors to our property. The Quality Deer Management Association is another case in point. This organization is the fastest-growing conservation group in the country today. The majority of its members are trying to improve their deer hunting through habitat development and proper herd management. Executive Director Brian Murphy estimates that QDMA members are actively managing between 12 and 15 million acres of land across North America. This is a big chunk of real estate. Are they all creating Leopold Landscapes? It's hard to say, but chances are they are doing something Leopold would be proud of.

14

Food Plot
Species Profiles
By Kent Kammermeyer

LEGEND

☀ DROUGHT TOLERANT

💧 TOLERATES WET CONDITIONS

🌿 EASY TO ESTABLISH

⚒ DIFFICULT TO ESTABLISH

pH TOLERATES WIDE pH RANGE

⬆N PRIMARILY NORTHERN

S⬇ PRIMARILY SOUTHERN

🌳 SHADE TOLERANT

🌱 SUSCEPTIBLE TO COMPETITION

🌾 SUSCEPTIBLE TO EARLY/
HEAVY GRAZING

Clovers

ALSIKE CLOVER (*Trifolium hybridum*)

OREGON STATE UNIVERSITY, FORAGE INFORMATION SYSTEM

ALSIKE CLOVER hails from northern Europe. It is a short-lived legume (about three years) that is well adapted to wet, heavy soil and is tolerant of flooded conditions and low pH. Alsike is a semi-erect perennial, 1 to 3 feet tall with pink and white flowers. Its usefulness in agriculture is short-rotation pastures, hay mixtures on wetlands, in areas with high precipitation, or areas that are poorly drained. Highest production occurs between May and September.

ADAPTATION/ESTABLISHMENT

Alsike can be grown in most areas of the United States and Canada that have sufficient moisture or wet soils. It will not, however, tolerate the hot summers of the Deep South. It produces well on soils that are either too cold and wet or too acidic or alkaline for red clover. Alsike is best established in early spring when soil moisture conditions are most favorable. In areas where irrigation is available or adequate rainfall is expected, late summer seedings are also successful. Seed should be broadcast at 8 to 12 lbs./acre and covered lightly (no more than ½-inch deep) by a drag or harrow. It can be drilled ¼-inch deep at 4 to 6 lbs./acre into a well-prepared seedbed or into a stand that has been killed by glyphosate (Roundup) or other herbicides. It is also a good candidate for frost seeding in late winter on dead vegetation when freezing and thawing will ensure good seed-to-soil contact. As with other clovers, do not forget to inoculate alsike with the proper strain (B) of inoculant (it uses the same strain as red clover and white clover). Planted alone, if no soil test is available, use 300 lbs./acre 8-24-24 on ground that has been in agricultural production and has built up phosphorus in the soil. New ground will require more (up to 500 lbs./acre 0-20-20).

VARIETIES/ MANAGEMENT

Like most other cool-season legumes, alsike clover should be planted in late summer or early spring with a grass such as timothy (5 lbs./acre) or perennial ryegrass (20 lbs./acre). Mixes with small grains (rye, wheat and oats) are also appropriate as long as the grain seeding rate does not exceed 50 lbs./acre total. When mixed, alsike seeding rate should be 6 to 8 lbs./acre broadcast and fertilizer should be 300 lbs./acre 19-19-19. Once established, alsike is resistant to heavy grazing pressure. Mow twice in summer, once in June and again in July. Hay removal is preferable, if possible. Fertilize again in August with 200 lbs./acre of 0-20-30. "Common" alsike clover is available from several suppliers. Aurora and Dawn are cultivars developed in western Canada for winter hardiness. Tetra was developed in Sweden for persistence and high yield. Alsike clover has its place in deer management as a specialty plant that thrives in low pH and wet soils, conditions that would not favor red clover. It is also a good candidate to follow glyphosate herbicide treatments in small woodland openings. Alsike is a must for areas that are too difficult, costly or impractical to apply lime. For that reason it would also work well in a mixture with birdsfoot trefoil (4 to 6 lbs./acre) and cereal rye (50 lbs./acre).

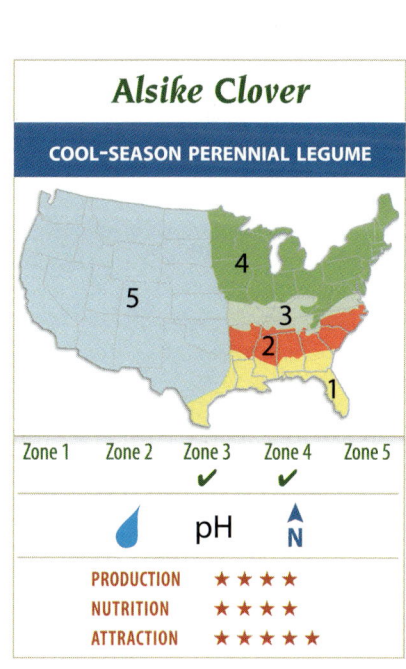

Oregon State University, Forage Information System

Alsike Clover

COOL-SEASON PERENNIAL LEGUME

Zone 1	Zone 2	Zone 3	Zone 4	Zone 5
		✔	✔	

pH

PRODUCTION	★ ★ ★ ★
NUTRITION	★ ★ ★ ★
ATTRACTION	★ ★ ★ ★ ★

ARROWLEAF CLOVER *(Trifolium vesiculosum)*

ARROWLEAF CLOVER is a reseeding, cool-season annual legume that is usually planted with small grains. It is native to the Mediterranean region and has good drought tolerance. Arrowleaf forage quality is high (20 percent protein), and digestible dry matter content is also very high (80 percent) at the peak of vegetative growth. Its greatest limitation is its high susceptibility to viruses and fungi (more about this later).

Leaves are non-hairy and arrow-shaped, 1½ to 2½ inches long with pronounced veins. Leaf marking ranges from none to a large, white, V-shaped mark. The large flowers are initially white turning pink to purple later. Flowering and seed production occur over a long period in spring and summer. Stems branch and curve upward to a height of 2 to 5 feet. The smooth, thick, hollow stems are often purple, becoming hard near maturity. Surprisingly, even these stems are grazed by deer.

ADAPTATION/ESTABLISHMENT

Arrowleaf is widely grown in the southern United States from Georgia to Texas and northward to Oklahoma, Arkansas, Tennessee, and North Carolina. Freeze-outs occur at temperatures between 0 and 10 degrees. Fall plantings north of this line will experience freeze-outs in some years. The plant is suited to a wide range of soil conditions from well to moderately well drained and from slightly acidic to slightly alkaline. It is not well suited to light-textured, sandy, droughty soil of low fertility or to poorly drained, wet soils.

For establishment, prepare a smooth, clean seedbed. Ideally, soil should be firmed with a cultipacker before and after planting. If not, smooth and pack with a heavy drag. Cover seed no deeper than ¼- to ½-inch deep. Plant at a rate of 15 lbs./acre and fertilize according to soil-test results. In lieu of a soil test, apply 300 lbs./acre of 0-20-20. Arrowleaf will tolerate soil pH between 5.0 and 7.5. However, best results are obtained when pH is between 5.8 and 6.5.

No-till drilling into plowed ground and dead stands (killed by frost or chemicals such as glyphosate) can be a very viable option. Reduce rates to 7 lbs./acre when planted alone through a no-till drill. In the mid-South, plant in September or March when moisture is available or predicted. Deep South planting time shifts to October (as long as enough growth is produced before winter) or February so seedlings can become fully established before warm-season weeds germinate. Inoculation with the correct Rhizobium bacteria (strain O) is essential in areas where arrowleaf has not been grown. This is a different strain of bacteria from many other common clovers.

VARIETIES/MANAGEMENT

As with other clovers, I rarely recommend planting arrowleaf in a pure stand. It makes sense to plant a legume/small grain mix because they are compatible as long as grain seeding rates are conservative. Another factor in mixes is guarding against a species-specific crop failure with a back-up plant. Consequently, a good late-winter/early spring mix (North or South) would be arrowleaf (10 lbs./acre), red clover (10 lbs./acre) and oats (50 lbs./acre). Do not overdo the rate of oats or it will shade out the clovers!

OREGON STATE UNIVERSITY, FORAGE INFORMATION SYSTEM

No-till drill rates would be 5 lbs./acre of arrowleaf, 5 lbs./acre of red clover, and 30 lbs./acre oats. The clovers in this mix will make it all the way through August or September with high production and high forage quality thus doubling as both cool- and warm-season forage. Fall planting mixtures (South) would include 10 lbs./acre arrowleaf, 10 lbs./acre crimson clover, and 50 lbs./acre of wheat, oats or rye grain. I do not recommend mixing arrowleaf with annual ryegrass because of the aggressive nature of ryegrass in year two and thereafter. Depending upon weed competition, year-two stands of a fall-planted mix will reseed with at least crimson and oats if stands are mowed in August. Arrowleaf has a hard seed and may not reappear until year three, or unless it is lightly disked in early September. Late-winter sown stands mowed in August will start year two in September with either red clover and/or arrowleaf and reseeded oats.

The most popular variety of arrowleaf is Yuchi, which is a mid-maturing variety of the long-season annual. Amclo is early maturing and Meechee is the latest maturing. All of these are vulnerable to viruses and fungi, which may not affect the stand for several years even if grown on the same ground. Arrowleaf leaves turn a distinctive purplish-red color in response to stress caused by disease or other factors. A new variety, Apache, is resistant to lethal wilt caused by viruses, has greater early-spring forage production (March) and flowers 10 to 14 days earlier than Yuchi. For those of you who have had problems establishing or maintaining Yuchi, Apache may be the answer.

Arrowleaf Clover

COOL-SEASON ANNUAL LEGUME

Zone 1	Zone 2	Zone 3	Zone 4	Zone 5
✔	✔	✔		

S ▾

PRODUCTION	★ ★ ★ ★
NUTRITION	★ ★ ★ ★
ATTRACTION	★ ★ ★ ★ ★

CRIMSON CLOVER (*Trifolium incarnatum*)

CRIMSON CLOVER may be the most popular annual clover planted for deer in the entire United States. Like many other clovers, crimson originated in the Mediterranean region. It is an important and colorful winter annual legume in the South and the Pacific coast, where winters are mild. It is also grown in some northern states as a fall or a summer annual, but it is not winter-hardy in the North. It has been used for a cover crop as far north as northern Maine. Do not confuse this plant with the perennial red clover. Crimson leaves have a more rounded tip and both stem and leaves have more hair than red clover. Crimson plants have dark green leaves and grow to a height of 1 to 3 feet. Brilliant crimson flowers on long heads mature in progression from bottom to top. Seed is rounded, yellow and about three times larger than most other clovers.

ESTABLISHMENT/MIXTURES

Although crimson is more acid tolerant than other clovers (pH range of 5.7 to 6.4), it will still require liming on many sites and soil types throughout the United States. Crimson should be inoculated with the proper strain of Rhizobium bacteria (strain R) just before planting. Note that this is a different strain than that required by other clovers or alfalfa.

Carefully follow the instructions for inoculating seed, as poor inoculation is one of the greatest causes of crimson clover failure in new plantings. Rapid fall growth is enhanced by planting on a firm, well-prepared seedbed by broadcasting, cultipacking or drilling with a grain drill. Seed should be covered no more than ¼-inch deep. Normal seeding rate is 20 lbs./acre in pure stands and 12 to 15 lbs./acre in mixture with cool-season grasses. Planting dates are August through October in the South and April in the North. It will not do well in extreme heat or cold.

Phosphorus and potassium are the most important fertilizer elements, but micronutrients and sulfur can also be limiting. Nitrogen is beneficial in early production especially when crimson is grown in association with small grains. Consequently (in lieu of a soil test), fertilizer at planting time may be estimated at 300 lbs./acre of 8-24-24 for a pure stand or 300 lbs./acre of 19-19-19 for a mixed stand.

Crimson can be mixed with rye, wheat or oats if rates of these small grains are held at about 50 lbs./acre. Adding arrowleaf clover (10 lbs./acre) to any of the above mixes adds variety and longevity to the mix in the South where winter temperatures remain above 10 degrees.

VARIETIES/MANAGEMENT

By far the most popular variety is Dixie reseeding crimson clover. The only drawback to crimson clover for deer is that it is a relatively short-season annual, which produces well from November through April (excluding mid-winter) in the South and April through June in the North. However, you can take advantage of this short season in several ways, especially in the South. Crimson can be plowed under before planting a summer crop of grain sorghum, corn, pearl millet or any grass, which can use the nitrogen fixed by the clover. Using minimum tillage, these same crops can be planted into crimson clover sod killed or partially killed by herbicides. The crimson left as mulch for a summer crop provides up to 70 lbs./acre nitrogen for use by grain sorghum or corn.

In the South, crimson can successfully reseed in September for several successive years by mowing in late August followed by light disking or even no disking, depending on soil conditions (usually heavy clay soil requires no disking, sandy requires disking). Check with your local wildlife biologist or county extension agent to determine if crimson is adapted to your area and will reseed without disking.

Crimson clover is a cheap, easy, high-quality, productive, palatable cool-season forage for deer. It starts fast, withstands heavy continuous grazing and produces a consistent, heavy seed crop with good reseeding potential.

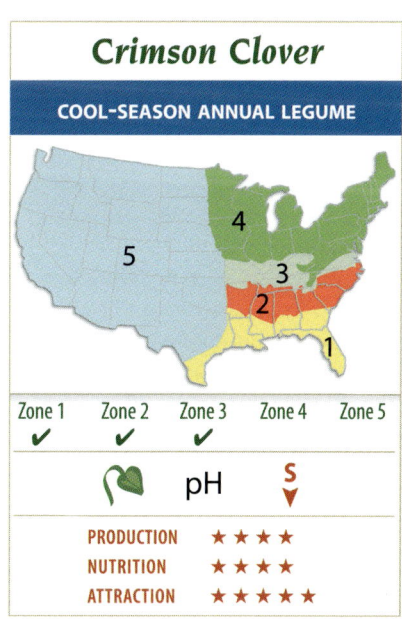

Crimson Clover

COOL-SEASON ANNUAL LEGUME

Zone 1	Zone 2	Zone 3	Zone 4	Zone 5
✔	✔	✔		

pH   S ▼

PRODUCTION	★ ★ ★ ★
NUTRITION	★ ★ ★ ★
ATTRACTION	★ ★ ★ ★ ★

KURA CLOVER *(Trifolium ambiguum)*

KEN ALBRECHT, UNIVERSITY OF WISCONSIN

KURA CLOVER is a spreading perennial clover originating in Caucasian Russia and Asia Minor (countries around the eastern shores of the Black Sea). It is also known as Caucasian, Pellett or honey clover (because it is a favorite of honey bees). Once established, it is a very hardy legume and will tolerate severe, continuous grazing and extreme cold. Caution must be exercised where it is planted, though it is not nearly as invasive as fescue, sericea lespedeza or Japanese honeysuckle.

Kura clover was first introduced in the United States in 1911 for honey production, but it was generally unknown until the late 1940s when its use in apiaries increased. Because of limited seed supplies, use of Kura clover has been restricted. The first United States variety, Rhizo, was released in 1990, and greater quantities of Kura clover seed are now available.

Kura has an extensive root and underground stem (rhizome) system. Initial regrowth in the spring consists of an upright stem containing a large, white-pink flower. The foliage is succulent and not hairy. Kura leaves are usually larger and more pointed than those of other clovers and commonly have white V-shaped markings. It is resistant to most viruses that attack white clover. It will produce yields roughly similar to red clover (4 to 8 tons/acre/year).

ADAPTATION/ESTABLISHMENT

Kura is adapted to the central and northeastern United States as far south as Kentucky and down the Appalachian Mountain chain (at higher elevations) as far south as Georgia. It is extremely winter hardy and has survived severe northern winters when other legumes (including alfalfa, birdsfoot trefoil and red clover) were killed by low and fluctuating temperatures. Stands have remained productive in Minnesota for more than 10 years.

Kura is adapted to a wide variety of soils. It tolerates low fertility, soil acidity, wet soils and some flooding. It is heat and drought tolerant because of its deep root system. It is a poor seed producer. It is highly frost tolerant but has early autumn dormancy. It is highest yielding in late spring and summer.

Kura's Achilles' heel is its poor seedling vigor and slow establishment phase. A pH range of 6.0 to 7.4 is optimum. Establishment must include inoculation with the proper Rhizobium strain (Trifolium Spec 3) and good cultivation with a uniform and firm seed-bed. Drilling or cultipacking are the preferred methods of obtaining good seed-to-soil contact at a shallow depth of ¼ to ½ inch. A seeding rate of 8 to 12 lbs./acre is recommended when planted alone. However, I do not recommend planting Kura alone for deer (see next section). The ideal planting time is early spring (April) or secondarily in late July or early August. Kura can be frost-seeded in winter but not with as high an establishment probability as red clover.

VARIETIES/MANAGEMENT

There are three varieties of Kura clover available in the United States, Cossack, Endura and Rhizo. Endura has shown the highest production (almost 5 tons/acre/year) in Kentucky trials. This was equivalent to alfagraze alfalfa production.

Recommended mixtures containing Kura would include a perennial grass or small grain and even the addition of another, quicker "fill-in" legume such as birdsfoot trefoil to nurse the slow-to-establish seedling Kura plants. Mix 8 to 10 lbs./acre Kura with 1 lb./acre timothy grass and add 3 to 4 lbs./acre birdsfoot trefoil. For an eventual pure stand with no perennial grasses use Kura (8 to 10 lbs./acre), spring wheat (50 lbs./acre) and trefoil (4 lbs./acre). Fall glyphosate treatment followed by no-till drilling in spring may be the ideal, precise, and most successful way to establish Kura mixes. When drilling, cut Kura and trefoil rates in half and mix in 30 lbs./acre wheat or the same 1 lb./acre timothy.

Kura is very similar to alfalfa in growth, production and quality but is easier to manage and tougher once established. Consequently it promises to be more persistent, especially under tough conditions.

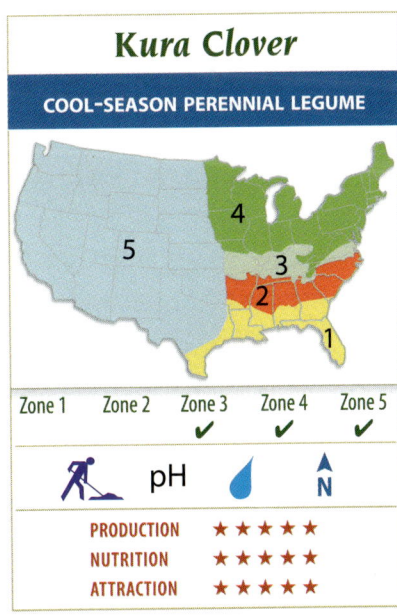

Kura Clover

COOL-SEASON PERENNIAL LEGUME

Zone 1	Zone 2	Zone 3	Zone 4	Zone 5
		✔	✔	✔

	pH		N

PRODUCTION	★ ★ ★ ★ ★
NUTRITION	★ ★ ★ ★ ★
ATTRACTION	★ ★ ★ ★

LADINO CLOVER (Trifolium repens)

There are currently three types of white clovers available to deer managers: small-leaf types, often called white Dutch clover or common white clover; intermediate-leaf types; and large- or giant-leaf types, called LADINO WHITE CLOVER. The large types (bred for high production) were originally cultivated in Northern Italy and later all around the world. There is a widespread misconception that ladinos are cattle clovers not suited for deer. This is false. Tall, long-stemmed clovers are fine for deer since the leaf is the main forage target, and tall growth makes them more competitive with grassy weeds. Ladinos are long-lived perennials in the northern United States but short-lived perennials or annuals in the Deep South. As such, including other improved, intermediate white clovers, they are arguably the best high-quality, low-maintenance, highly productive perennial forages available to deer managers in the United States

Ladinos are characterized by very leafy plants 8- to 12-inches tall that spread by stolons, or runners, and form shallow roots at nodes. Leaves are smooth, not hairy, and usually marked with a white "V." White flowers are clustered into heads, and seeds are extremely small.

ADAPTATION/ESTABLISHMENT

Ladino is adapted throughout the eastern United States from Canada south through Florida and westward until production becomes limited by low rainfall in the Great Plains, picking up again in the Northwest. Although it is not productive on droughty soils, it will survive considerable dry weather. Once established, ladino is tolerant of moderate soil acidity. It is tolerant of wetter soils and is highly responsive to potassium fertilizer. Under ideal conditions, Ladinos can produce over 10,000 lbs./acre/year of high-quality forage.

Ladino grows well in association with cool-season, perennial grasses such as perennial ryegrass and timothy. It will not do well with fescue, orchardgrass, bermudagrass or bahiagrass. In most of the United States, I recommend mixing ladino clover with one of the annual grains such as wheat, rye, or oats because the above cool-season perennial grasses are generally not good deer forage except in the North. Inoculation with live Rhizobium bacteria (strain B) that helps clover fix nitrogen is critical to seedling survival, and soil pH is critical to inoculant survival. Buy pre-inoculated ladino with the clay/lime coating, and be sure soil pH is above 6.0 at planting. Broadcast rate in the South is 5 lbs./acre ladino mixed with 7 lbs./acre red clover and 50 lbs./acre wheat (or rye or oats) planted in September to early October. An alternative month is late February to early March for a ladino/red clover/oats mixture. In the far North, plant pre-inoculated ladino (5 lbs./acre) with red clover (7 lbs./acre) and perennial ryegrass (20 lbs./acre) or timothy (5 lbs./acre). Plant in September or April. Ladino can be mixed with red clover and frost-seeded in late winter. Fertilize according to a soil test. In lieu of a soil test, keep nitrogen levels at less than 60 lbs./acre to avoid grass competition, and apply plenty of phosphorus and potassium (300 lbs./acre of 19-19-19 or 300 lbs./acre 8-24-24). Ladino clover production will be slow the first fall, but high production will begin in early spring and continue through October or November for several years thereafter. While the ladino starts slowly, developing a root system and nodules to fix its own nitrogen, the red clover and the grasses in the recommended mixes provide immediate forage production for deer in the first fall. These companion plants also act as a nurse crop by diverting grazing pressure away from new ladino seedlings.

VARIETIES/MANAGEMENT

Varieties in the United States which are in widespread use include California ladino, Osceola, Regal, Tillman, Advantage, Will, Tripoli, Alice and Patriot (a hybrid). I have used all of the above varieties in north Georgia, and all produce well and are utilized heavily by deer. Both Osceola and Patriot are noted for their persistence. New cultivars and hybrids that are even more persistent should be available in a few years.

Management of ladino clover is dependent on grass management and weed control. Ladino planted with perennial grasses should be mowed two or three times per summer, with the final mowing in late August. Fertilizer should be applied once per year in September with 300 lbs./acre of 0-20-30. The same management technique is used for ladino planted with annual grasses, but fewer mowings may be needed depending on weed competition. If everything goes well, the second year stand should be a mixed stand of ladino and red clover with the third year being pure ladino. Wild grasses like crabgrass, johnsongrass, bermudagrass, bahiagrass, foxtail, fescue or ryegrass can become a problem competing with clover. Refer to Chapter 10 for guidance on eliminating grasses in legume crops.

In my opinion, using a perennial for deer plots is the way to go! Ladino clovers fit the bill for a productive, high-quality perennial plant that is tops on the deer preference list at 30 percent protein and 60 to 80 percent digestibility.

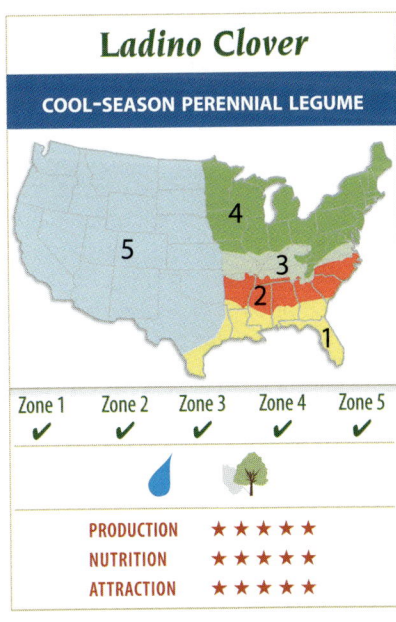

Ladino Clover

COOL-SEASON PERENNIAL LEGUME

Zone 1	Zone 2	Zone 3	Zone 4	Zone 5
✔	✔	✔	✔	✔

PRODUCTION	★ ★ ★ ★ ★
NUTRITION	★ ★ ★ ★ ★
ATTRACTION	★ ★ ★ ★ ★

DURANA WHITE CLOVER (*Trifolium repens*)

KENT KAMMERMEYER

There has long been a need for a persistent, productive, long-lived clover that is highly competitive in a mixed stand with perennial grasses or other aggressive plants. Along comes DURANA WHITE CLOVER, the product of Dr. Joe Bouton, renowned plant breeder formerly of The University of Georgia (he went on to head the Noble Foundation in Oklahoma). To improve grazing tolerance of white clover, he collected several types of naturalized clovers that had survived hot, dry summers in several Georgia locations. Plants were subjected to heavy grazing with grass competition, productive survivors were crossed, and a promising entry called GA43 (later named Durana) was selected for further development. Durana has smaller leaves than ladino clovers but produces more runners, or stolons, which allow aggressive spreading and excellent grazing tolerance. Durana produces flowers profusely for long periods making it a more dependable reseeder. Parent material from Durana was also crossed with a virus-resistant ladino clover to form a variety named Patriot. In performance tests, both compared very favorably with Regal ladino (an industry standard). Durana is not as productive as Regal ladino during the establishment year but catches up to it in year two. Both produce 2 to 5 tons of forage per year at 25 to 30 percent protein levels and up to 80 percent digestibility (indicating lower lignin levels). The difference is that Regal succumbs to perennial grasses in a couple of years while Durana can persist for five years or more.

ADAPTATION/ESTABLISHMENT

This cool-season, perennial legume is adapted from east Texas across the South to the Atlantic Coast and north of a line from central Georgia to central Texas. Below this line, it will do well on sandy loam or heavy soils. It is adapted to the Pacific Northwest, the Upper

Midwest and New England. I suspect it will thrive in Canada, but this is unknown.

Durana will grow in low pH (down to 5.4) but like all other clovers will thrive in a pH of 6.0 or above. Get a soil test to tailor your fertilizer application for your soil. Prepare a smooth seedbed (disked 4 to 6 inches deep) and broadcast 5 lbs./acre Durana mixed with 7 lbs./acre red clover (Cinnamon Plus, Redlan-Graze II, Redland III or Bulldog) and 50 lbs./acre of wheat (or oats or rye where appropriate). In lieu of a soil test, apply 300 lbs./acre of 19-19-19 or equivalent. Cultipack or drag the mix so that clover seed has good soil contact and a firm seedbed but is not more than ¼-inch deep. In the North, August and April are the best months for planting, but in the South, September and late February are ideal. For all spring plantings, always substitute oats for wheat. Durana is sold pre-inoculated with a coating of lime and selected Rhizobia bacteria (strain B) for optimal nitrogen fixation. I have drilled Durana into grasses killed by glyphosate with great success in both spring and fall. Cut clover rates to 3 lbs./acre and small grains to 30 lbs./acre when using a drill.

VARIETIES/MANAGEMENT

As mentioned, Patriot white clover is a close relative of Durana with better production but probably somewhat less persistence. One smart option would be to mix them 50:50 for the best of both worlds. Both are exclusively marketed by Pennington Seed Company of Madison, Georgia (*www.penningtonseed.com*).

For Durana management, unhook your plow and hook up your mower. Depending on weed coverage, mow the Durana (down to 4 to 5 inches) one to three times each summer. Try to avoid mowing during droughts. If weed competition is not a problem, mowing once in late August is sufficient. Fertilize once per year in September with a no-nitrogen fertilizer such as 0-20-30 or 0-20-20 at 300 to 400 lbs./acre.

After several years of field tests, University of Georgia agronomists declared unrivaled persistence. Meanwhile, I have seen more than 30 different plots of Durana clover on public and private lands (including a 1½-acre patch on my own property) and despite harsh conditions (competition, drought, overgrazing and cold) have encountered very few that I would consider a failure. Most of the others are vigorous, thriving and exceeding expectations. Some are going into their third year. Grassy weed management is the key to longevity of Durana stands (*see Chapter 10 for details*).

Durana is resistant to grazing, more persistent, more drought tolerant, more acid tolerant, more aggressive with grasses and weeds and has more stolon density than any other clover. My agronomist friend, Dr. Bill Sell, has a Durana stand that is 3 years old and thriving in a soil pH of 5.4 with no fertilizer. That is one tough clover!

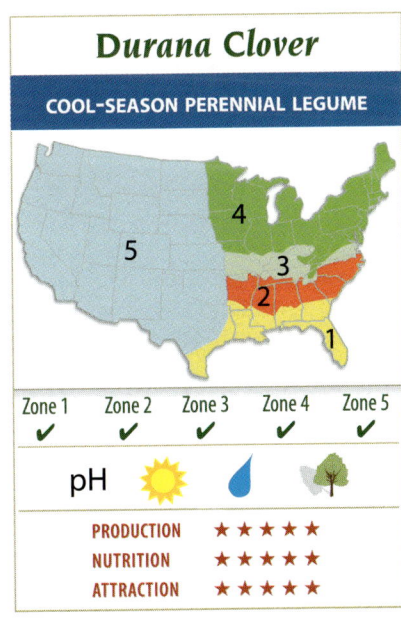

Durana Clover

COOL-SEASON PERENNIAL LEGUME

Zone 1	Zone 2	Zone 3	Zone 4	Zone 5
✔	✔	✔	✔	✔

pH ☀ 💧 🌳

PRODUCTION	★ ★ ★ ★ ★
NUTRITION	★ ★ ★ ★ ★
ATTRACTION	★ ★ ★ ★ ★

RED CLOVER (*Trifolium pratense*)

OREGON STATE UNIVERSITY, FORAGE INFORMATION SYSTEM

RED CLOVER (also known as June clover, peavine clover, and cowgrass) originated in the eastern Mediterranean region and Asia Minor. It is a short-lived perennial usually persisting for two to three years. Red clover is erect-growing with leafy plants 2 to 3 feet tall. Leaves and stems are hairy with oblong to wedge-shaped leaflets often marked with a white "V." Flowers are clustered into large, pinkish-violet (not red) heads that produce blooms anytime from June through August. Red clover should not be confused with crimson clover, a winter annual.

ADAPTATION/ESTABLISHMENT

Red clover does best in the northern and central United States, but with good management, it will perenniate in the upper South. In the Deep South, it may survive only as an annual. It is adapted to a wide range of climatic and soil conditions. It is fairly drought tolerant and tolerates more soil acidity (down to a pH of 5.5) and poorer soil drainage than alfalfa but is less tolerant of wet conditions than white clover. Agronomists use red clover for hay or pastures. In combination with cool-season grasses and other clovers, it makes an excellent low-maintenance, low-cost, high-quality food plot for deer. In research in Tennessee during the summer of 2003, red clover was preferred by deer and produced more biomass than all other perennial cool-season forages. Red clovers have been called "cattle clovers," but nothing could be further from the truth. Red clover is a productive, palatable forage for deer.

Red clover is best for deer plots when planted in August (North) to October (South) broadcast at 5 to 7 lbs./acre mixed with white clover (5 lbs./acre) and winter wheat, rye or oats (50 lbs./acre total). Red clover also is an excellent choice for frost seeding/drilling into grain sorghum/corn stubble, dormant warm-season grasses or weeds, fallow ground, heavily grazed cool-season grasses, or fall-seeded winter wheat from February (South) to April (North). Timing and competition are critical when frost-seeding red clover mixes.

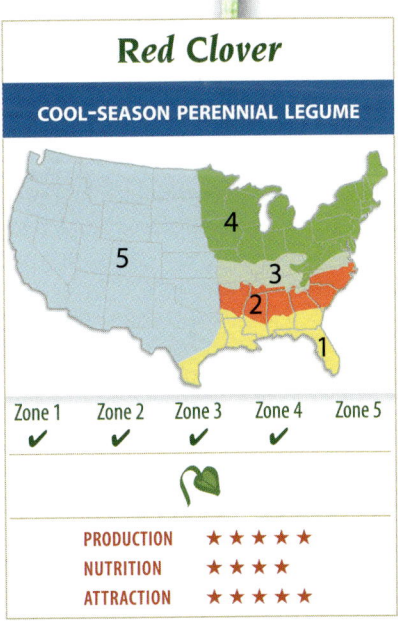

Good soil contact is also necessary and is usually provided by freezing and thawing of wet ground and late-winter precipitation. The objective of this technique is to provide the red clover mix with an early start when conditions are favorable for germination and subsequent spring growth. In addition to broadcast frost seeding, red clover can certainly be established by no-till drilling or by conventional plowing/tilling methods during the same time period.

Red clover has a long growing season and is one of the best-yielding clovers, producing from April to October in the North and March to November in the South. Red clover produces more grazing than ladino clover during summer but will not tolerate continuous close grazing over long periods of time. Annual production can be 5 tons or more dry weight per acre with protein levels of 15 to 30 percent depending on season. Optimum pH levels should be maintained between 6.0 and 7.0. Like all clovers, red clover is responsive to phosphorus and potassium fertilizer and must be inoculated at planting with a live bacteria culture (strain B) or purchased pre-inoculated and kept reasonably cool.

Many diseases, especially funguses like powdery mildew, northern and southern anthracnose, crown rots and root rots can attack red clover along with viruses or insects. Varieties have been developed that are resistant to one or more of these diseases.

VARIETIES/MANAGEMENT

My personal experiences with red clover in north Georgia have been very positive. It is a great companion with ladino or arrowleaf clovers and any small grain (wheat, rye, oats). Deer use has been very heavy for eight to 10 months of the year, especially in early spring and late summer. I have had a mixture of red clover, arrowleaf clover and oats reseed and persist for three years by mowing once in August and fertilizing in September every year with 100 lbs./acre 0-46-0 and 100 lbs./acre 0-0-60. I have used the Kenland, Kenstar, Redland III, Cinnamon Plus, Bulldog and Cherokee varieties with good success. Other varieties include Concord, Red Gold, Greenstar, Red Star, Start and others. The Cherokee variety is best for the Deep South. Check with your local county agent for varieties best adapted to your area.

Red Clover

COOL-SEASON PERENNIAL LEGUME

Zone 1	Zone 2	Zone 3	Zone 4	Zone 5
✔	✔	✔	✔	

PRODUCTION	★ ★ ★ ★ ★
NUTRITION	★ ★ ★ ★
ATTRACTION	★ ★ ★ ★ ★

225

SUBTERRANEAN CLOVER *(Trifolium subterranean)*

OREGON STATE UNIVERSITY, FORAGE INFORMATION SYSTEM

Just like varieties of apples, corn, pears and peaches, clover varieties fall in and out of favor over the years depending on current research and subsequent publicity. SUBTERRANEAN CLOVER (subclover) is one of these. At one time it was thought to contain enough phytoestrogens to inhibit horse foaling (current research suggests otherwise) and fell out of favor in Australia where it was commonly used. It was given new life in the 1980s by researchers in Louisiana who found it very suitable for planting in the shade of thinned pine stands. Currently, it is quiet on the subclover front, but going back to one of my favorite phrases, "there is a clover for everyone," subclover is for people with shade problems in the South and West.

Subclover is the common name for three clover subspecies native to the Mediterranean region. Most varieties grown in the United States are the subterranean species. Subclover has a low growth habit, forming a dense sod that seldom exceeds a 10-inch height. Flowering and seed development in subclover are different from other clovers. After pollination, the flower develops in a burr, and the stem bearing the burr bends downward, placing the seed in the soil surface. Consequently, grazing can continue during this time without reducing seed production. In fact, seed production is reduced if subclover is not kept grazed down to 2 to 4 inches. The stoloniferous growth habit of subclover makes it well suited for close-grazing animals like deer.

ADAPTATION/ESTABLISHMENT

Subclover works well in western states, especially along the coast, throughout the Deep South, and in the Atlantic coastal area. It generally will not withstand winter temperatures below 10 degrees (similar to arrowleaf clover). Subclover has the largest seed of any cool-season clover. Consequently, it is quick to emerge and has excellent seedling vigor. Recommended seeding rates range from 16 to 20 lbs./acre broadcast. Good stands have been obtained by drilling less than 10 lbs./acre in a pure stand on a clean, firm seedbed. Planting depth is critical. Seeds should not be placed deeper than $\frac{1}{2}$ inch. Productive seasons are from October to November and March to May. By far the biggest advantage of using subclover is its shade tolerance. One study showed that it produced 92 percent of its potential under 50 percent shade and performed well under 75 percent shade. It is also tolerant of heavy grazing, resistant to acidic soil conditions, and is highly nutritious. Disadvantages include low production, unreliable reseeding, intolerance of poor drainage and intolerance of drought. This clover grows rapidly when night temperatures are above 55 degrees and grows very slowly when night temperatures are below 40 degrees.

OREGON STATE UNIVERSITY, FORAGE INFORMATION SYSTEM

Like other annual clovers, subclover should be seeded in the fall from September to October. Seed must be inoculated with a specific subclover inoculant (WR strain). Fertilize at planting with 300 lbs./acre of 8-24-24.

VARIETIES/MANAGEMENT

Varieties include Mt. Barker, Woogenellup, Tallarook, and Nangeela. Mt. Barker appears to be the best variety for the South and Mid-Atlantic. There are two very specific uses for subclover with the most common one being planted under thinned pines. This can be accomplished by burning or disking in September followed by broadcasting or drilling of subclover. Basal areas (plantation densities) of 40 sq.ft./acre and 80 sq.ft./acre showed 2,000 to 3,000 lbs./acre clover production while a 120 sq.ft./acre basal area reduced yield to 1,500 to 2,000 lbs./acre. It can also be overseeded with ryegrass on perennial-grass pastures or drilled in warm-season, perennial hay fields. Logging roads lined with standing timber are another application.

As with many other clovers, I do not recommend planting pure stands of subclover. One mix for shade would be 10 lbs./acre subclover, 25 lbs./acre cereal rye, 30 lbs./acre wheat and 3 lbs./acre white clover. Subclover does well with any cereal grain and vetches.

Year-two management must include either light disking or burning in September or October to release seeds lying in the soil. Subclover reseeds better on heavy soils. This is true of all annual, reseeding clovers.

If your deer property has lots of pines but few openings, you may be able to get a lot of mileage from subclover plantings under pine canopy. A word of caution: due to denser shade and heavy leaf fall, attempts to plant subclover in dense, mature hardwoods are quite likely to fail.

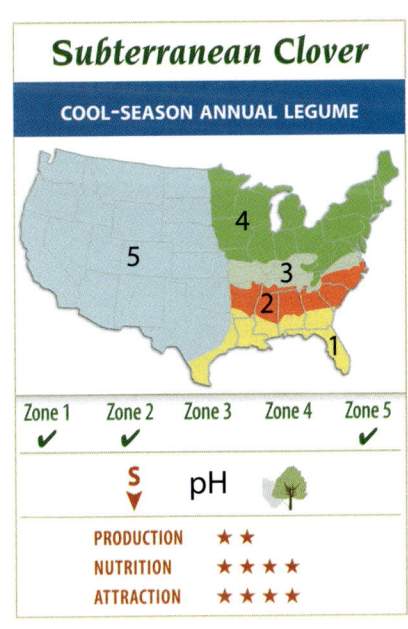

Subterranean Clover

COOL-SEASON ANNUAL LEGUME

Zone 1	Zone 2	Zone 3	Zone 4	Zone 5
✔	✔			✔

S ↓   pH

PRODUCTION	★ ★
NUTRITION	★ ★ ★ ★
ATTRACTION	★ ★ ★ ★

Other Legumes

ALFALFA *(Medicago sativa)*

ALFALFA originated near Iran but related forms are found scattered over central Asia and into Siberia. It was first introduced into the eastern United States by colonists in 1736. Known as the "Queen of Forages," alfalfa is the oldest and one of the most palatable and nutritious cultivated forage crops. It is rich in protein, vitamins and minerals. Alfalfa has a very high yield potential (5 to 6 tons dry weight per acre) compared with that of other forage crops. Alfalfa is a herbaceous perennial legume. A mature plant may have 5 to 25 stems which usually reach a height of 15 to 25 inches. Stems are branched and slender and bear three leaflets which are linear, oblong, or obovate oblong and are toothed toward their tip. Alfalfa is grown in many areas of the United States, accounting for nearly 30 million acres of production – mostly for hay. For best production, it requires a well-drained soil with nearly neutral pH (6.5 to 7.0) and good fertility. It does not do well in poorly drained or acidic soil or areas where adequate water is not available. Alfalfa is used primarily as a hay crop. With careful management and selection of varieties, it can be used successfully as a food plot for deer.

OREGON STATE UNIVERSITY, FORAGE INFORMATION SYSTEM

ADAPTATION/ESTABLISHMENT

Alfalfa requires a deep, permeable soil with an adequate moisture supply. It is sensitive to poor drainage and compacted soil conditions that restrict root growth. Alfalfa does not tolerate acidic soils (pH below 6.2), especially in the seedling stage. A good seedbed for alfalfa is finely pulverized, leveled and firmed to the seeding depth and contains soil moisture near the surface.

Most alfalfa seeding in the United States occurs in August to September or March to April. Northern ranges usually mean August or April, while southern plantings do better in September or March. Fall plantings should be planted at least six weeks before freezing. For best seedling survival, drill or sow seeds approximately ¼-inch deep. Seedling emergence is greatly reduced when seeds are planted deeper than ½ inch. Seeding rates are 15 to 20 lbs./acre for drilling and 20 to 25 lbs./acre when broadcasting. Mixing with small grains is not recommended because of competition in the early seeding stage. Alfalfa can be mixed with clover (red or ladino) at reduced rates (5 lbs./acre clover to 15 lbs./acre alfalfa), but this is also risky due to early competition. All alfalfa seed should be inoculated (strain A) immediately prior to seeding or purchased pre-inoculated. Inoculated seed should be kept cool until planted.

VARIETIES/MANAGEMENT

Until recently, alfalfa could not withstand heavy continuous grazing such as would be expected from a high deer population grazing in small, isolated food plots. With the introduction of grazing-tolerant varieties, this has changed, and many small field plantings of alfalfa for deer have been successful in recent years. For deer food plots, besides selecting a variety that was developed to resist heavy grazing, varieties of alfalfa are available with specific characteristics for cold tolerance and insect and disease resistance. Dormant, moderately dormant and non-dormant cultivars are available for the different climatic regions. Selecting the right alfalfa variety from the hundreds available can be bewildering. Go to www.alfalfa.org and click on "Variety Leaflet" for the most recent edition of ratings. A few of the recommended grazing varieties you will see in these ratings include Alfagraze (north and central United States), Amerigraze 401 (north and central), Amerigraze 702 (southeast) and Amerigraze 701 (southwest). Better yet, consult your county agent, seed dealer or consultant for varieties that will do well in your area.

Alfalfa is a heavy user of plant nutrients. Careful pre-planning is very important in establishing alfalfa. Applications of fertilizer and lime should be based on soil test results. A pH of 6.5 to 7.0 is necessary. Phosphorus, potassium, sulfur (if necessary) and boron should be broadcast and incorporated prior to seeding. Nitrogen (N) application is not necessary but, if applied, should not exceed 40 lbs./acre.

More than 20 diseases are serious problems for alfalfa in the United States. These include fungal and bacterial wilts, leaf spots, crown and root rots, viruses and nematodes. Resistant varieties are available for most of the diseases and nematodes listed. There are a number of insect pests that are problems for alfalfa in the United States. These include the potato leafhopper, alfalfa weevil, several aphids and the alfalfa plant bug. Depending upon severity of infestation, chemical control of insects may be necessary to maintain a healthy, productive stand. Weeds can be a serious problem with alfalfa, especially in spring-planted stands. In the fall plantings, preparing a smooth, weed-free seedbed is essential. Use of pre-emergent herbicides may be necessary. Watch for warm-season weed competition the following spring and treat accordingly with herbicides.

Alfalfa is an excellent food plant for deer. However, it is not a panacea or a miracle plant. It is dormant from November to April in most of the United States and is therefore a poor choice by itself for cool-season forage. Small grains and clovers do better in this period. Alfalfa is expensive and somewhat difficult to establish. It requires careful management including strict attention to pH and fertility, chemical spraying for insect or weed control, and removal of excess growth for hay, if possible. It is highly productive, palatable, high quality and persistent. Alfalfa stands, well managed, can be productive for five or more years.

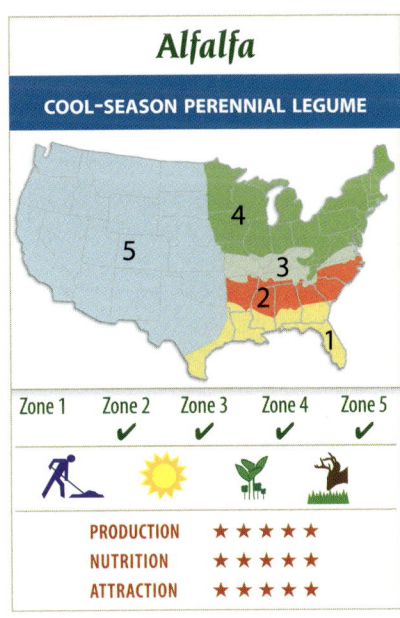

Alfalfa

COOL-SEASON PERENNIAL LEGUME

Zone 1	Zone 2	Zone 3	Zone 4	Zone 5
	✔	✔	✔	✔

PRODUCTION ★ ★ ★ ★ ★
NUTRITION ★ ★ ★ ★ ★
ATTRACTION ★ ★ ★ ★ ★

ALYCECLOVER (*Alysicarpus vaginalis*)

KENT KAMMERMEYER

There is a great need in deer management for high-quality, grazing-resistant summer forage. ALYCECLOVER is one good choice to fill this need. It is native to tropical areas of the Orient. It is not a true clover but is an erect annual legume with a thin stem, rounded leaves and pink flowers. This plant should not be confused with Alsike clover, another warm-season annual (better adapted to the northern United States) or with Alice clover, a cool-season perennial white clover from New Zealand.

Alyceclover is primarily adapted to the Gulf Coast area but will grow well in the mid-Atlantic region, too, if there is adequate summer rainfall. It is best adapted to well-drained, sandy soils but will also do well on clay soils. Best production occurs from June through September. It maintains quality well in late summer when there can be a fairly significant stress period for deer related to low-quality vegetation.

Alyceclover is tolerant of moderate soil acidity but does better at pH above 6.0. It responds well to phosphorus fertilization.

ADAPTATION/ESTABLISHMENT

Seeding rate is 15 to 20 lbs./acre in May or June. Establishment is somewhat slow, and weed competition may be a problem in the sensitive small seedling stage. For this reason, on sites with significant weed potential of species such as crabgrass or other summer annual grasses, sowing in middle or late June may be more successful.

Alyceclover does well in a 50:50 mixture with aeschynomene (American jointvetch) at 10 lbs./acre each. Both require inoculation with the proper strain of Rhizobium bacteria (strain EL) at planting to ensure that nitrogen fixation of these legumes will take place properly. Fertilize by soil test or, in lieu of soil test, apply 300 lbs./acre of 8-24-24 at planting. This mixture may be the most successful way to go with alyceclover, especially in the northern limits of its adaptability. If summer weather is dry or heavy deer grazing takes place immediately after planting, alyceclover may be lost, but the jointvetch should persist since it is more resistant to droughts and less sensitive to grazing in the seedling stage. Both produce high-quality growth until the first frost, and both are very resilient under heavy grazing after establishment (about one month after planting).

Lawrence Pierce planted these legumes in a mixture with great success when he was the biologist at Burnt Pine Plantation in Georgia. He says they make an excellent summer forage as well as a great place to bowhunt in the September archery season. He was unsuccessful, however, in his attempts to get them to reseed and double crop with wheat.

VARIETIES/MANAGEMENT

Alyceclover should not need much attention after planting, except for weed control or management. If weed encroachment threatens the stand, there are two solutions – mowing and chemical spraying. Mowing is probably most appropriate for broadleaf competition, and herbicides are more suited to controlling grass competition. Wait at least a month after establishment before doing either one. See Chapter 10 for guidance on using grass-selective herbicides.

If alyceclover seed matures and shatters, a volunteer crop can be produced in succeeding years. However, it may be difficult or impossible to get seed production before frost because of heavy grazing by deer even in September. This is the problem Lawrence had.

If the stand is relatively weed-free, a fall crop such as wheat or rye mixed with any of the clovers (crimson, ladino, red or arrowleaf) can be broadcast or drilled at first frost to get a quick, easy cool-season crop on the same acreage. Mow the dead stand down on top of the broadcast seeding but leave it standing if a no-till drill is used.

The alyceclover/jointvetch combination may provide more high-quality summer forage for deer than virtually any other annual summer legume, including some of the peas and beans. It's worth a try if you are not in a drought-prone area.

Alyceclover

WARM–SEASON ANNUAL LEGUME

Zone 1	Zone 2	Zone 3	Zone 4	Zone 5
✔	✔	✔	✔	

PRODUCTION	★ ★ ★ ★
NUTRITION	★ ★ ★ ★
ATTRACTION	★ ★ ★

AMERICAN JOINTVETCH (*Aeschynomene americana*)

AMERICAN JOINTVETCH is a warm-season annual legume native to the Southeast. There is great confusion surrounding this plant since it is not a vetch nor is it a cool-season forage as are the true vetches. Moreover, it is commonly referred to by at least three different names, including aeschynomene (pronounced *ash-uh-nom-uh-nee*), jointvetch and deervetch. There are two or three closely related species, including one which is considered endangered, sensitive jointvetch, and one which is recommended for seeding in bahiagrass pastures in Florida. This species profile concentrates on American jointvetch, which is a vigorous erect annual legume with pinnately compound leaves attaining a height of 3 to 6 feet.

ADAPTATION/ESTABLISHMENT

Jointvetch is most adapted to wet soils in Coastal tropics or subtropics. It tolerates low fertility and moderately acid pH (5.5 to 6.0). Although erect and tall when not grazed, it develops a branched, low-growth habit under grazing. In recent years, many wildlife managers have found out that jointvetch is much more widely adaptable than once believed. It has also prospered on dry upland sites in Mountain and Piedmont regions and well-drained sandy soils. It is one of the few warm-season legumes which is highly palatable (20 to 25 percent crude protein) but can withstand heavy grazing pressure by deer, and this is probably its greatest asset. If jointvetch flowers and produces hard seed before frost, it is possible to get natural reseeding the following spring. Heavy deer grazing, however, may keep it from going to seed in adequate numbers before frost.

Jointvetch can be planted beginning in April in the Deep South through May and June in virtually the entire eastern United States. It may not be a good choice to plant in the more drought prone areas of the central and western United States. Broadcast rate is 20 lbs./acre, and like all legumes, seed must be inoculated (strain EL) at planting. Cover seed ¼- to ½-inch deep and fertilize with 300 lbs./acre of 0-20-20.

Jointvetch can be successfully mixed with other summer forages for an effective warm-season food plot. Alyceclover (not a true clover) is also resistant to overgrazing and can be successfully mixed with jointvetch with a seeding rate of 10 lbs./acre each. Both are highly nutritious and palatable to deer and both provide excellent brood rearing habitat for quail and wild turkeys. Jointvetch can be successfully mixed with grain sorghum as long as the seeding rate of sorghum is kept low at 5 lbs./acre or less to keep from shading out the jointvetch. Apply more nitrogen and potassium fertilizer (350 lbs./acre 19-19-19) when grain sorghum is used.

VARIETIES/MANAGEMENT

According to QDMA founder Joe Hamilton, one of the best uses of jointvetch occurs in intensive pine management where it can be planted between pine rows after a row thinning or in firebreaks. Being quite shade tolerant, it will do especially well in these narrow strips or breaks if they are limed (usually 1 to 2 tons per acre) and fertilized with 300 lbs./acre of 0-20-20. Jointvetch is very responsive to phosphorus. There may be enough seed production each year to regenerate the stand, however it will probably not be dependable enough to count on.

Jointvetch is one of the few warm-season legumes which can withstand deer grazing pressure in small fields well enough to reach maturity and provide high-quality grazing all summer long, especially during the late summer stress period (most other warm-season legumes need protection in early stages with repellents or fencing). While it is well adapted to wet soils, it has proven highly adaptable, even withstanding moderate drought conditions on shallow upland soils. Commercial seed sources are somewhat difficult to find because of recent contamination with the seeds of tropical soda apple.

Glenn jointvetch is a variety from Australia which was originally collected on the coast of Mexico. It does well in low-lying coastal country subject to periodic waterlogging. It also grows on well-drained soils receiving more than 50 inches of annual rainfall.

Lee perennial jointvetch (also from Australia) is noted for more leaf growth earlier and later than annual jointvetches. It is also suited to seasonally wet tropics with greater than 40 inches of annual rainfall.

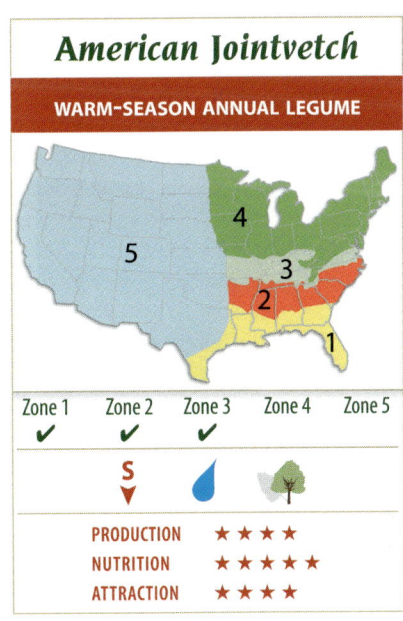

American Jointvetch

WARM-SEASON ANNUAL LEGUME

Zone 1	Zone 2	Zone 3	Zone 4	Zone 5
✔	✔	✔		

PRODUCTION	★ ★ ★ ★
NUTRITION	★ ★ ★ ★ ★
ATTRACTION	★ ★ ★ ★

AUSTRIAN WINTER PEA (*Pisum sativum*)

CRAIG HARPER

AUSTRIAN WINTER PEA, sometimes called "black pea" and "field pea," may be the ultimate cool season "ice-cream plant" for deer, ranking very high on deer preference lists. It is an annual legume with very good nitrogen-fixing capabilities. This and related pea species are native to the eastern Mediterranean region and western Asia.

Austrian winter pea is a low-growing, viny legume which can fix more than 200 lbs./acre/year of nitrogen under good conditions. It has hollow, slender, and succulent stems, 2 to 4 feet long. Foliage is pale green, and the flowers are usually purple, pink or reddish. The leaf consists of one to three pairs of leaflets and terminal, branched tendrils. Pods are 1½- to 2½-inches long with three to five round, dark-colored seeds. Seed color is commonly gray with purple or brown mottles. Seed size is large with test weights of 55 to 60 lbs./bushel.

ADAPTATION/ESTABLISHMENT

As its name implies, Austrian winter pea has good winter hardiness and can be successfully grown in the entire United States and parts of Canada. However, during severe winters when the small pea plants are exposed to long periods of sub-zero weather without snow cover, they may be winter killed. The winter pea can also be grown spring-seeded as a summer annual in the northern half of its range and maybe even further south. Normal planting dates are August to October (moving north to south). The pea is somewhat slow starting and vulnerable to overgrazing. Broadcast seed at 30 to 40 lbs./acre and cover ½- to 1-inch deep. Be sure to inoculate with Rhizobium bacteria specific to peas (strain C), and apply 0-20-20 fertilizer at 300 lbs./acre incorporated well into the soil. Austrian winter pea is sensitive to acidic soil and grows well in a pH of 6.0 to 7.5. Production can be 3,000 to 4,000 lbs./acre forage. It maintains extremely high-quality foliage and stems with protein levels in the 25- to 30-percent range (similar to white clover). It grows best on loam or clay-loam soils, although it will do well on sand with adequate rainfall.

VARIETIES/MANAGEMENT

Varieties include Granger and Sioux. Several varieties of lentils are also closely related to Austrian winter pea. For deer management, stick with the original. With Austrian winter

OREGON STATE UNIVERSITY, FORAGE INFORMATION SYSTEM

pea, more than with any other cool-season deer food-plot plant, it is important to ask the question, "What is the main purpose of this food plot?" If the answer is to attract and harvest deer in this plot in the fall, then these peas should be an integral part of your planting program. However, these peas are quite vulnerable to overgrazing, especially in small plots. For this reason and others, I would never recommend planting Austrian winter peas in a pure stand. There are many possible combinations for mixtures including ladino clover (5 lbs./acre), red clover (5 lbs./acre), wheat (50 lbs./acre) and Austrian winter peas (20 lbs./acre). Austrian winter peas (25 lbs./acre) can also be paired with rye (50 lbs./acre), or oats (50 lbs./acre), or arrowleaf clover (10 lbs./acre), or crimson clover (10 lbs./acre).

Austrian winter peas are especially suited to no-till drilling into summer plantings weakened by cold weather or killed with glyphosate. These include bahia grass, crabgrass, Bermuda grass, browntop millet, jointvetch, alyceclover, soybeans and cowpeas. When drilling in the fall, mix 20 lbs./acre Austrian winter peas with 25 lbs./acre wheat or rye, and drill 1-inch deep. The small grains will try to act as a nurse crop, which in bigger fields and lower deer populations may allow the Austrian winter peas to escape overgrazing. Fertilize with 300 lbs./acre 19-19-19 for best results.

One late December, I went out to one of my Austrian winter pea mixtures to get photographs of the peas. The mix was planted in early September and included 50 lbs./acre wheat, 10 lbs./acre crimson clover, 10 lbs./acre hairy vetch and 10 lbs./acre Austrian winter peas. The field was only one quarter of an acre. At last check in November, everything was doing fine. However, this December trip would yield no Austrian winter pea photographs – they were gone! There was light to moderate grazing on the wheat, clover and vetch, but the deer had selectively knocked out the Austrian winter peas over the course of less than a month. I do not have a high deer population on my property (25 to 30/square mile). Oh well, this experience reinforces the value of mixtures for deer managers!

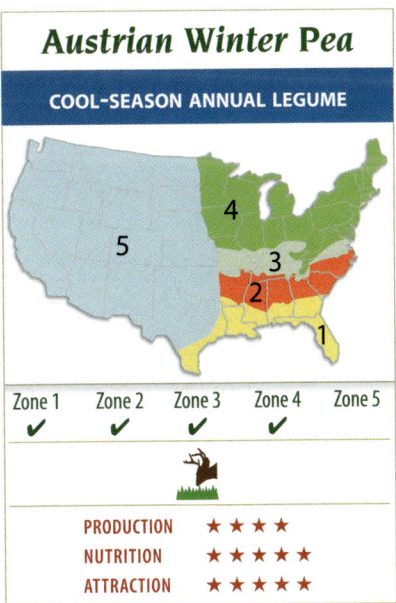

Austrian Winter Pea

COOL-SEASON ANNUAL LEGUME

Zone 1	Zone 2	Zone 3	Zone 4	Zone 5
✔	✔	✔	✔	

PRODUCTION	★ ★ ★ ★
NUTRITION	★ ★ ★ ★ ★
ATTRACTION	★ ★ ★ ★ ★

BIRDSFOOT TREFOIL *(Lotus corniculatus)*

BIRDSFOOT TREFOIL is near the top of deer preference lists, ranking below alfalfa and clover. It is a warm-season perennial legume from the Mediterranean region that is adapted to poorly drained or low pH soils. It can reseed itself, is resistant to root rots and insects, and responds well to fertilization. As with other forage legumes, trefoil is most productive on fertile, well-drained soils with a pH above 6.0. However, it has the ability to produce relatively high yields and quality on land that is too acidic or otherwise marginal for alfalfa production. For this reason, it is often referred to as "poor man's alfalfa." Compared with alfalfa, trefoil is more short-lived, has finer stems and more leaves. It grows 12 to 30 inches tall, depending on whether it is a prostrate or erect variety. Flowers are bright yellow, and the brown to purple seedpods radiate from the stem branch, resembling a bird's foot.

OREGON STATE UNIVERSITY, FORAGE INFORMATION SYSTEM

ADAPTATION/ESTABLISHMENT

Birdsfoot trefoil can withstand severe winters and cold temperatures. Varieties are adapted to Canada, the northern United States, the Midwest, the Pacific Northwest, and upper Southeast down to mid-state areas of the Carolinas, Georgia, Alabama, and Arkansas.

Seed at the rate of 10 lbs./acre in pure stands or mixed with a perennial grass such as timothy (5 lbs./acre) or perennial ryegrass at 15 lbs./acre. If a seeder/cultipacker or no-till grain drill is used, the seeding rates can be cut in half. Seeding can be done in late August or September in the North or October in the South, or better yet, in March in the South, or April in the North when more rainfall is usually available for the young seedlings. One problem with trefoil is weak seedling vigor when establishing stands.

Because it has a slow growth rate and small seed size, good seeding practices and weed control are essential. Seed should be covered lightly at ¼-inch deep. Like all legumes,

it should be inoculated with the proper strain (K) of Rhizobium bacteria before planting so that it can properly fix atmospheric nitrogen. Use the proper inoculum – those available for clovers or alfalfa will not work. For good establishment and production, use 300 lbs./acre of 0-20-30 fertilizer well incorporated at planting. If possible, lime to bring pH up to 6.0 or higher.

CHRIS EVANS, THE UNIVERSITY OF GEORGIA, WWW.FORESTRYIMAGES.ORG

VARIETIES/MANAGEMENT

There are about 25 varieties of birdsfoot trefoil available in the United States. Varieties are generally characterized by growth habit into two types, Empire and European, and both are referred to as "broadleaf trefoils." Empire-type trefoils may be better adapted for deer food plots since they have fine stems. Dawn and Empire are high-yielding Empire types that have performed well in Pennsylvania tests. European-type varieties (usually better adapted to hay) now have new varieties (AU Dewey, Fergus, Norcen, and Tretona) that are high yielding and persist better under heavy grazing pressure. Erect growth may also allow these varieties to persist better with strong weed competition.

Watch trefoil carefully for the first three months, especially if seeded in early spring, to look for and correct weed competition. If the companion grass gets too tall and begins to shade the new trefoil seedlings, mow as needed. Fertilize once per year with 300 lbs per acre of 0-20-30 in September.

Birdsfoot trefoil is superior to alfalfa in both production and quality on soils that have marginal fertility (especially low pH) and production capabilities. Poor seedling establishment has been a major complaint, but careful management at seeding by cultipacking or no-till drilling can reduce this problem considerably. Birdsfoot trefoil will persist for several years. When the stand fades, it can be lightly disked in September or April to reestablish the stand from existing seeds in the soil. Trefoil is a good choice for deer plots, especially where low pH is a problem and lime application is impractical.

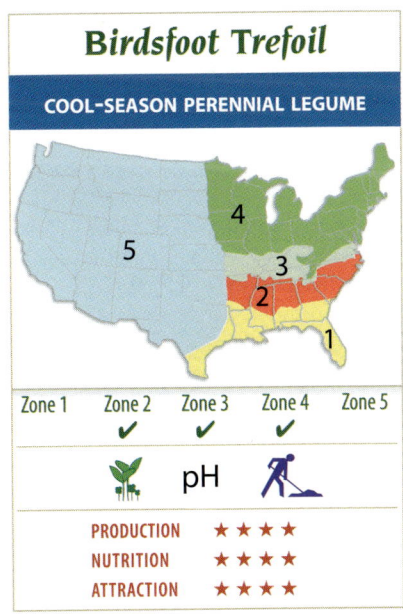

Birdsfoot Trefoil

COOL-SEASON PERENNIAL LEGUME

Zone 1	Zone 2	Zone 3	Zone 4	Zone 5
	✔	✔	✔	

| 🌱 | pH | 🚶 |

PRODUCTION	★ ★ ★ ★
NUTRITION	★ ★ ★ ★
ATTRACTION	★ ★ ★ ★

BURGUNDY BEAN *(Macroptilium bracteatum)*

BURGUNDY BEAN is a warm-season legume native to South America. It is potentially a short-lived perennial in the subtropics but will most likely be an annual in all of the United States except parts of the Deep South. Burgundy bean was selected for use as a short-term pasture plant on heavy alkaline soils in the subtropics. It replaces the more tropically adapted butterfly pea in subtropical regions because of its greater tolerance of cooler temperatures. It is also an alternative to alfalfa in the subtropics. It is known for its adaptation to heat and drought. In a measurement of forage quality, burgundy bean showed 20 percent protein, slightly less than alfalfa's 22 percent.

These beans are an erect and climbing hairy perennial (in the subtropics). Leaves are trifoliate with leaflets 1½- to 3-inches long and 1½- to 2-inches wide, hairy on both sides. Flowers are purple-red in color, and fruit is in a purple, linear pod, 2- to 6-inches long with nine to 17 seeds. Seeds are almost cylindrical, 1½-inches long and 1¼- to 1½-inches in diameter. They are brown, black or tan in color and almost always mottled.

RANS THOMAS

Burgundy beans shown growing among sorghum and sunflowers – a good warm-season combination.

ADAPTATION/ESTABLISHMENT

Burgundy bean seed was mostly collected from plants growing in sandy to medium-textured soils, but the plant adapts well to heavy clays. While the pH of these soils has most often been near neutral to alkaline, it has also been collected on soils with pH of 4.5. The ideal soil characteristic required for the bean is a slightly acidic to alkaline soil. Burgundy bean can be grown throughout the United States, but their greatest area of adaptation is in the central and southern United States because warm soil is needed for rapid germination. Consequently, in the majority of the United States, the beans can be planted in warm soil (over 60 degrees) anytime after the last threat of frost. August-planted beans – if not killed by overgrazing – will provide forage until the first frost but will not have time to go to seed.

In good growing conditions, burgundy bean can produce in excess of 2 to 3 tons/acre/year dry weight in the South. Yields in the first year are often in this range if sufficient moisture is available.

Burgundy bean is tolerant of drought, low fertility and soil acidity. Having a deep tap-root, it does well on sandy soil. It needs good drainage and will not do well on wet soils. It is easily established in prepared seed beds in warm soil. Recommended depth of sowing is about 1½ inches, although burgundy bean does re-establish well from seed that is near the surface. Seedlings grow rapidly, although they compete poorly with some weeds species and well-established grasses. Burgundy bean is sold pre-inoculated and coated. Recommended planting rate for coated seed is 5 to 8 lbs./acre. Application of 50 to 100 lbs./acre of phosphorus (100 to 200 lbs./acre of triple super phosphate [0-46-0]) at sowing improves performance on most soils.

VARIETIES/MANAGEMENT

Although burgundy bean is less vulnerable to early overgrazing than many other peas and beans, it must be carefully watched and managed. Planting in large fields is one way to ensure increased longevity of any bean planting for deer. Once the bean gets past about 30 to 45 days, it is even more resistant to grazing and will show resilient re-growth. Burgundy bean is extremely palatable and is preferentially grazed. Although Juanita (a climbing form) is strongly perennial, Cadarga (an erect form) is less so and relies far more upon seed production and seedling recruitment to persist in areas of the subtropics.

Use of repellents such as Milorganite, repellent fencing such as PlotSaver, electric fencing or reversible fencing may be required to protect young seedlings for 30 to 60 days to allow stand establishment. See Chapter 9 for details on specific methods to establish warm-season legumes when facing deer grazing pressure.

Planting burgundy bean mixed with other plants is extra insurance against a crop failure caused by overgrazing. Burgundy bean forms good associations with corn and grain sorghum. Sow beans at 5 lbs./acre with corn (10 lbs./acre) or grain sorghum (7 lbs./acre). For any of the grass mixes, increase the nitrogen component by using 300 lbs./acre of 19-19-19. Burgundy bean can also be mixed with low rates of buckwheat, cowpeas or soybeans.

The rapid growth and establishment of burgundy bean means that it can be mixed with butterfly pea, which is comparatively low yielding in its first year but can persist longer in the subtropics. Burgundy bean and butterfly pea are the components of Buck Beans marketed by Tecomate Seed Co. Burgundy bean is marketed exclusively by Heritage Seeds of the Royal Barenbrug Group, which includes Barenbrug USA.

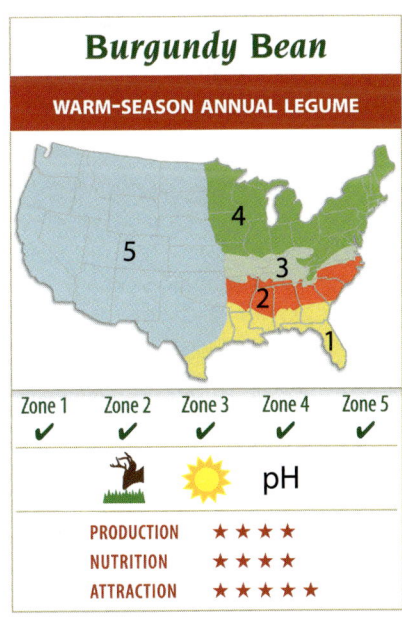

Burgundy Bean

WARM-SEASON ANNUAL LEGUME

Zone 1	Zone 2	Zone 3	Zone 4	Zone 5
✔	✔	✔	✔	✔

pH

PRODUCTION	★ ★ ★ ★
NUTRITION	★ ★ ★ ★
ATTRACTION	★ ★ ★ ★ ★

COWPEAS *(Vigna unguiculata)*

KENT KAMMERMEYER

COWPEA, also known as iron-and-clay pea and black-eyed pea, is a warm-season legume that came to the United States from Ethiopia. It is an annual, though it can potentially be a strong reseeder. Cowpea is known for its viny, weak stems, large triangular shaped leaves, yellow bloom, and curved pods. If there ever was a warm season "ice cream" plant for deer, cowpeas would be a top contender. As a matter of fact, it is so palatable to deer, it is often immediately overgrazed by deer in small and medium-sized fields. There are some ways to prevent this (*discussed below*).

ADAPTATION/ESTABLISHMENT

Cowpeas can be grown in the entire United States, but its greatest area of adaptation is the central and southern United States, because warm soil is needed for germination and maturity of peas in 90 to 100 days. Consequently, in the majority of the country, cowpeas can be planted from May to August. August-planted peas (if not killed by overgrazing) will provide forage as well as bow-season attraction in September and October but will not have time to go to seed.

Cowpeas are moderately tolerant of drought, low fertility and soil acidity but do better in the pH range of 5.5 to 7.0. Cowpeas need good drainage. Seeds are drilled in rows at 40 to 60 lbs./acre or broadcast at 60 to 90 lbs./acre. For best production, inoculate with fresh pea inoculant (strain EL) and apply a complete fertilizer such as 19-19-19 at 200 lbs./acre.

VARIETIES/MANAGEMENT

Due to its vulnerability to overgrazing, cowpeas must be carefully watched and managed. In one study in east Texas, cowpeas showed a markedly higher utilization

than lablab in July, August and September. Even at very low deer densities, deer utilized cowpeas heavily (76 to 96 percent) and exhibited a preference over lablab. Of the common varieties of cowpeas (Thorsby Cream, Tory, Wilcox, Iron-and-Clay, and Catjang), Catjang (also known as Oklahoma game-bird pea) reportedly exhibits a little more deer resistance in the early seedling stage. This is one way to increase longevity of a cowpea planting for deer. Once the pea gets past about 30 to 45 days, it is somewhat resistant to grazing pressure and will show resilient regrowth.

Use of repellents such as Milorganite, repellent fencing such as PlotSaver, electric fencing or reversible fencing may be required to protect young seedlings for 30 to 60 days to allow stand establishment. See Chapter 9 for details on specific methods to establish warm-season legumes when facing deer grazing pressure.

Finally, planting cowpeas mixed with other plants is extra insurance against a crop failure caused by overgrazing. Thin the planting rate to 25 lbs./acre and plant with grain sorghum (5 lbs./acre), corn (10 lbs./acre), or alyceclover (15 lbs./acre). Cowpeas can also be mixed with Peredovik sunflowers (25 lbs./acre) or buckwheat (25 lbs./acre) but remember that all of these are vulnerable to deer overgrazing.

For a bowhunting attractant plot, plant a mixture of cowpeas (20 lbs./acre), sweet blue lupine (20 lbs./acre), buckwheat (20 lbs./acre) and oats (50 lbs./acre) in August. Frost and deer grazing will get the cowpeas and buckwheat, but the oats and lupine will overwinter in the southern half of United States, providing a bonus of late-winter and early spring grazing. Another combination mix for August/September planting is cowpeas (40 lbs./acre) mixed with cold-tolerant oats (40 lbs./acre) and either red clover in the North (10 lbs./acre) or arrowleaf clover in the South (10 lbs./acre).

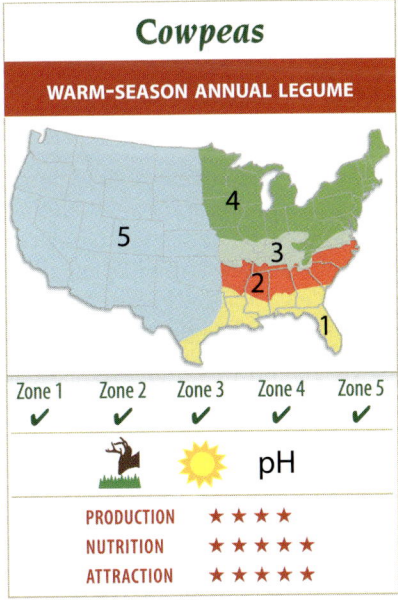

Cowpeas

WARM-SEASON ANNUAL LEGUME

Zone 1	Zone 2	Zone 3	Zone 4	Zone 5
✔	✔	✔	✔	✔

pH

PRODUCTION	★ ★ ★ ★
NUTRITION	★ ★ ★ ★ ★
ATTRACTION	★ ★ ★ ★ ★

HAIRY VETCH *(Vicia villosa)*

TES RANDLE JOLLY

The vetches are distributed throughout the temperate zones around the world. There are about 150 species of vetch, about 25 of which are native to the United States. However, HAIRY VETCH and other vetches in commercial use are all native to Europe.

This cool-season annual legume is a spindly, climbing, viny plant (3 to 7 feet tall) with compound, elliptical-shaped hairy leaflets terminating in a tendril. Flowers are mostly blue-violet occurring as 20 to 32 florets. Seedpods are hairy and flat, containing round black or mottled brown seeds, which mature in early summer.

ADAPTATION/ESTABLISHMENT

Hairy vetch, also called sand vetch, is the most winter-hardy vetch and the only one that can be fall-seeded and reach maturity the following July in the Midwest. Consequently, hairy vetch can be grown in all but the extreme northern United States. It is an important cover crop because of its wide range of adaptability and consistently high rates of nitrogen fixation and forage production.

Although vetch can be top-sown under some conditions in late summer to early fall, plowing is essential on heavy soils, firmly-packed soils or where there is a heavy weed infestation. Plant vetch in August in the North and September in the South at 25 to 35 lbs./acre. Be sure to inoculate the seed with the proper strain (C) of fresh inoculant. Good stands are obtained from planting seed at a depth of ¼ to ½ inch. Vetch does not require nitrogen fertilizer when planted alone and grows best in soils high in potassium. Consequently, in lieu of a soil test, fertilize at planting with 300 lbs./acre of 0-20-30. Hairy vetch is more tolerant of acidic soils than most legumes. For best results, soil pH should be between 5.8 and 6.5. Vetch is fairly drought tolerant and winter-hardy with medium palatability (lower than most clovers, higher than most grasses). It is resistant to grazing and has moderate shade tolerance. Vetch has a hard seed that lasts up to five years in the soil, and it produces 1½ to 3½ tons/acre of forage dry weight.

VARIETIES/MANAGEMENT

The beauty of planting hairy vetch for deer is its ability to consistently reseed and to fix large amounts of nitrogen (50 to 120 lbs./acre) for a follow-up crop of something like corn, grain sorghum or millet. Be aware, however, that it is a fierce competitor in the spring, laying over in a mat that can choke out competition and become difficult to mow or plow. For best results, mix vetch (15 lbs./acre) with a small grain (wheat, rye, or oats at 50 lbs./acre). Add crimson clover (10 lbs./acre) or Yuchi arrowleaf clover (10 lbs./acre) in the South. Due to its vigorous growth and climbing ability, vetches rarely have any serious weed problems, especially when seeded in late summer or early fall. Depending on the ground cover and height, mowing in August may be required for reseeding in year two and thereafter. Fertilize annually in September with at least 200 lbs./acre of 0-20-30.

On the down side, vetches can be vulnerable to several diseases and nematodes, including funguses, root rot, gray mold, false anthracnose, downy mildew, stem rot, and root-knot nematode. Resistant varieties may offer the best disease control. Use disease-free seed and rotate out of reseeding vetch when disease problems become evident.

Although hairy vetch is the most winter-hardy of the vetches, other varieties can do a good job as a cover crop but may not consistently reseed. These include common vetch (cahaba white vetch) and bigflower vetch. Hairy vetch also doubles as a quail and turkey planting due to its insect production and early seed production when few other desirable plants have yet produced a hard seed.

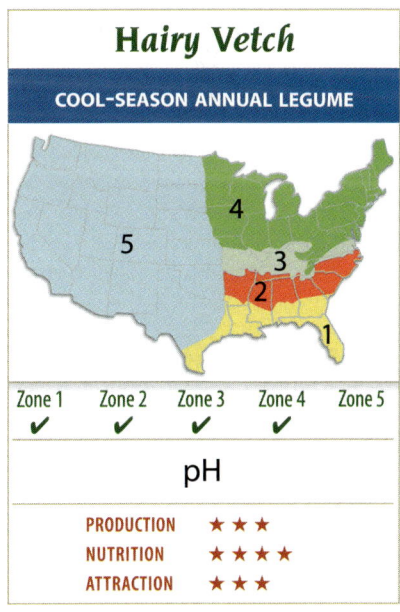

Hairy Vetch

COOL-SEASON ANNUAL LEGUME

Zone 1	Zone 2	Zone 3	Zone 4	Zone 5
✔	✔	✔	✔	

pH

PRODUCTION	★ ★ ★
NUTRITION	★ ★ ★ ★
ATTRACTION	★ ★ ★

COMMON (KOBE) LESPEDEZA *(Kummerowia striata)*
KOREAN LESPEDEZA *(Kummerowia stipulacea)*

JOHN D. BYRD, MISSISSIPPI STATE UNIVERSITY, WWW.FORESTRYIMAGES.ORG

KOBE and KOREAN LESPEDEZA were introduced into the United States from China, Japan and Korea in the mid-1800s. Both can be valuable, high-quality deer forage plants in middle to late summer. Do not confuse these annual lespedezas with the shrubby perennial lespedezas such as sericea or bi-color lespedeza.

Korean lespedeza is larger, coarser and earlier maturing than Kobe. It also has broader leaflets. At maturity, the leaves of Korean turn forward so the branch tips resemble small cones, but the leaves of Kobe do not turn forward. The hairs on the stem of Korean lespedeza point upward while those of Kobe point downward. In oriental countries, native stands of these plants are sometimes grazed or harvested for hay, but it is rarely planted. Interestingly, the plant seems to be even more ideally suited to conditions in the southern United States than in its area of origin. These warm-season annual legumes germinate in spring, grow throughout the summer, then make seed and die in autumn.

ADAPTATION/ESTABLISHMENT

Korean lespedeza, of which there are several varieties, matures in early fall and is best suited for the upper South and lower Midwest. Kobe lespedeza (an improved variety of striata or common) is more disease resistant, persists longer in autumn and has been the preferred annual lespedeza in the South.

Annual lespedezas can be used as an erosion control plant on bare, eroded soil such as logging decks or top sown on a controlled burn area or firebreaks. It grows surprisingly well on poor soils. They can be grown with grasses including perennial ryegrass and timo-

thy. While this is an excellent erosion-control mix, the addition of the perennial grasses may not be the best choice for deer food plots. Planted alone, the broadcast rate is 25 to 35 lbs./acre or drill 15 to 25 lbs./acre in February or March. Use de-hulled, scarified seed for late-winter planting. In a grass mixture, reduce rates to 25 lbs./acre broadcast or 15 lbs./acre drilled. Add 2 lbs./acre partridge pea for added deer and quail benefit as well as beautiful yellow blooms in August. Kobe and partridge pea can also be planted without grasses. They are both consistent re-seeders. Seed can be covered with ¼- to ½-inch of soil, but will often become established without being covered if adequate moisture is present and competition is dead or burned.

VARIETIES/MANAGEMENT

For zones where Kobe is adapted, a new, improved variety called Marion is now available. Marion is a good seed producer, good yielder and more resistant to diseases than the other annual lespedeza types.

Lespedezas are slow starters but produce abundant forage from May to October (Kobe and Marion) and June to October (Korean). All three varieties produce seed in late summer and reseed readily if properly managed. Forage yields of over 6,000 lbs./acre (dry matter) have been reported for grass/annual lespedeza mixtures.

The real value of annual lespedezas to deer is in middle to late summer, when it is highly productive and has crude protein levels of about 16 percent. It will tolerate fairly heavy deer grazing, but heavy grazing may substantially reduce seed production. An added bonus is that the seed is an excellent quail food.

For reclamation projects, surface broadcasting on controlled burns, and bare soil in logging operations, it is hard to beat the annual lespedezas for ease of establishment, low maintenance, and low fertilizer and lime requirements.

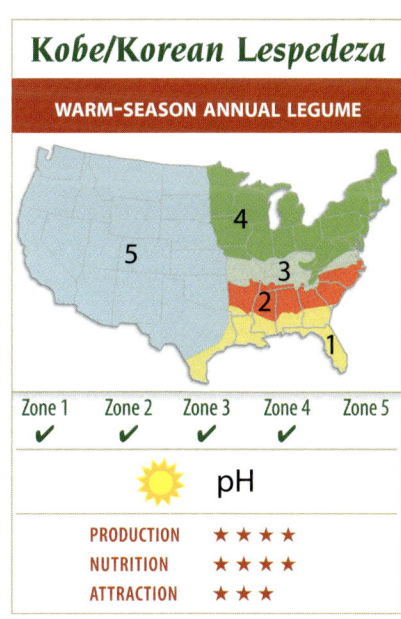

Kobe/Korean Lespedeza

WARM-SEASON ANNUAL LEGUME

Zone 1	Zone 2	Zone 3	Zone 4	Zone 5
✔	✔	✔	✔	

☀ pH

PRODUCTION	★ ★ ★ ★
NUTRITION	★ ★ ★ ★
ATTRACTION	★ ★ ★

LABLAB (*Lablab purpureus*)

RANS THOMAS

LABLAB is a warm-season annual legume with twining vines and purplish stems with three large leaflets. It has flowers in long clusters that are pea-shaped and white, pink or purplish. Its fruit is a flat, curved, maroon or purplish pod with three to five black seeds. Originating in tropical Africa, hyacinth bean and Dolichos lablab are other names for it. It is one of a group of three highly preferred, grazing-sensitive, summer annual legumes commonly planted for deer in the United States (the others are cowpea and soybeans). Planted in large fields or protected by a fence or repellent, lablab is drought resistant and highly productive at 2,000 to 6,000 lbs./acre production and 22 to 27 percent protein.

ADAPTATION/ESTABLISHMENT

Lablab is quite drought tolerant once established, but it will not grow in wet soils. It is extremely tolerant of soil texture, growing in deep sands to heavy clays provided there is good drainage. It will grow in a wide range of pH from 5.0 to 7.5 but prefers a pH between 6.0 and 7.0. Plant at 15 to 20 lbs./acre at a depth of ½ to 1½ inches. Inoculate with the cowpea strain (EL) of Rhizobium to encourage good root nodulation, which allows the plant to fix its own nitrogen (N) from the air. Failure to inoculate will cause poor growth on most soils. In the absence of a soil test, fertilize with 300 lbs./acre of 0-20-20. Plant in March in the Deep South and June in the North. As with soybeans, lablab planted early in the South will produce a mature bean in late summer if the deer grazing pressure allows it to flower and develop a seed pod. Late-planted lablab in the North may not have time to reach maturity before frost, but this is no great disadvantage, because the value of this plant is in the forage provided by leafy growth.

RANS THOMAS

VARIETIES/MANAGEMENT

Lablab can be seeded in mixes very similar to soybeans (refer to *Varieties and Management* for soybeans). Thin the rate of lablab to 5 lbs./acre and mix with 10 lbs./acre Egyptian wheat, 10 lbs./acre corn, or 5 lbs./acre grain sorghum. This should produce a weed-free legume/small grain mix which is highly compatible because of the ability of the lablab to produce over 200 lbs./acre N, some of which is available for growth and production of the grains.

However, all of this discussion is frivolous if you cannot get this plant past the deer herd for at least 30 to 45 days. Use of repellents such as Milorganite, repellent fencing such as PlotSaver, electric fencing or reversible fencing may be required to protect young seedlings for 30 to 60 days to allow stand establishment. See Chapter 9 for details on specific methods to establish warm-season legumes when facing deer grazing pressure. Early planted stands (when natural growth in nearby woodlands is highly palatable and nutritious) will help keep deer out of your lablab patch until it is tough enough to take the pressure. This will also depend on the size of your deer herd. It will certainly be easier to maintain a lablab patch all summer with a deer herd of less than 20 deer/square mile than with a herd of more than 40 deer/square mile.

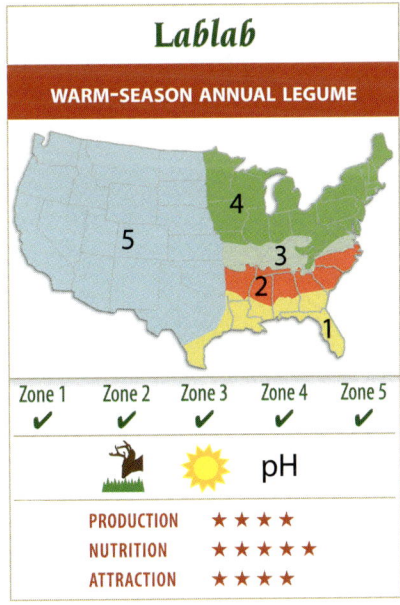

Lablab

WARM-SEASON ANNUAL LEGUME

Zone 1	Zone 2	Zone 3	Zone 4	Zone 5
✔	✔	✔	✔	✔

pH

PRODUCTION	★ ★ ★ ★
NUTRITION	★ ★ ★ ★ ★
ATTRACTION	★ ★ ★ ★

LUPINES *(Lupinus* spp.)

KENNETH M. GALE, WWW.FORESTRYIMAGES.ORG

Use of blue LUPINE by deer can range from heavy to none and everything in between, depending on variety and other factors. It doubles as valuable brood-rearing cover and a food source for turkeys and quail. Many species of lupines are native to the United States, but the three commercially available, cultivated, large-seeded species originated in the Mediterranean region. These are commonly known as blue, white and yellow lupines, named for the color of their flower. Blue lupines have been most commonly grown in the United States. White lupine is the most winter-hardy, and yellow lupine is grown as a summer annual for grain in Northern Europe, Australia and New Zealand. Lupines, which are in the legume family and fix nitrogen (N) from the soil, were an important green manure and grazing crop in the Deep South in the 1940s and 1950s — it was used as a follow-up crop to cotton to add nitrogen to the soil. Cheap N fertilizer and disease problems have limited its agricultural use. However, there has been increasing interest in summer production of lupines for grain in the Upper Midwest. Forage production of lupine is 1 to 2 tons/acre.

Lupines are erect-growing winter annuals 3 feet or more in height with coarse, hollow stems, fingerlike leaves and a mass of colorful, blue, white or yellow flowers closely packed in spikes 6 to 8 inches long. The seeds are round like a small soybean. Lupine foliage tests about 25 to 30 percent protein. The plant requires a growing season of five months or longer free from serious drought. If lupine is sown in the fall, winter temperatures must drop no lower than about 10 degrees.

ADAPTATION/ESTABLISHMENT

Fall plantings of lupines are limited to the South because of cold intolerance. Spring plantings (March in the South and April or May in the North) are appropriate all the way to the Canadian border. Deer managers should be able to grow this plant pretty much anywhere that receives adequate rainfall. Lupines thrive on moderately acidic soils as well as loamy soils with good drainage. Ideal pH is 6.0 to 6.5. The large seeds are sown alone, broadcast at about 100 lbs./acre and covered about ½-inch deep. As with all legumes, inoculate with the proper Rhizobium bacteria (strain H) at planting. In lieu of a soil test, use 200 to 300 lbs./acre of 0-20-20. Lupine can be no-till drilled (cut the rate to 50 lbs./acre) or broadcast and covered by a cultipacker or drag. Seedling vigor is good, but the plant establishes slowly and should not be grazed heavily until about 60 days after planting. For this reason, it should be planted in a mix with nurse crops to divert early grazing. One mix might include oats (50 lbs./acre) plus red clover (5 lbs./acre) and lupine (50 lbs./acre). It might even be advantageous to add chicory (2 lbs./acre), especially on poor sites. For these mixes where N is necessary, standard fertilizer rates of 300 lbs./acre of 19-19-19 should apply. Although I cannot document the success of this technique, it should be possible to get a second year from this mixture by mowing in August (and possibly light tilling) to germinate remaining oat and lupine seeds. However, because of viruses, funguses and insects, it is not recommended to grow lupine more than two years in the same field.

VARIETIES/MANAGEMENT

Selection of variety can be extremely important with lupines. Most lupines are high in alkaloids, which repel insects and make the plants unattractive to grazing animals. Lupines high in alkaloids are bitter and are often avoided by grazing animals. "Sweet" blue lupine (low alkaloid) is recommended for deer and turkey food plots. Sweet lupines have been developed for grain production in the United States and Australia. Depending on deer density, sweet blue lupines are subject to early overgrazing. Prevent this by planting fields over 3 acres in size using mixtures to divert early grazing pressure or employing repellents and/or fencing. Research needs to be conducted using high-alkaloid lupines for deer plots to reduce palatability and take pressure off of young seedling plants yet still maintain moderate deer use. Meanwhile, low-alkaloid, winter-hardy (to about 10 degrees), disease-resistant varieties have been developed in south Georgia including Frost and Tif-blue-78. Hope, developed in Arkansas, is a high-alkaloid, cold-tolerant variety. Sweet blue lupine is a major component of Turkey Gold Strut & Rut Southeast Fall Mix sold by the National Wild Turkey Federation. It can also be purchased from Wannamaker Seed Co. (*www.wannamakerseeds.com*).

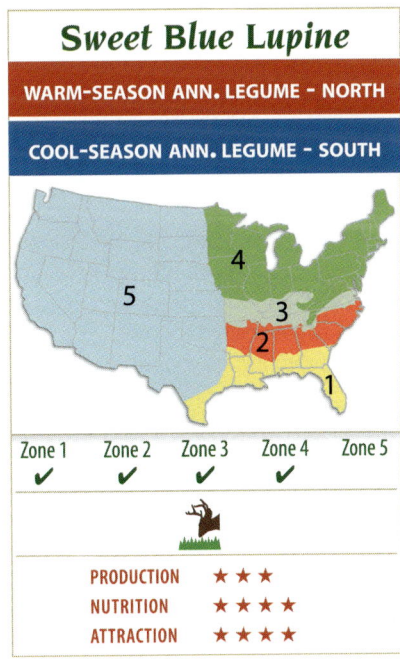

Sweet Blue Lupine

WARM-SEASON ANN. LEGUME - NORTH

COOL-SEASON ANN. LEGUME - SOUTH

Zone 1	Zone 2	Zone 3	Zone 4	Zone 5
✔	✔	✔	✔	

PRODUCTION	★ ★ ★
NUTRITION	★ ★ ★ ★
ATTRACTION	★ ★ ★ ★

SOYBEANS *(Glycine max)*

Agronomists have been working on SOYBEAN varieties for decades. Back in the old days, forage soybeans were the ones to grow for both forage and grain production. Over the past few decades, soybean grain has become an extremely valuable dietary concentrate for animals. Soybeans are also used in a wide range of industrial products, especially oils. Consequently, the current focus of most soybean breeding programs is on grain production.

Deer managers need forage-type soybeans for their warm-season food plot programs. Like cowpeas and lablab, soybeans are a highly preferred warm-season annual legume with trifoliate leaves branching out in all directions. The stems, leaves and pods are covered with short fine hairs. Small white or purple flowers originate where the leaf joins the stem. Flowers become short pods containing the beans. Soybeans can be erect or sometimes viny, climbing over erect plants. Despite mainstream emphasis on grain production, the United States Department of Agriculture has developed improved varieties of forage soybeans. Containing 25 to 35 percent protein, these plants are developed for tall, leafy growth and can climb or vine.

ADAPTATION/ESTABLISHMENT

Soybeans are adapted to well-drained, medium-textured soils such as sandy loams and clay loams. In the absence of a soil test, use 300 lbs./acre of 0-20-20 and maintain a pH between 5.8 and 7.0. Always inoculate seed with the appropriate Rhizobium (strain S). Broadcast at 60 to 85 lbs./acre in pure stands (cover ½- to 1-inch deep) or drill at 50 lbs./acre. Plant as early as April in the Deep South or as late as June in the North or as a follow-up to wheat or other spring grain anywhere in the United States. Forage soybean varieties mature later than grain varieties – up to 140 days. Consequently, forage soybeans planted late in the North will not produce mature beans before frost. Where the growing season is long enough and beans are planted early, forage soybeans can produce a bonus crop of 30 to 40 bushels/acre of beans for fall consumption by deer, turkey or quail. Forage production of some varieties ranges from 3 to 7 tons/acre of dry matter depending on rainfall and variety.

SCOTT BAUER, WWW.FORESTRYIMAGES.ORG

VARIETIES/MANAGEMENT

I recommend planting soybeans in a mixture. In addition, they are vulnerable to overgrazing in the early seedling stage and must be planted in big fields (5 to 10 acres or more) or protected in some way.

Use of repellents such as Milorganite, repellent fencing such as PlotSaver, electric fencing or reversible fencing may be required to protect young seedlings for 30 to 60 days to allow stand establishment. See Chapter 9 for details on specific methods to establish warm-season legumes when facing deer grazing pressure. Planting a 1- or 2-acre soybean patch that is unprotected is asking for trouble, since you may lose the entire patch just days after germination. Earlier-planted beans (when native woodland plants are at peak nutrition and palatability) also guard somewhat against overgrazing.

For deer, forage varieties are definitely important. Good choices include Tyrone, Laredo or Quail Haven, which are specifically bred for tall growth, up to 6 or 7 feet, and climbing or vining. Good choices for mixtures include Quail Haven (20 lbs./acre), Tyrone (35 lbs./acre) or Laredo (40 lbs./acre) with either corn at 10 lbs./acre, Egyptian wheat at 15 lbs./acre, or grain sorghum (a tall variety such as KS989) at 5 lbs./acre. This legume/small grain combo is advantageous because the nitrogen-fixing ability of legumes benefits the grasses. An added advantage is that the beans will climb the grass stalks and form a dense, weed-free stand which provides both food and cover for deer. Deer trails through the stand will show removal of leafy top growth within reach all summer long, which will continuously encourage new leafy bean growth without hurting the grasses — they will be consumed as grain in the fall and winter. This all works great if you can get the beans past the deer for the first 30- to 45-day period.

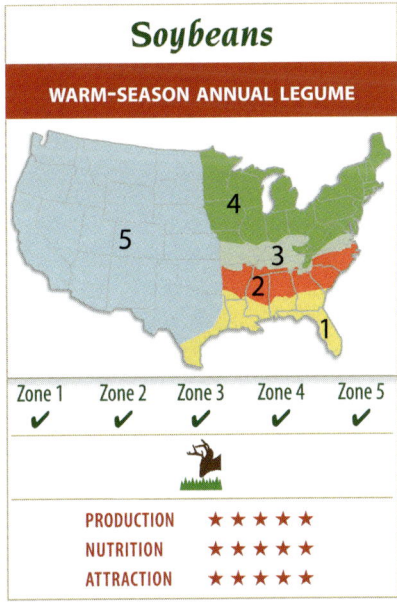

Soybeans

WARM-SEASON ANNUAL LEGUME

Zone 1	Zone 2	Zone 3	Zone 4	Zone 5
✔	✔	✔	✔	✔

PRODUCTION	★ ★ ★ ★ ★
NUTRITION	★ ★ ★ ★ ★
ATTRACTION	★ ★ ★ ★ ★

SPECIES PROFILES

Other Legumes

SWEETCLOVER (*Melilotus* spp.)

DAVE POWELL, USDA FOREST SERVICE, WWW.FORESTRYIMAGES.ORG

There are three species of SWEETCLOVER, two yellow and one white. White sweetclover is native to Europe and western Asia. It was probably introduced into North America by early settlers and was first recorded in the United States in 1739. Its widespread use as bee pasture, cow pasture, hayfield, and for soil stabilization hastened its spread across North America. Today it is found in all of the contiguous United States, Alaska and Hawaii, and every Canadian province and territory.

Sweetclover (both yellow and white) is primarily biennial. First-year plants are entirely vegetative growth (usually a single stem). Second-year plants have a strongly-developed taproot which can exceed 50 inches in depth, and they have up to 10 upright or ascending flowering stems from three to 8½ feet in height. The fruit is a one-seeded pod. Sweetclover is noted best for its ability to improve soil structure through its tremendous root growth.

ADAPTATION/ESTABLISHMENT

Sweetclover is adapted to clay or loam soils in the United States and Canada. It is extremely drought-tolerant, heat-tolerant and winter-hardy but intolerant of soil acidity. Like alfalfa, sweetclover requires a soil pH near 7.0. Sweetclover can obtain phosphorus from relatively unavailable soil phosphates and is able to grow on soils where alfalfa, red clover, or white clover often fail. Except for its high lime requirements, it is similar to lespedeza in its ability to tolerate low fertility soils.

Sweetclover produces more vegetative growth the first year than most legumes because it grows uninterrupted until freezing weather. However, it resumes growth in spring later than alfalfa, red clover or alsike clover.

Seed can be planted in spring or autumn at 10 to 15 lbs./acre. Seed must be inoculated (strain A) and scarified since a large percentage of the seeds have a hard seed coat and can remain viable in the soil for more than 20 years (the seed should already be scarified when you buy it – chemically or mechanically treated so that the seed coat is scarred to aid germination – but ask the supplier to be sure). Minimum fertilizer is needed for establishment. Something like 300 lbs./acre of 0-20-30 would suffice on most sites if a soil test were unavailable. Sweetclover has a digestible crude protein level of 31 percent, and crude protein content of hay often exceeds 15 percent on a dry-matter basis. Pure stands may add up to 70 lbs./acre nitrogen to the soil.

VARIETIES/MANAGEMENT

Seeded sweetclover grows rapidly, quickly providing vegetative cover on disturbed areas. Its chief rehabilitation use is for erosion control and revegetation of mined lands where low pH is not an issue or is heavily corrected by lime. It incorporates large amounts of nitrogen (N) and organic matter into the soil, which is made available to succeeding plants. New seedlings are sensitive to heavy early grazing, but grazing in mid-fall and mid-spring is beneficial to the plant and root growth. First-year sweetclover plants have a "special growth period" at the end of summer when rapid root growth and food storage occur. The period of best sweetclover production is May to August.

Yellow sweetclover blooms earlier, produces less plant matter but more roots, has shorter smaller stems, withstands drought conditions better during seeding, is a better hay producer the second year, and is also a better seed producer than white sweetclover. Certified Norgold seed produces a variety that is low in coumarin, which reduces the bitter taste of the clover and the potential risk of sweetclover disease.

Sweetclover is often interseeded into fall-planted small grains just before the period of spring freezing and thawing. Sweetclover and red clover seedlings withstand lower spring temperatures than alfalfa seedlings. Despite being a biennial legume, it can be terminated the following spring after planting to quicken the rotation back to grain sorghum or corn. Usually May is the perfect month for the rotation change. In the North, sweetclover can be interseeded (broadcast or drilled) with grain sorghum at planting. In a drill, the rates are about 4 lbs./acre sorghum and 6 lbs./acre sweetclover. Proper seedbed preparation and quick emergence of the sorghum and sweetclover are critical for shading out weeds. In deer management, sweetclover's chief use is as a palatable soil builder on highly-eroded, mined mineral soils with no organic matter and high pH (either natural or amended with lime).

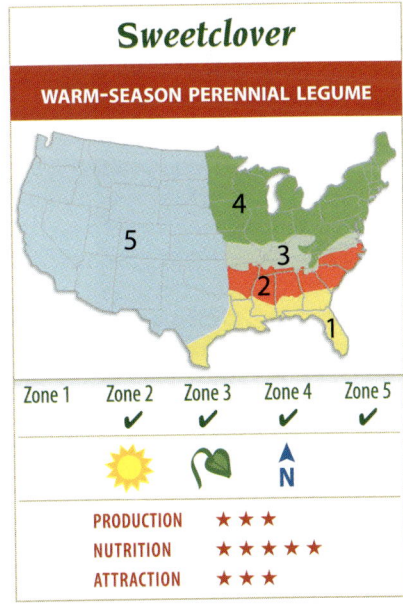

Sweetclover

WARM-SEASON PERENNIAL LEGUME

Zone 1	Zone 2	Zone 3	Zone 4	Zone 5
	✔	✔	✔	✔

PRODUCTION	★ ★ ★
NUTRITION	★ ★ ★ ★ ★
ATTRACTION	★ ★ ★

Grains

CORN *(Zea mays)*

Look at the top of a deer's forage preference list and you will find corn. CORN helps fill the need for fat-building carbohydrates before winter. The nutritional value of corn is well documented, especially by the cattle folks. What corn lacks in protein, 5 to 8 percent, it makes up for in fat (4 percent) and carbohydrates (75 percent).

Before you jump on the corn bandwagon, a word of caution is in order. Corn is used by over 100 species of wildlife, many of which can decimate a small cornfield before deer even find it. I know – it has happened to my sweet corn patch repeatedly. Those other 100 species include raccoons, crows, squirrels, possums, beavers, bears and blackbirds.

Corn is also drought

KENT KAMMERMEYER

Weed control is a challenge when growing corn, but the Roundup Ready variety can help. This Roundup Ready corn was planted in April, and the photo was taken in September. Following label instructions, two applications of glyphosate were applied at about three weeks and six weeks after planting. As you can see, weeds were not a problem in this field.

prone, has high fertility requirements, and needs chemical weed control for best results. Nevertheless, if you want the best for deer, you have the equipment, and you can get it past the other critters (using big fields of 3 acres and larger), then try corn in your deer food plot.

ADAPTATION/ESTABLISHMENT

First, locate the best soil on your property. Bottomland is best, but flatter uplands will do. Droughts are hard on corn, so soil moisture is critical, especially during the tasseling and silking stages. Plant when your soil temperature reaches 60 degrees or above, which is usually March in the Deep South, April in the central United States and May or June in the North. Measure the temperature at a depth of 1 inch at 7 a.m. Corn will germinate slowly at 55 degrees. Corn can be planted by conventional plowing and planting in rows, broadcast planting in a prepared seedbed, or no-till drilling into dead mulch. Corn plants need to be 7 to 12 inches apart which translates into 5 to 10 lbs./acre. Broadcast rate would be 10 to 15 lbs./acre. Conventional row planting is recommended for the best results. Plant 1- to 2-inches deep or shallower in cool soils. Germination occurs in six to 10 days.

Plenty of fertilizer is needed. For a yield of 100 bushels/acre, depending on your native soil fertility, you probably need 100 lbs./acre of nitrogen, about 50 lbs./acre of phosphorus and over 50 lbs./acre of potash. This translates to 300 lbs./acre of 19-19-19 at planting and

KENT KAMMERMEYER

an additional application of 100 to 150 lbs./acre of ammonium sulfate (34-0-0) about four weeks later. Corn will mature in about 70 to 120 days, depending upon variety.

VARIETIES/MANAGEMENT

If you plan to eat some of your corn patch yourself, then obviously use sweet corn varieties that suit your palate. But if you do this, count on lots of damage from non-target species like raccoons and beavers who share your preference for sweet corn. Otherwise, use field corn, cow corn, or any variety suited for cattle feed. Don't use white corn or silage corn varieties.

If you expect high yields, weed control will be necessary. Atrazine is a common, effective chemical for weed control in corn, which can be pre-plant incorporated or applied post-emergent with boom sprayers. There are many other herbicides approved for use on corn. If chemicals are not used, you can cultivate your corn at about four weeks after germination, at the same time you apply your dose of ammonium sulfate. Roundup Ready corn is also now available, which is tolerant of glyphosate, allowing you to kill weeds without harming the corn (if label directions are followed carefully). Also, glyphosate is not soil active, unlike traditional herbicides used for corn. See Chapter 10 for more on Roundup Ready technology.

If you don't have the planting equipment, then you will have to broadcast your corn seed and fertilizer. If you do this, then I recommend reducing the corn rate to 5 to 7 lbs./acre and mixing with 5 lbs./acre of a tall, bird-resistant grain sorghum such as KS989. This will give you two advantages – two-tiered shade for better weed control and a buffer crop in case of drought, depredation or insect damage to the corn. Grain sorghum is a close relative of corn and provides similar nutritional value. For additional food value and weed control, you can mix in cowpeas, forage soybeans or lablab at a rate of 25 lbs./acre.

Bigger fields are better by far. Your fields are too small when you lose newly planted corn seed to crows, turkeys, squirrels, or skunks digging up the kernels. There also is a cumulative learning effect when corn is grown in the same small fields for several years. There are no commercial crow repellent applications available to treat corn seed before planting.

Corn is a great crop for deer if you can pull it off successfully. I have grown it for 20 years and have had good years and bad. In the good years, your corn should last at least into early winter before being entirely consumed.

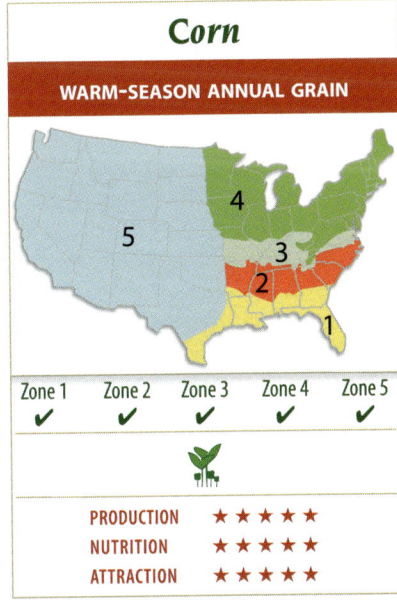

Corn

WARM-SEASON ANNUAL GRAIN

Zone 1	Zone 2	Zone 3	Zone 4	Zone 5
✔	✔	✔	✔	✔

PRODUCTION	★ ★ ★ ★ ★
NUTRITION	★ ★ ★ ★ ★
ATTRACTION	★ ★ ★ ★

GRAIN SORGHUM *(Sorghum bicolor)*

KENT KAMMERMEYER

GRAIN SORGHUM (also called milo) is a member of the grass family like its relative, corn. There are grain varieties, syrup varieties, silage and hay varieties that are all coarse-stemmed, erect annuals, 4- to 15-feet tall. Grain varieties, however, are really the only ones beneficial to deer. They are relatively short-growing with large seed heads. Do not plant sorghum sudan, sweet sorghum or cane sorghum for deer!

Grain sorghum is widely adapted across the United States and can be planted in any state provided that the growing season is long enough to allow maturity before frost (maturity is 90 to 120 days). It is very drought tolerant, making it an excellent substitute for corn in drought-prone areas, especially in the Midwest and Southwest. It is grown commercially on large acreages in Texas, Kansas and Nebraska and is not tolerant of acidic soils, doing best at a pH between 6.0 and 7.5. The seed head of sorghum is preferred by deer, and they sometimes heavily utilize seed in the "dough" stage in August and/or fully mature stage in mid-fall to late winter, depending upon the variety, the annual acorn crop (including timing of acorn drop) and other food supplies.

ESTABLISHMENT/MIXTURES

Grain sorghum is best as a deer food plot when planted in April (Deep South), May (Central) or June (North). Broadcast alone at 10 lbs./acre or drill alone at 5 lbs./acre. Seeding rates of more than 10 lbs./acre will produce poor, spindly seed heads. Broadcast seed should be covered ½- to 1-inch deep. Fertilizer at planting should be broadcast at the rate of 400 lbs./acre of 19-19-19 or according to soil test results. Grain sorghum has a moderate fertility requirement but is a heavy nitrogen user and produces best with 80 to 100 lbs./acre of actual nitrogen. Under optimum conditions and fertility, it can produce 80 bushels/acre of seed. Under normal conditions, you should expect 50 to 60 bushels/acre.

Grain sorghum food plots are more beneficial to deer when planted as a mixture. Several mixes have been successful, including sorghum broadcast at 7 lbs./acre mixed with one of the following: aeschynomene (15 lbs./acre), Quail Haven soybeans (25 lbs./acre), Catjang pea (25 lbs./acre), iron-and-clay pea (25 lbs./acre), or corn (5 lbs./acre). The addition of a legume such as aeschynomene (also called deer vetch or jointvetch) or any of the peas and beans improve the quality and attractiveness of the stand. The soybeans and peas will actually climb up the sorghum stalk, increasing total deer forage and suppressing weeds. In addition, legumes reduce the need for expensive nitrogen fertilizer by about half because they fix nitrogen utilized by the grain sorghum. In summer, deer will freely roam through the mixed planting ignoring the sorghum plants while selectively browsing on the legumes, thus providing both warm- and cool-season forage in the same stand.

I use grain sorghum mixes as a follow-up, rotation planting behind faded-out clover stands to use leftover nitrogen and shade out noxious weeds. Often, two years of this sorghum mix will be followed by another clover planting.

When the seed heads of sorghum mature, deer will bite them off, sometimes taking the entire seed mass in one mouthful.

VARIETIES/MANAGEMENT

If available, bird-resistant varieties (with reddish seed heads) do better for deer than light-headed varieties. Because the bird-resistant varieties contain tannic acid, they are not as palatable to deer at early maturity (the dough stage) and last longer into fall. Weather gradually reduces the tannic acid and increases palatability. Bird-resistant varieties also prevent damage by migrating blackbirds and other songbirds in September.

Also, tall-growing varieties are better than shorter ones because of better tolerance to weed problems. Tall-growing varieties (alone or mixed with legumes) do a great job of shading competition like fescue, crabgrass, bermuda or other summer weeds like sicklepod or cocklebur. Johnsongrass, because it is so tall and competitive, can present a real problem for grain sorghum and may need to be treated with herbicides prior to planting (*see Chapter 10*). WGF (Wild Game Food) sorghum is a short-growing (3 feet tall) sorghum that may be vulnerable to weeds unless cultivation or chemicals are used. KS989 (formerly the old Savannah 5 variety) is a 5- to 6-foot tall bird-resistant sorghum very suitable for deer. It is also known as Cooper's Wildlife Sorghum and is available at www.cooperseeds.com.

Grain sorghum pests include anthracnose, leafspots, lesser cornstalk borer and the sorghum midge. The midge, which attacks the grain in the seed head, is probably the worst of the three but should not present problems unless sorghum is grown in the same field for three or more years. Overall, I recommend that grain sorghum mixes should be the backbone of your summer food plot program. Try it!

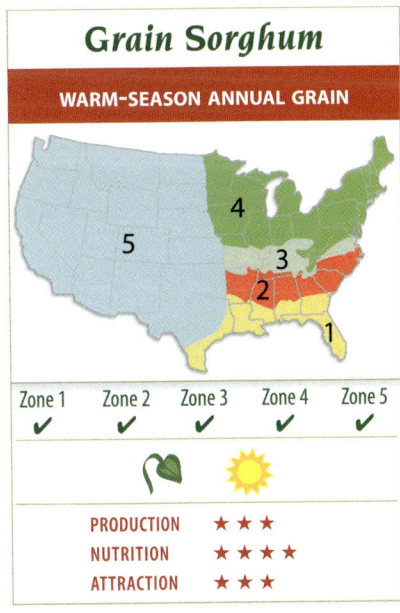

Grain Sorghum

WARM-SEASON ANNUAL GRAIN

Zone 1	Zone 2	Zone 3	Zone 4	Zone 5
✔	✔	✔	✔	✔

PRODUCTION	★ ★ ★	
NUTRITION	★ ★ ★ ★	
ATTRACTION	★ ★ ★	

OATS *(Avena sativa)*

KENT KAMMERMEYER

OATS may be the best deer attractant of five annual small grains grown in the United States. Oats average about 3 feet tall and have mainly been grown for grain, pastures, hay or silage. Oats can produce 1 to 4 tons/acre of high quality (10 to 25 percent protein), cool-season forage that is highly digestible in early stages of growth. In palatability tests using horses, oats were consistently selected above ryegrass, rye, wheat or triticale. Similar tests with deer have been inconclusive.

ADAPTATION/ESTABLISHMENT

Oats are sensitive to cold (they will winter-kill at temperatures between 0 and 10 degrees), so the Southeast (Zones 1 and 2) is the only area where oats should be planted in the fall, except as a hunting-season attractant in a fall mix. Early spring plantings can be successful over the entire United States where moisture conditions are favorable. Oats can be frost-seeded into tilled soil or no-till drilled as long as there is adequate soil moisture and good seed-to-soil contact. Drill at 1- to 1½-inch depths. Oats tolerate heavy grazing but are not tolerant of poor drainage or drought. Oats have excellent seedling vigor but are sensitive to pH and fertility. Your pH needs to be corrected to above 6.0. Despite their high quality and production, I recommend mixing oats with another grain or, even better, legumes. This guards against possible freeze-outs, saves on nitrogen, and adds to the quality and longevity of the planting. My favorite oat mixes (drilled) are oats (30 lbs./acre), red clover (5 lbs./acre) and arrowleaf clover (5 lbs./acre) in the South and oats (30 lbs./acre), red clover (5 lbs./acre) and white clover (3 lbs./acre) in the North. Drill rates are roughly doubled when seed is broadcast. Best time to plant is either September or late February to early March in the South and April in the North. A good fall mix for the South is 50 lbs./acre oats, 5 lbs./acre white clover, 1 lb./acre chicory and 20 lbs./acre blue lupine.

VARIETIES/MANAGEMENT

Oat mixes will be heavily used by deer as soon as they germinate until well into midspring. By middle to late summer, oat seeds mature and are eaten by deer and turkey along with the clover. However, oat seeds have a tough husk, which protects the seed, and many of them will remain uneaten by late

summer. In late August, mow the oat/clover mixes close to the ground. Depending on the vigor and percent cover of the clovers, oats will usually reseed after late-summer rains and produce a second or even third year mixed stand of oats and clover. Even if the oats are killed by cold, they will have provided high-quality fall grazing, and you will be left with a pure clover stand. Not a bad deal at all!

Unless you live in the Deep South or coastal areas, the main thing to look for in selecting oats for deer is cold tolerance. Several Southern varieties have been successfully selected for cold tolerance, including Buck Forage, Buck Magnet, Arkansas 833, Arkansas 604, Rodgers, Harrison and Chapman. Spring oats performing well in Pennsylvania trials include, but are not limited to, Blaze, Rodeo, Jay, Armor, Judd and Chaps. For better seed utilization, choose naked (no hull) oats from Wannamaker Seed Co. (*www.wannamaker-seeds.com*) Ask your county extension agent, wildlife biologist, or seed dealer for suggestions on oat varieties suited to your area.

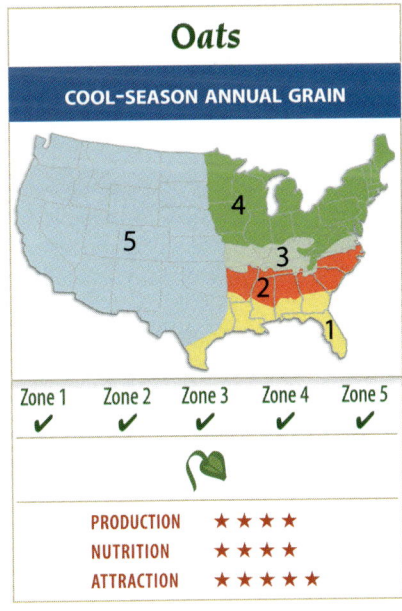

Oats

COOL-SEASON ANNUAL GRAIN

Zone 1	Zone 2	Zone 3	Zone 4	Zone 5
✔	✔	✔	✔	✔

PRODUCTION	★ ★ ★ ★
NUTRITION	★ ★ ★ ★
ATTRACTION	★ ★ ★ ★ ★

RYE (*Secale cereale*)

RYE, a cool-season annual bunchgrass, is grown in every state in the United States, often when conditions are unfavorable for wheat. It is the most popular of the small grains for cattle forage and is the most cold tolerant cereal grain used for wildlife planting in the country. Rye is more cold tolerant than oats or wheat and tolerates low fertility and acidic soil better than any other small grain. Rye can also be grown in a wider range of environmental conditions. Do not confuse cereal rye with annual or perennial ryegrass – they are totally different plants.

Rye grows 2 to 4 feet tall, depending on variety, grazing pressure and fertility. Seed heads are spikes, and leaf sheaths are hairy. Leaf color is more blue-green and leaves are less erect than other small grains.

Deer eat the tender, nutritious foliage (12 to 25 percent protein) in fall, winter and early spring. Of the three small grains, however, most deer managers would rank rye third in preference or palatability to oats and wheat. This varies by region, soil fertility and other factors.

Less than 50 percent of the rye grown in the United States is harvested for grain, with the remainder as pasture, hay or as a cover or green manure crop. In addition to contributing organic matter, rye reduces soil erosion and enhances water penetration and retention. Furthermore, some evidence suggests that rye could be exploited for weed control since residues of fall-planted, spring-killed rye reduces total weed biomass by 60 percent to 95 percent when compared to controls with no residue. Rye residues modify the physical and chemical environment during seed germination and plant growth.

ESTABLISHMENT/MIXTURES

Rye is usually planted in September in the North or October in the South. Spring-planted rye should be planted as early as possible (February in the South and as soon as thaw in the North). If planted alone, 90 to 120 lbs./acre is recommended. Planted in mixtures, no more than 60 lbs./acre (one bushel/acre) should be broadcast. Drill rates would be roughly half of the above broadcast rate. I wouldn't consider planting rye alone for deer, with one possible exception. When it is too late or too cold to plant anything else, rye serves as an ideal late fall/early spring season cover crop that will germinate and grow in colder, poorer, more acidic soil. Under these conditions, it will feed deer and also hold the soil together, preventing erosion. Otherwise, in the South, mix rye with one or more legumes such as arrowleaf clover (10 lbs./acre) and crimson clover (10 lbs./acre). In the North or South mix rye with red clover (5 lbs./acre), white clover (5 lbs./acre), and Austrian winter peas (20 lbs./acre). In the North, add birdsfoot trefoil (5 lbs./acre). Rye is also very compatible with wheat (30 pounds of each per acre) plus any of the above legumes. My favorite mix is rye (30 lbs./acre), wheat (30 lbs./acre), Durana white clover (5 lbs./acre), Cinnamon Plus red clover (7 lbs./acre), and chicory (2 lbs./acre). Besides adding palatability, production and protein to the mix, the legumes make perfect companion plants for the rye by fixing nitrogen in the soil (some of which is used by the rye). On the flip side, the rye acts as a nurse crop for the legumes for the first month or two after planting by producing vigorous early growth, which takes the brunt of the early deer grazing pressure while the legumes develop a root system. Rye may reseed on its own when mowed in August and produce a second-year crop mixed with its companion legumes.

Like all other small grains, rye will achieve greatest forage and seed production when soil is limed to raise the pH above 6.0. A complete fertilizer applied according to soil-test results at planting (example: 300 lbs./acre 19-19-19) is recommended whether planted alone or in a mix.

VARIETIES/MANAGEMENT

There are dozens of rye varieties planted across the United States. Some have been bred for forage production – these are probably the most appropriate for deer – and others for seed production. Good forage varieties include but are not limited to Wintergrazer 70, Wrens Abruzzi (spring), Wintermore, Maton, Bonel (spring), Florida 401 (spring), Elbon, Winter King, Wheeler, Dacold, Aroostook and others. Check with your local extension agent for forage varieties adapted to your area.

Fewer diseases attack rye than other cereal grains. Rye is attacked by the same insects that attack other small grains, but serious crop losses are not common. Varieties with high forage production can produce about 3 tons of forage per acre (dry weight) and 60 to 80 bushels per acre of grain if best management practices are followed. These include using a higher seeding rate for forage production and sowing the crop early for deeper roots and greater ability to use soil moisture. If grazing production to ease the cool-season stress period is your goal, apply additional nitrogen (100 lbs./acre 34-0-0) in late winter. Do not apply the spring top-dressing if you have planted the legume mix! The key to getting good rye forage yields is selecting a variety that fits your situation. Do not use "combine run" rye, which is not inspected and can contain several species of noxious weeds that you will end up fighting for years to come. See Chapter 8 for more details on selecting grain seed.

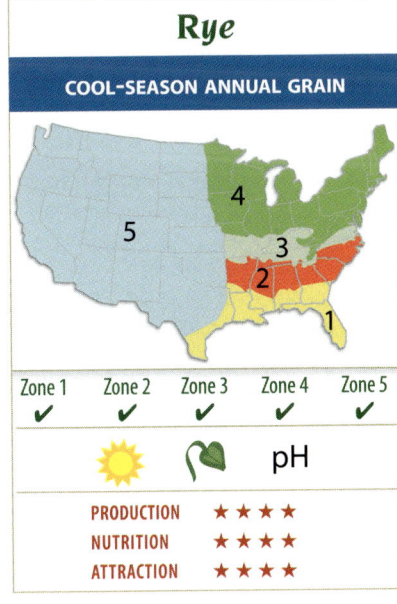

Rye

COOL-SEASON ANNUAL GRAIN

Zone 1	Zone 2	Zone 3	Zone 4	Zone 5
✔	✔	✔	✔	✔

☀ 🌿 pH

PRODUCTION	★ ★ ★ ★
NUTRITION	★ ★ ★ ★
ATTRACTION	★ ★ ★ ★

TRITICALE *(Triticosecale* spp.)

TRITICALE is a hybrid cross of rye and wheat that traces all the way back to Scotland in 1885. There are dozens of varieties in two main groups having either winter or spring growth habit and varying in height. They generally have larger seed heads than wheat, and most cultivars have prominent awns (spike-like hairs projecting from each seed) like rye. Early varieties produced excellent forage yields but were not winter hardy. Now, winter wheats are being used as parents, which has resulted in varieties being available that have good winter hardiness. These are most appropriate for deer management. Some varieties have grain yields similar to wheat. Triticale also has protein values similar to wheat (20 to 25 percent) when grazed as a young tender plant in the fall or early spring, which makes it well suited as pasture for cattle or deer. Triticale is the least popular of the small grains for cattle forage and grain production, but some agronomists rate it a higher-quality grazing forage than barley, oats, wheat or rye, in that order. Triticale forage yields are highly variable depending on variety, climate and rainfall with production ranging from 1 to 3 or more tons per acre, often similar to that of oats.

ESTABLISHMENT/MIXTURES

Triticale is usually planted in August to September in the North or September to October in the South, generally two to three weeks earlier than wheat. Spring-planted triticale should be planted as early as possible (February in the South and as soon as thaw in the North). If planted alone, 75 to 100 lbs./acre is recommended. Planted in mixtures with legumes, no more than 50 lbs./acre should be broadcast. Drill rates would be roughly half of the above broadcast rate. I would not consider planting triticale alone for deer, opting instead to plant in mixtures with other small grains and legumes. Unlike rye, triticale is not tough enough to use for late planting, poor or acidic soils and erosion control.

Consequently, mix triticale at 25 lbs./acre with oats or wheat (25 lbs./acre) and one or more legumes such as arrowleaf clover (10 lbs./acre) and crimson clover (10 lbs./acre) in the South. In the North or South, mix the small grains (50 lbs./acre) with red clover (7 lbs./acre), white clover (5 lbs./acre) and Austrian winter peas (20 lbs./acre). One promising fall attractant mix is triticale (25 lbs./acre), oats (25 lbs./acre), Durana white clover (5 lbs./acre) and Redland Max or Cinnamon Plus red clover (7 lbs./acre). Besides adding palatability, production and protein to the mix, the legumes make perfect companion plants for the triticale and oats by fixing 100 or more lbs./acre of nitrogen in the soil, some of which is used by the small grains. In an almost symbiotic relationship, the small grains act as a nurse crop for the legumes for the first month after planting by producing vigorous early growth, which takes the brunt of the early deer grazing pressure. Meanwhile, the legumes expend energy developing a root system and root nodules capable of fixing nitrogen.

Like all other small grains, triticale will achieve greatest forage and seed production when soil pH is above 6.0. A complete fertilizer applied according to soil test at planting (*example*: 300 lbs 19-19-19 or 400 lbs./acre of 13-13-13) is highly recommended whether triticale is planted alone or in a mix.

VARIETIES/MANAGEMENT

There are dozens of triticale varieties planted across the United States. Some have been bred for fall and winter forage production and are probably the most appropriate for deer. The most common cultivars have been bred for spring forage production and still others have been bred for maximum seed production. Good fall and winter forage varieties include but are not limited to Florida 201, Beagle 82 and Trical 102 in the South and Nutriseed 2-2-4 or 6-6-2, Tritigold-22, and WB-UW26 in the North. The following winter-hardy varieties may be appropriate for North and South, but be aware that these are grain varieties, not forage varieties: Alzo, Danko Presto, Kitaro, Lamberto, NE422T, NE426GT, Sorento, Trical 815 and Vero. Check with your local agricultural extension agent for forage varieties adapted to your area.

Fewer diseases affect triticale than wheat, but it is somewhat more susceptible than its other parent, rye. Triticale is attacked by the same insects that attack other small grains, but serious crop losses are not common. Varieties with high forage production can produce about 3 tons/acre of dry-weight forage and 60 to 80 bushels per acre of grain if best management practices are followed. If forage production to ease the cool-season stress period is your deer management goal, apply additional nitrogen in late winter (100 lbs./acre 46-0-0). Do not apply this top dressing if you have planted the legume mix! The key to getting good fall triticale forage yields is selecting a variety that fits your climate and determining whether you want an attractant plot, a nutrition plot or both.

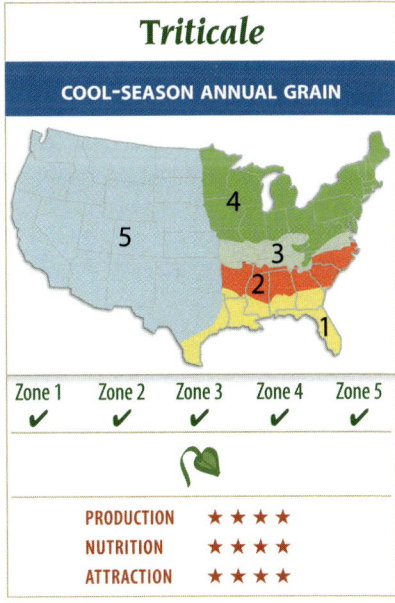

Triticale

COOL-SEASON ANNUAL GRAIN

Zone 1	Zone 2	Zone 3	Zone 4	Zone 5
✔	✔	✔	✔	✔

PRODUCTION	★ ★ ★ ★
NUTRITION	★ ★ ★ ★
ATTRACTION	★ ★ ★ ★

WHEAT *(Triticum aestivum)*

KENT KAMMERMEYER

Grown practically everywhere in the United States, WHEAT is one of the most valuable wildlife plants in the nation. The source of man's "staff of life" is also the mainstay for wild creatures, especially deer. Deer eat the tender, nutritious (15 to 25 percent protein) foliage in fall, winter and spring as well as the mature seed when available in late spring and summer. Wheat is more cold tolerant than oats but not as tolerant of cold or acidic soil as rye. Of the three small grains, most experts would rank wheat as second in preference or palatability to oats, with rye ranking third.

Originating in Eurasia, wheat is one of the cool-season annual bunch grasses that grow 2 to 4 feet tall, depending on variety, grazing pressure and fertility.

ESTABLISHMENT/MIXTURES

Wheat is usually planted in September in the North or October in the South. If planted alone, 90 to 120 lbs./acre is recommended. Planted in mixtures, no more than 60 lbs./acre (one bushel/acre) should be broadcast. Drill rates would be roughly half of the above broadcast rate. Personally, for deer, I would never consider planting wheat alone with one possible exception. Wheat fields serve as an ideal nursery for common ragweed, a natural deer forage. Generally, the best ragweed crops develop and mature in the stubble of the grazed seed heads. Deer browse ragweed quite heavily all summer, and ragweed provides

264

excellent quail and turkey habitat. Otherwise, in the South, mix wheat with one or more legumes such as arrowleaf clover (10 lbs./acre) and crimson clover (10 lbs./acre). In the North or South, mix it with red clover (5 lbs./acre), white clover (5 lbs./acre), chicory (1 lb./acre) and Austrian winter peas (20 lbs./acre). In the North, add birdsfoot trefoil (3 lbs./acre). Besides adding palatability to the mix, the legumes make perfect companion plants for the wheat by fixing nitrogen in the soil (some of which is used by the wheat). On the flip side, the wheat acts as a nurse crop for the legumes for the first month or two after planting by producing vigorous early growth, which takes the brunt of the early deer grazing pressure while the legumes develop a nitrogen-fixing root system.

As with all other small grains, wheat will achieve greatest forage and seed production when soil is limed to raise pH above 6.0. A complete fertilizer applied according to soil test at planting (300 pounds of 19-19-19, for example) is highly recommended whether planted alone or in a mix.

VARIETIES/MANAGEMENT

There are dozens, if not hundreds, of wheat varieties planted all across the United States. Some have been bred for forage production, and these are probably the most appropriate for deer. Others have been bred for seed production and others for resistance to fungus, mildew, root rot, rust and Hessian fly — and every combination thereof.

Agricultural Extension agents should be consulted concerning diseases in a local area before growing wheat. Varieties that are resistant to disease and fungus should be selected for your local area. Disease-resistant varieties with high forage production can produce about 6,000 pounds of forage (dry weight) and 60 to 80 bushels/acre of grain if the best management practices are followed. These include using a higher seeding rate for forage production and sowing the crop early for deeper roots and greater ability to use soil moisture.

If maximum grazing and grain production is your goal, apply at least 1 pound of nitrogen for every bushel of your yield goal and then topdress the crop in early spring with 0.75 pounds of nitrogen per bushel of yield goal. Do not apply the spring top dressing if you have planted the legume mix. The key to getting good wheat forage yields and grain yields is selecting a variety that fits your situation and operation. Do not plant "combine run" wheat, which is not inspected and can contain several species of noxious weeds. Recleaned seed or feed seed is cheap, but it also has no guaranteed germination. The risk of noxious weeds is usually lower, but it depends on how it was "cleaned." Centrifugal cleaning and use of sieves or screens can eliminate noxious weeds, but there are no guarantees.

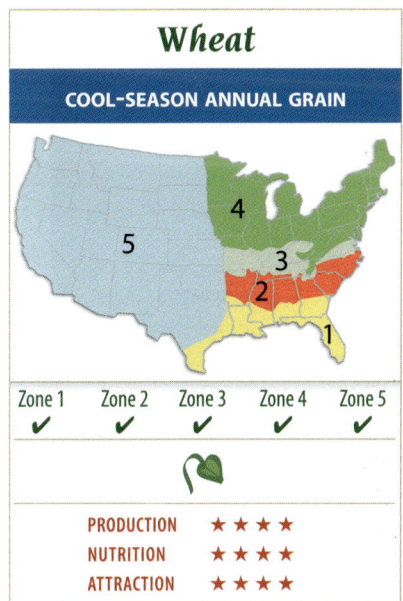

Wheat

COOL-SEASON ANNUAL GRAIN

Zone 1	Zone 2	Zone 3	Zone 4	Zone 5
✔	✔	✔	✔	✔

PRODUCTION	★ ★ ★ ★
NUTRITION	★ ★ ★ ★
ATTRACTION	★ ★ ★ ★

Grasses

ANNUAL and PERENNIAL RYEGRASS (*Lolium* spp.)

RYEGRASSES were brought to the United States from Europe and are now grown and planted throughout the country. These bunch grasses have two basic types – annual and perennial. Both have shiny, dark green, smooth leaves and grow 2 to 3 feet tall. Annual ryegrasses are primarily adapted to the South but will grow in the North, especially if planted in early spring. It is less winter hardy than tall fescue or orchardgrass. Perennial ryegrass is better adapted to the central and northern United States. Ryegrass tolerates wet, poorly drained soil but has a high moisture requirement, good nutritive quality, high production (4 tons forage/acre), and is responsive to nitrogen. It is tolerant of moderate soil acidity. Natural reseeding of annual ryegrass is so common it is usually problematic for future food plots on the site (*more on this below*). Best production of ryegrass occurs from late winter through May.

ESTABLISHMENT/MIXTURES

Seeding rate is 10 to 15 lbs./acre in mixtures or 20 to 30 lbs./acre alone. September is generally the best month to plant but October overseeding of warm-season grasses can be successful. March or April can be a good month to frost-seed perennial ryegrass or establish a stand of annual ryegrass to go to seed especially in the North. Ryegrasses can be seeded alone or used in mixtures with cereal grains (rye, wheat, oats) or clovers. Ryegrass is a "throw-and-grow" seed because it can be sowed without tillage if moisture conditions are favorable and good soil contact occurs. It is easily seeded and established on burned stubble. I recommend never establishing ryegrass alone. Always mix with legumes to improve the quality of the stand for deer and lower the nitrogen requirement.

One popular mix that works in many climates and soil types is ryegrass (15 lbs./acre), ladino clover (5 lbs./acre), and red clover (7 lbs./acre). This can be sowed in September or early spring. Another mix appropriate in the South is ryegrass (15 lbs./acre), crimson clover (10 lbs./acre), and arrowleaf clover (10 lbs./acre).

VARIETIES/MANAGEMENT

Even though I have suggested ryegrass mixtures above, I include this word of caution: without careful planning and management, ryegrass can be an aggressive pest! Do not sow annual ryegrass on ground that you need for other crops, you may have it forever! In many parts of the country, ryegrass is an aggressive reseeder and when allowed to mature and produce seed every year, it will out-compete every other cool season forage. You can slow this process or prevent it with grass-selective herbicides or repeated late spring and early summer mowing before seed matures, which greatly reduces seed production. You may now be wondering why ryegrass is even mentioned in this book, and here's why – because of its ease of establishment, tolerance of tough conditions (including shade and acidic or wet soils), and reseeding ability, ryegrass is an option for remote sites with poor soil conditions and a lack of access for equipment to improve those poor conditions. This includes small, remote hunting plots established with hand tools. Again, if you intend to upgrade these sites to different forages later, do not establish ryegrass in them.

When ryegrass exceeds 3 to 6 inches, forage quality and palatability rapidly declines. Mixed stands of ryegrass (especially perennial ryegrass) and clover can be maintained for five to eight years without replanting if regular mowing or grass selective herbicides are used. If not, life of the mixed stand is reduced by about half.

Varieties of annual ryegrass to plant for deer include Marshall, Passerel, Big Daddy, Rustmaster and Gulf. Perennial ryegrass variety selection may be much more important than annual ryegrass selection because of cultivar selection for early or late maturity, rust or drought resistance, or winter hardiness. Check with your local county extension agent or seed dealer for varieties adapted to your area. Linn is the most widely available and economical variety. Barenburg USA (*www.barusa.com*) offers seven perennial varieties, which range from early to late maturity and are winter hardy or drought resistant or crown rust resistant.

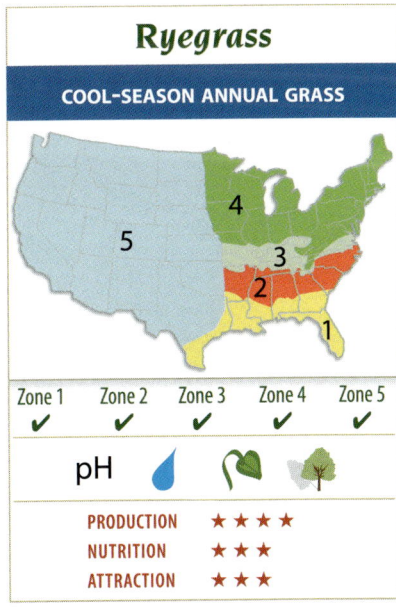

Ryegrass

COOL-SEASON ANNUAL GRASS

Zone 1	Zone 2	Zone 3	Zone 4	Zone 5
✔	✔	✔	✔	✔

pH			

PRODUCTION	★ ★ ★ ★
NUTRITION	★ ★ ★
ATTRACTION	★ ★ ★

TIMOTHY GRASS *(Phleum pratense)*

TIMOTHY is a perennial cool-season grass that is relatively late flowering and best adapted to cool, humid climates. The perennial bunchgrass originated in northern Europe and grows 2 to 4 feet tall. It normally matures two to three weeks later than tall fescue, orchardgrass and smooth bromegrass. Timothy is very palatable to deer, cattle and horses. Consequently, it is often selectively grazed and sometimes disappears when seeded with less palatable species. At certain stages of development, generally from middle to late spring, timothy is intolerant of intensive grazing as it transitions through vegetative growth to flowering and seed production. This should not be a problem in deer plots, since deer generally get off the plots in midspring and concentrate on foraging the spring greenup in woodlands. Timothy is well known as a prime horse hay crop.

ADAPTATION/ ESTABLISHMENT

Timothy is best adapted to the fertile, moist medium-heavy soils of the Pacific Northwest, and to the Great Lakes States and New England States. It can do well down to the northern area of Oklahoma, Arkansas, Georgia,

OREGON STATE UNIVERSITY, FORAGE INFORMATION SYSTEM

and North Carolina, especially in the higher elevations of the Appalachian Mountains. Timothy is easy to establish and is used extensively for revegetation of forest land and for erosion control in many areas. The seeding rate is 6 to 8 lbs./acre with a clover, or trefoil in August (North) or September (Central). The mix can also be planted in late winter or early spring (March in the central United States, April in the North). It is tolerant of low fertility and low pH but responds well to fertilizer and lime.

I have seen success with a mixture of Barliza timothy (5 lbs./acre), BG-34 perennial ryegrass (15 lbs./acre), Will ladino clover (5 lbs./acre), and Start red clover (10 lbs./acre). For best results, pH should be above 6.0 and adequate fertilizer applied at planting (300 lbs./acre of 19-19-19). After initial establishment, manage it as a deer plot by mowing twice per year, once in early bloom stage (late May or June) and again in August. Remove the hay if possible. Fertilize with 0-20-30 in September (200 to 300 lbs./acre) or use triple super phosphate (0-46-0) at 100 lbs./acre and muriate of potash (0-0-60) at 150 lbs./acre. Keep nitrogen off the timothy mix after establishment to favor the legume crop planted with it (clover, trefoil).

VARIETIES/MANAGEMENT

For deer and other wildlife, late-maturing varieties withstand spring grazing pressure better and remain palatable longer than common timothy. The Climax variety is productive, rust resistant and widely adapted. The same is true for a couple of European varieties marketed by Barenbrug USA (*www.barusa.com*). Barliza and Bart timothy are both very persistent with high yields under grazing. They withstand heavy grazing pressure and mature late.

Timothy is often considered among the highest quality cool-season bunchgrasses. Tests in Pennsylvania show timothy to be more preferred by deer than orchardgrass when both were mixed with alfalfa. I have seen the same marked preference in Georgia. Timothy produces from April through October in the North but typically shows low production from August to October.

More advice on timothy: I would not recommend planting it alone. For deer, use it as a combination, high-quality nurse crop for legumes and a companion nitrogen user to prevent nitrogen buildup in soils with crops of pure legumes. A companion grass like timothy takes up a niche that might otherwise be invaded by less desirable grasses like crabgrass or fungus-infected fescue. So, plant your timothy but manage the stand for clover, or birdsfoot trefoil. Timothy/clover or timothy/alfalfa mixes may be perfect for you if you grow hay commercially.

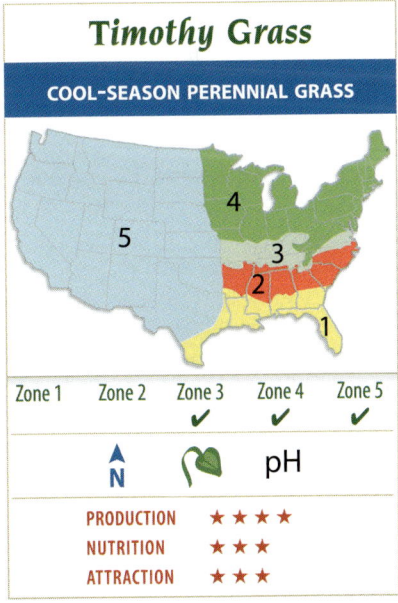

Timothy Grass

COOL-SEASON PERENNIAL GRASS

Zone 1	Zone 2	Zone 3	Zone 4	Zone 5
		✔	✔	✔

N   pH

PRODUCTION	★ ★ ★ ★
NUTRITION	★ ★ ★
ATTRACTION	★ ★ ★

Brassicas

CANOLA (rapeseed) *(Brassica napus and rapa)*

OKLAHOMA FARM BUREAU

CANOLA is a modern, high-quality form of rapeseed and as such is a member of the brassica family, which includes rape and turnips. Despite being used in Europe since the 13th century, there is a need for continued research on the value, utilization, production and palatability of canola/rape for whitetails in the United States. Canola, bred from these earlier plant cousins, is a relatively new crop and is more commonly known as double-zero or double-low oilseed rape. It is rapidly gaining value as an agronomic crop with winter rapeseed forage having crude protein of 21 to 33 percent. Its seed when crushed contains 40 percent vegetable oil, and the oilmeal that remains contains about 33 percent protein, 8 percent fat and 10 percent fiber. The oil from improved varieties has important potential in the human diet as cooking oil, while the oilmeal is an important source of protein for animals. Canola is distinguished from other forms of rapeseed by its low level of erucic acid (a fatty acid with adverse human health effects) and glucosides (toxic sulfur compounds in oilmeal that may injure livestock).

Canola can provide livestock producers (and deer managers) with fast-growing, high-yielding, quality fall pasture. Like forage rape, canola can be very useful for extending the grazing season into November through January when other forages are less productive or dormant. However, grazing of canola can require careful management. Canola is a short-season, leafy brassica whose stems and leaves are ready to graze 60 to 90 days after establishment. It is very important to note here that canola (and all brassicas) should not be planted more than two consecutive years on the same plot to prevent insect and root disease problems.

ADAPTATION/ESTABLISHMENT

Canola is adapted to the entire United States and Canada. In the North it can be planted in fall (August) or spring (April). In the South, it should be planted in the fall

(September). Tolerant of cold, drought and heat, canola can provide valuable feed when other crops are less productive. Canola requires good soil drainage and a pH between 5.5 and 7.5. It does best in a pH above 6.0. Seed should be planted in a firm, moist seedbed. Canola can be broadcast at 6 to 8 lbs./acre or drilled at 4 to 5 lbs./acre in 6- to 7-inch rows. It is important not to plant the seed too deep (¼ inch). As with turnips, many managers are successful top sowing the tiny seed on bare soil just before an expected rainfall. For best production and highest quality forage, 80 to 100 lbs./acre of nitrogen is required, along with about 30 to 50 lbs./acre of phosphorus and potassium. Consequently, if planted alone, fertilize with 200 lbs./acre of 19-19-19 or equivalent plus 200 lbs./acre ammonium sulfate (34-0-0) or 150 lbs./acre urea (46-0-0). If mixed with legumes, you can skip the extra nitrogen. Properly fertilized, canola's crude protein levels range from 21 to 33 percent in canola leaves. Total digestible nutrients (TDN) average about 70 percent and dry matter tested about 15 percent. This translates to a very high quality, highly digestible forage with very high moisture content.

MANAGEMENT/VARIETIES

Well-fertilized, well-managed stands of canola can produce 1½ to 2 tons of forage per acre over a relatively short grazing season from October to January (moving north to south in the United States). As far as management, it is very important to plant canola early — from August in the North through September in the South. Later-planted canola may not fully mature before cold weather and may be subject to early overgrazing. Reports on deer use of canola nationwide have varied from "killed by overgrazing as a small seedling" (less than two weeks old) to "hardly grazed at all" and everything in between. It is generally more preferred by deer than rape. This is where we need more research. Experts recommend not allowing grazing for 60 to 80 days due to the potential for overgrazing. Deer commonly hit canola hard in November and December, removing all leafy forage in a short time. Livestock producers remove their livestock at this time to allow 30 days or more of regrowth for a second grazing period.

Deer managers obviously cannot do this, so the planting is basically exhausted in late fall or early winter. For this reason, I recommend strip planting canola and other brassicas such as turnips, kale or rape next door to clover mixes, especially in fields one acre or larger. Mixing canola with clovers, chicory, and/or wheat is another option, but it's tricky. Be very careful on rates, not broadcasting more than 2 lbs./acre canola (its quick, leafy growth produces a lot of shade on nearby seedlings), 2 lbs./acre chicory, 5 lbs./acre red clover and 30 lbs./acre wheat. There are dozens of good canola varieties available split into broad categories of winter or spring plantings. Remember, do not plant canola or any other brassica for more than two consecutive years on the same ground! To do so is asking for serious disease and insect problems.

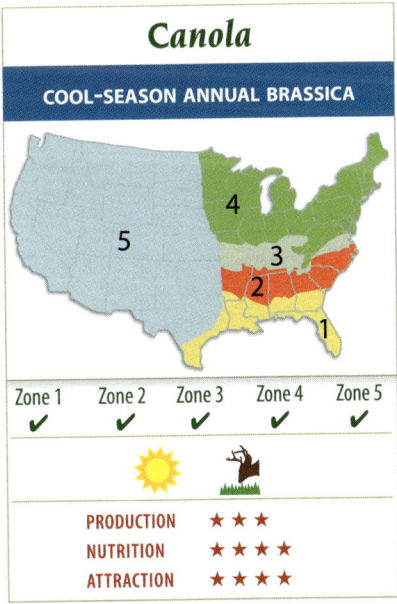

Canola

COOL-SEASON ANNUAL BRASSICA

Zone 1	Zone 2	Zone 3	Zone 4	Zone 5
✔	✔	✔	✔	✔

PRODUCTION	★ ★ ★	
NUTRITION	★ ★ ★ ★	
ATTRACTION	★ ★ ★ ★	

SPECIES PROFILES

Brassicas

KALE *(Brassica oleracea)*

The three main species of forage brassicas used for late fall pasture are rape, kale and turnip. KALE is a cold-hardy green that is high in nutritive value. It is not well adapted to hot weather. The best quality is produced where summers are cool or when kale is grown into the fall or winter. Dry matter yields of kale range from 4,500 to 7,100 lbs./acre. Crude protein of kale leaves ranges from 18 to 25 percent, which is very similar to rape. Kale is slower growing than rape and requires a longer growing season to reach its full grazing potential (rape is faster at accumulating forage for browsing). However, it can provide excellent winter browse just like rape. Kale is of particular interest when a large amount of forage is desired for winter grazing. In this situation, managers need to allow for a long growing period (five to six months) in order to give kale time to slowly reach its potential yield.

ADAPTATION/ESTABLISHMENT

Kale is adapted across the entire United States and into Canada. It produces best in the northern states where summers are cool. However, it can be planted in late summer in Florida. The preferred time of planting in most of the United States is June or July. Plant at 4 to 5 lbs./acre and plan on leaf maturity for maximum yield to occur in 110 to 150 days in November, December or January. Plant kale seeds ¼-inch deep in well-drained loams high in organic matter. Clay or sandy soils will do okay. The desirable pH is between 5.5 and 6.5. If the pH is too high, manganese is unavailable, which results in a marbled or mottled appearance of the leaves.

General fertilizer recommendations for kale are 60 to 100 lbs./acre of nitrogen, 80 to 120 lbs./acre of phosphorus, and 60 to 120 lbs./acre of potassium. In other words, 300 lbs./acre of 19-19-19 at planting would be a minimum application, with 400 pounds producing better growth. Other elements needed include 1 to 4 lbs./acre of boron, 60 to 120 lbs./acre of magnesium, and trace amounts of copper and zinc. Get a soil test to be sure of these requirements in your soils.

VARIETIES/MANAGEMENT

Varieties of kale greens are of two types. Scotch types have gray-green and very curled and crumpled leaves while Siberian types are blue-green and less curled. Both dwarf and tall types are available with the dwarf types being preferred. Widely adapted varieties include Premier, Vates and Siberian. In New Zealand, Kapeti kale has shown high yields, high percent utilization, high stem utilization, and improved club root resistance. Most preference tests reveal kale varieties sandwiched between the higher-preferred rape and the lower-preference turnip varieties. However, all are close relatives, and it would not surprise me that other trials would show different results. Other varieties would include Darkibor, Dwarf Siberian, Vates Blue Curled, Dwarf Curled Scotch, Blue Ridge, Dwarf Green Curled, Improved Vates, Redbor, Starbor, Tall Scotch and Vates Dwarf Blue.

Just like rape, kale would be best suited for deer as a mixture with other brassicas and even chicory or clovers as long as the brassica rate is held low enough (less than 2 lbs./acre) to prevent shading of the clover and chicory companion plants. Better yet, divide your food plot in half, planting one strip in a rape/kale/turnip mix and the other half in a clover/small grain mix. This will assure survival of all varieties and species in the plot with both strips serving a specific function. The brassica function, of course, would be late-fall and early winter grazing after the clover mix goes dormant.

There are numerous commercial mixes on the market today that include kale. Best management of a kale stand would include application of additional nitrogen at 30 to 60 days after establishment (100 to 150 lbs./acre of 34-0-0). Just like rape, do not plant kale or other brassicas on the same ground for more than two successive years to prevent serious fungal disease problems.

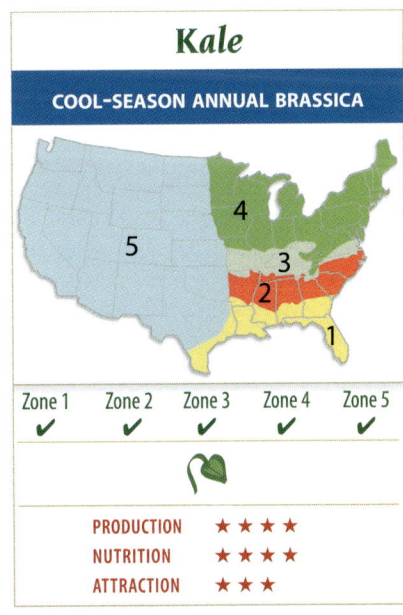

Kale

COOL-SEASON ANNUAL BRASSICA

Zone 1	Zone 2	Zone 3	Zone 4	Zone 5
✔	✔	✔	✔	✔

PRODUCTION	★ ★ ★ ★
NUTRITION	★ ★ ★ ★
ATTRACTION	★ ★ ★

FORAGE RAPE *(Brassica napus)*

CRAIG HARPER

Rape (the leafy greens in this blend) works well in food plot mixes. This well-planted, healthy mix includes dwarf essex rape, ladino clover and chicory. Note that the seeding rate of rape in this mix was kept low to prevent the leafy rape from shading the other species.

RAPE is a member of the brassica family. Brassicas include cabbage, cauliflower, canola, kale, radish, turnip, rutabaga and swede. They have been used extensively in Europe, Australia, New Zealand and even Canada for livestock grazing and, more recently, for deer farming.

Annual rape cultivars can provide deer managers with fast-growing, high-yielding, quality fall forage. Rape can be very useful for extending the grazing season into November through January when other forages are less productive or dormant. Do not confuse forage rape with oil-seed rape or canola. Forage rape is a short-season leafy brassica whose stems and leaves are ready to graze 30 to 90 days after establishment. It is important to note here that most common rape varieties (and other brassicas) should not be planted more than two consecutive years on the same plot to prevent root disease and pest problems. However, many of the improved varieties entering the United States market from New Zealand have increased disease and pest resistance.

ADAPTATION/ESTABLISHMENT

Rape is adapted to the entire United States and Canada, although it does not do well in semi-tropical regions of south Florida. Cold, drought and heat tolerant, rape can provide valuable feed when other crops are less productive. Rape requires good soil drainage and a pH between 5.3 and 6.8. It grows best in soil with a pH above 6.0. Seed should be planted in a firm, moist seedbed. Rape can be broadcast at 4 to 9 lbs./acre or drilled at 2 to 6 lbs./acre in 6- to 8-inch rows. It is important not to plant the seed too deep, no deeper than ¼ inch. Many managers are successfully top-sowing the tiny seed (just like turnips) on bare soil just before an expected rainfall. For the best production and highest-quality forage, 70 to 90 lbs./acre of nitrogen is recommended, along with about 50 to 60 lbs./acre of phosphorus and potassium. If planted alone, fertilize with 300 lbs./acre or 19-19-19 or an equivalent, plus 100 lbs./acre ammonium sulfate (34-0-0). If mixed with legumes, you can skip the ammonium sulfate. Properly fertilized, crude protein levels range from 18 to more than 30 percent in rape leaves. Total digestible nutrients (TDN) average about 70 percent, and dry matter tested about 15 percent. This translates to a very high-quality, highly digestible forage with a high moisture content.

VARIETIES/MANAGEMENT

Well-fertilized, well-managed stands of rape can produce 1½ to 4 tons of forage per acre over a relatively short grazing season ending from October to January, moving north to south in the United States. As for management, it is very important to plant rape early — from July in the North through September in the South. Later planted rape may not fully mature before cold weather and may be subject to early overgrazing. Reports on deer use of rape nationwide have varied from killed by overgrazing as small seedlings (less than two weeks old) to hardly grazed at all and everything in between (more research will help us understand this variability).

Experts recommend not allowing grazing for 60 to 90 days for dwarf rape varieties, which are probably better suited for deer management due to the potential for overgrazing. Giant types have higher yields and are more palatable but may be more subject to early overgrazing than dwarfs.

After several freezes, deer commonly eat rape heavily in November and December, removing all leaves in a short time. Livestock producers remove their livestock when this happens to allow 30 days or more of regrowth for a second grazing period. Deer managers cannot do this, so I recommend strip-planting rape next to clover mixes, especially in fields 1 acre or larger. Mixing rape with clovers, chicory and/or oats is another option but a low seeding rate is required. To prevent the rape from shading out the other species, broadcast no more than 1 to 2 lbs./acre rape, 1 to 2 lbs./acre chicory, 5 lbs./acre red clover, and 30 lbs./acre wheat. The most common rape variety is dwarf essex rape, though many improved varieties are available in commercial blends from a number of the well-known food plot seed companies.

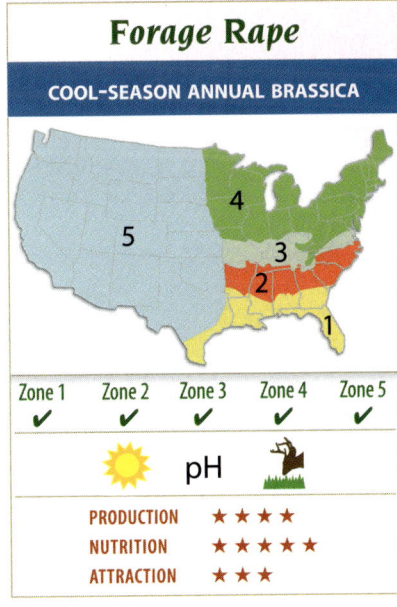

Forage Rape

COOL-SEASON ANNUAL BRASSICA

Zone 1	Zone 2	Zone 3	Zone 4	Zone 5
✔	✔	✔	✔	✔

☀ pH 🦌

PRODUCTION	★ ★ ★ ★
NUTRITION	★ ★ ★ ★ ★
ATTRACTION	★ ★ ★

TURNIPS (*Brassica rapa*)

CHARLES ALSHEIMER

Like kale and rape, TURNIPS are another member of the brassica family. Other close relatives of turnips include rutabagas and Swedes. In the late 1970s, researchers began to demonstrate the potential of turnip as pasture. The development of varieties with partially exposed roots made the roots more available as pasture rather than harvesting or storing. Turnips (and rutabagas) are cool-weather crops providing roots, stem, and leaf growth for rotational grazing or strip grazing 90 or more days after seeding. The leaves can be grazed from mid-September until January depending on critical low temperatures and snow cover. Top growth generally will survive temperatures between 15 to 20 degrees while bulbs will be about 5 degrees hardier. Depending upon variety and fertility, turnips yield 1½ to 5 tons per acre of dry matter including the bulb. The tops have 17 to 24 percent crude protein while roots commonly contain 12 to 15 percent protein.

Like other brassicas, turnips are not generally an "ice cream" plant for deer. As a matter of fact, use of turnips by deer varies greatly. Some reports have it grazed early and hard, others indicating it going virtually untouched by deer and everything in between. Many growers indicate it takes deer two or three years to figure out turnips, at which time they get hooked for life. Some northern turnip plots look like mine fields in December, as hungry deer paw up turnip bulbs. A more common scenario nationwide, however, is heavy utilization of top growth in late fall and early winter but little use of bulbs.

ADAPTATION/ESTABLISHMENT

Turnips are both cold hardy and drought tolerant, making them adapted to virtually the entire United States and Canada. They can be planted late – even as a second crop – and provide high-quality grazing late in the fall. In the North, plant turnips in July or early August to provide grazing from September to November. In the South, August or September plantings will accomplish the goal of vigorous root growth during periods of low temperatures (40 to 60 degrees) in the fall. The leaves maintain their nutritional quality even after repeated exposure to frost. Turnips grow best in loamy, fertile and slightly acidic soil (pH 6.0 to 6.5). Turnips will do okay in heavy clay but not in wet or poorly drained soils. Turnip seed is small and should be seeded into a fine, firm seedbed with adequate moisture for germination. Turnips can be top-sown or no-till drilled into a sod by applying 2 quarts per acre of glyphosate at least three days prior to seeding. Drill at $1\frac{1}{2}$ to $2\frac{1}{2}$ lbs./acre. Broadcast at 3 to 4 lbs./acre followed by

CHARLES ALSHEIMER

cultipacking. The seed should never be covered more than ¼-inch deep. Fertilize at planting with 300 to 400 lbs./acre of 19-19-19. Top dressing with 100 to 150 lbs./acre ammonium sulfate (34-0-0) at 30 to 60 days will increase production and utilization of the top and especially the bulb. Boron and/or sulfur may be needed, but only a soil test can reveal this.

VARIETIES/MANAGEMENT

Weeds are generally not a problem once the turnip crop is established. A weed-free seedbed at planting (using plowing or chemicals) is sufficient for turnips to get the jump on competition by shading. Turnips are ready for grazing when forage is about 12 inches tall or 90 to 110 days after planting. Earlier grazing will hurt production of both top-growth and bulb. Of course, this is out of the control of most deer managers depending on alternative food supplies of deer and their palatability. Timing of the planting (to coincide with first frosts occurring 90 to 110 days after planting) will go a long way toward managing the deer grazing pressure for late fall and maximum production of top growth and bulb.

There are many varieties of turnips including those selected for forage (more top growth and less bulb). Forage varieties include Barkant, Seven Top, Typhon, Rondo, Dynamo, Samson, Forage Star, All Top, Pasja, Appin, Green Globe, York Globe, and Sirius. Purple Top and Royal Crown have bigger bulbs and less top growth, but similar total production as the forage varieties.

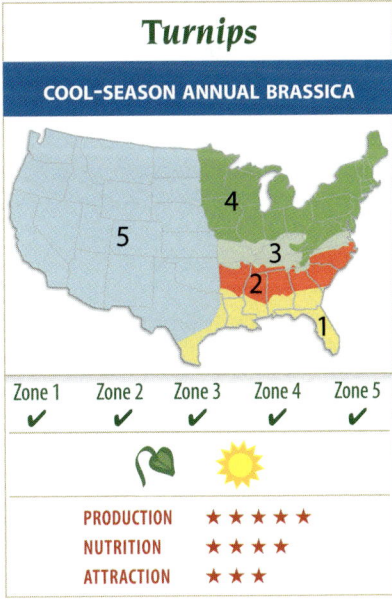

Turnips

COOL-SEASON ANNUAL BRASSICA

Zone 1	Zone 2	Zone 3	Zone 4	Zone 5
✔	✔	✔	✔	✔

PRODUCTION ★ ★ ★ ★ ★
NUTRITION ★ ★ ★ ★
ATTRACTION ★ ★ ★

Others

SPECIES PROFILES

Others

BUCKWHEAT *(Fagopyrum esculentum)*

BUCKWHEAT has been grown in America since colonial days, and the crop was once common on farms in the northeast and central United States. Buckwheat is an annual that can grow from 2 to 5 feet tall. The plant has a single, erect stem and usually has many branches. Leaf blades are 2- to 4-inches long and triangular or heart-shaped. The plant has a shallow taproot and numerous short side roots.

ADAPTATION/ESTABLISHMENT

Buckwheat can be grown virtually anywhere in the United States and Canada except in extremely dry climates. It is a high-quality forb-like plant with protein levels ranging from 20 percent to 9 percent. It grows best under cool, moist conditions and can mature in 10 to 12 weeks. When planted later in the season, maturity can occur in six to nine weeks. Although best planted soon after the last frost, the crop can be planted from April until September in the South. Germination is best at 80 degrees soil temperature, but it will germinate at any temperature between 45 and 105 degrees. Yield of early plantings can sometimes be adversely impacted by hot, dry weather during bloom. Good yields are 1½ to 3 tons/acre over a short period of productivity.

Buckwheat tolerates a wider variety of soil conditions than almost any other crop. However, expect a poor yield on heavy, wet soils. In the Deep South, the crop is often sown on poorly or hastily prepared land or rough, stony areas where good preparation is impossible. Even under these conditions, buckwheat can still produce fair crops, but it does respond well to good seedbed preparation. If established weeds are controlled with an appropriate non-selective herbicide (such as glyphosate), the crop can be seeded in stale seedbeds or in crop residues using a no-till drill.

If soil test levels of phosphorus and potassium are medium or above, additional applications of phosphorus and potash will not be needed. In lieu of soil tests, apply 100 to 300 lbs./acre of 3-12-12 or 5-10-15, or apply about 100 to 150 lbs./acre of 8-24-24. Buckwheat does not need a lot of nitrogen. Nitrogen should be limited to 10 to 20 lbs./acre. Buckwheat tolerates a wide range of soil acidity. However, if pH is below 5.5, lime will be beneficial to raise pH to 6.0 or better. If planted alone, drill at 36 to 50 lbs./acre or broadcast at 60 lbs./acre and cover no deeper than 2 inches. Germination generally occurs in about six days.

VARIETIES/MANAGEMENT

In most cases, seed of unknown or no variety designation will be all that is available. Recognized varieties, if available, include Japanese, Silverhull, Common Gray, Mancan, Manor, Royal and Tokyo (a smaller-seeded variety). Tartary buckwheat (also known as Indianwheat and Duckwheat) is a separate species that is smaller, more slender and considered hardier than buckwheat. It is sometimes planted and flooded for ducks.

Buckwheat has an excellent "rotational effect." Root residues make phosphorus more available to the follow-up crop, and residues also return considerable levels of phosphorus to the soil. Buckwheat also makes an excellent "smother crop" to suppress weeds because it is a good competitor, germinates rapidly, and the dense leaf canopy soon shades the soil. The rapid growth soon smothers most weeds. Buckwheat is a useful crop for control of quackgrass, thistle, creeping jenny, leafy spurge, Russian knapweed and perennial peppergrass. Because of buckwheat's early competitiveness, it should not be used as a companion crop for establishing cool-season legumes. If buckwheat is used in any mixture, seeding rate should be cut to 20 lbs./acre and

mixed with tall grain sorghum (5 lbs./acre) or corn (10 lbs./acre) plus cowpeas (25 lbs./acre) or soybeans (25 lbs./acre). If any of these mixes are used, increase fertilization to 300 lbs./acre of 19-19-19. If seed are allowed to mature and the plant is mowed, it will reseed and produce another stand.

Deer use of buckwheat leaves and blooms is often heavy. Some use of the mature seed has been reported. However, it may take deer a year or two to discover and begin using buckwheat. Once they begin use, overgrazing wipeouts may occur in fields less than 3 acres. One of the best food plots of wheat and white clover I ever grew, and this despite a drought, was planted right after I mowed and plowed under a stand of buckwheat in August and planted clover in September. Did buckwheat account for some of the clover success in this field? I think so because of its rotational effect and improvements of soil structure.

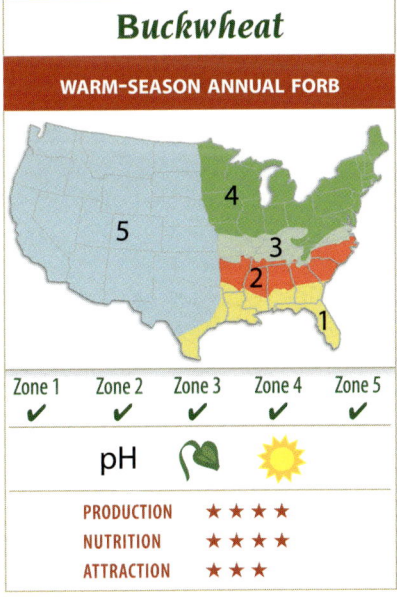

Buckwheat

WARM-SEASON ANNUAL FORB

Zone 1	Zone 2	Zone 3	Zone 4	Zone 5
✔	✔	✔	✔	✔

pH

PRODUCTION	★ ★ ★ ★
NUTRITION	★ ★ ★ ★
ATTRACTION	★ ★ ★

SPECIES PROFILES

Others

FORAGE CHICORY *(Chicorium intybus)*

FORAGE CHICORY is a broad-leaved perennial herb in the sunflower family that looks similar to common plantain. It can be grown on well-drained or moderately-drained soils having medium to high fertility. Chicory has good seedling vigor and a deep taproot, which makes it quite drought tolerant. Though it remains green in a flat rosette through winter (much like dandelion), its productive season is April through October when it can average production of 50 lbs./acre/day, providing valuable spring and summer forage for deer. If managed properly, chicory produces leafy growth similar in nutrition and mineral content to alfalfa or cool-season grasses. Protein levels range from 10 percent to 32 percent depending on growth stage and soil fertility.

First introduced in the United States in the late 1700s, chicory has since become a common roadside weed in the central and northern United States. During the Civil War, chicory root was used as a coffee substitute, and it is still used as a coffee additive in some areas. Wild chicory produces low forage yields. Despite being relatively new in the United States, forage chicory has been used in agriculture for more than 300 years. It originated in central Europe, but much of the breeding for improved forage has been done in New Zealand where it has produced in excess of 10 tons of forage per acre.

ADAPTATION/ ESTABLISHMENT

Chicory is widely adapted to most climate conditions in the United States where it needs to be sown by early August to develop a deep root before winter. In the South, it can be planted in September. Possible exceptions are the deep sands of the southeastern Coastal Plains and Canada (or the extreme northern United States). It will grow in a pH as low as 5.0 but prefers 6.5 to 7.0. Seed may be either drilled or broadcast, although drilling is preferred, because it results in a uniform planting depth. Chicory seed should be planted ¼- to ½-inch deep. Cultipacking the seedbed before and after planting is recommended for best seed-to-soil contact. When planted alone, a rate of 4 to 5 lbs./acre is recommended. However, I do not recommend planting chicory alone. Because of potential grazing and fertility management problems (including high nitrogen needs for good growth), chicory needs to be part of a mixture with a legume and an annual or perennial grass. One mix would be 2 lbs./acre chicory, 5 lbs./acre ladino clover, and 50 lbs./acre wheat (or 20 lbs./acre perennial ryegrass). Another possibility is 2 to 3 lbs./acre of chicory along with clovers (5 to 10 lbs./acre), small grains (30 to 50 lbs./acre) and a brassica (2 lbs./acre). Fertilize according to a soil test or use 300 lbs./acre of 19-19-19 at planting.

VARIETIES/MANAGEMENT

Chicory requires a high level of fertility for maximum production. It is also quite responsive to nitrogen (N) fertilization. However, if chicory is planted with alfalfa or clover, annual N applications can be restricted to limit the effect the N has on reducing nitrogen fixation of the legume. Chicory can produce up to 4.5 to 6 tons/acre/year of dry forage with careful grazing management. The digestibility of chicory leaves is very high – generally between 90 and 95 percent!

Grazing management can be extremely important with chicory, as it is with the brassicas. Fall-planted chicory should not be heavily grazed until the following spring, hence the advantage of the mixture of nurse crop plants of legumes and small grains. In spring and summer, chicory grows vigorously and will attempt to produce flower stems in late spring and early summer. Management practices which do not allow the flower stems to exceed 6- to 10-inches in late May (grazing or mowing to a 1½-inch stubble height) will reduce the amount of stem bolting (rapid stem growth). Rest periods longer than 25 days allow stems to bolt. In other words, if the deer don't do it for you, delay bolting by periodic mowing. Once bolting has occurred, the production potential of plants is reduced for the remainder of the grazing season or until the stems are mowed. Controlled grazing or mowing can sustain a productive chicory stand for up to seven years or more.

By far the most popular and widely available forage chicory is Puna from New Zealand. Other commercially available varieties are Good Hunt, Forage Feast and Choice. All of the major seed companies produce blends containing chicory.

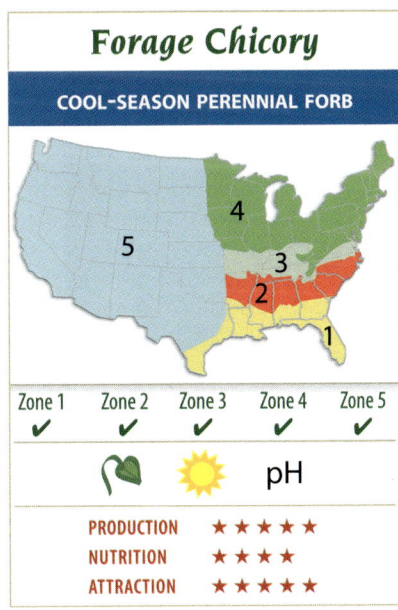

Forage Chicory

COOL-SEASON PERENNIAL FORB

Zone 1	Zone 2	Zone 3	Zone 4	Zone 5
✔	✔	✔	✔	✔

pH

PRODUCTION	★ ★ ★ ★ ★
NUTRITION	★ ★ ★ ★
ATTRACTION	★ ★ ★ ★ ★

SMALL BURNET (*Sanguisorba minor*)

The USDA refers to SMALL BURNET as a "very desirable forage for elk, deer, antelope and birds either as herbage or seed." It is an excellent choice in seed mixes for erosion control and beautification. In terms of human consumption, the leaves can be added to salads, cold drinks, vinegar, butter and cream cheese to add a pleasant, cucumber-like flavor.

Small burnet is a hardy, long-lived, introduced evergreen perennial forb (a non-woody plant other than a grass, sedge or rush). It has a thick base of branched stems with a prominent taproot. It has nine to 17 oval, coarsely toothed, four-inch-long leaflets. Height varies from 6 inches (with low rainfall or droughty sites) to 2 feet where rainfall is adequate. Red flowers are closely packed at the top of head-like spikes 3 to 8 inches long with no petals. The seed is oblong, less than ¼-inch long, woody and warty.

ADAPTATION/ESTABLISHMENT

Small burnet is adapted to the West, Upper Midwest, Northeast and Southeast, as well as southern Canada. Deer managers should be able to grow this plant almost anywhere that receives more than 14 inches of rainfall per year. Small burnet does best on well-drained soils and infertile to disturbed soils. It has excellent cold and drought tolerance but is not tolerant of poor drainage, flooding or high water tables. It needs a pH between

6.0 and 8.0 and is usually best used in open areas, but it will tolerate semi-shaded conditions.

Small burnet can be drilled or broadcast and covered no more than ½-inch deep by the drill, cultipacker or drag. Like many other food-plot plants, I would not recommend planting small burnet alone but always as a component of a mix. It can be seeded in late summer or late winter as long as moisture conditions are favorable. For this reason, late winter may be the preferred time in the West and Southeast. Seedling vigor is excellent, but the plant establishes slowly and should not be grazed heavily until the second growing season. For this reason, it should be planted in a mix with nurse crops to divert early grazing pressure by deer. One mix might include wheat (50 lbs./acre), white clover (3 lbs./acre), red clover (5 lbs./acre) and small burnet (3 lbs./acre). It might even be advantageous to add chicory (2 lbs./acre) and birdsfoot trefoil (3 lbs./acre), especially on poor sites where small burnet will do well but is slow to establish.

Best results will be achieved by liming and fertilizing based on soil-test recommendations, but if a soil test is not possible, apply fertilizer at a rate of 300 lbs./acre of 19-19-19.

Varieties/Management

Growth of small burnet begins in early spring, and flowers appear in late May through June. Plants have been known to persist for more than 20 years on western rangeland. As with other species, plant life can be prolonged if it is permitted to set seed at least every other year. Weed control will improve establishment and longevity. See Chapter 10 for help on weed control, especially grasses. Stands can also be mowed in late summer to set back competition and rejuvenate burnet plants. If clover persists with small burnet, fertilize with 0-20-30 once per year in late summer to early fall. If all you have left are small burnet and chicory, apply 200 lbs./acre of 19-19-19.

A variety named Delar is a selected release from seed originating in Europe. It was developed by the USDA for outstanding seed and forage production, cold tolerance and palatability. Deer use of small burnet is extremely variable, ranging from little or no use to heavy use and everything in between. To my knowledge, the only commercial bagged seed mix available that contains small burnet is Imperial Whitetail Extreme marketed by the Whitetail Institute in Pintlala, Alabama (*www.whitetailinstitute.com*).

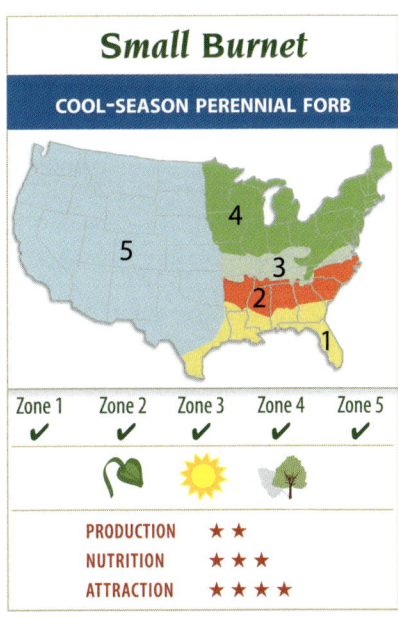

Small Burnet

COOL-SEASON PERENNIAL FORB

Zone 1	Zone 2	Zone 3	Zone 4	Zone 5
✔	✔	✔	✔	✔

PRODUCTION	★ ★	
NUTRITION	★ ★ ★	
ATTRACTION	★ ★ ★ ★	

SUGAR BEETS (*Beta vulgaris*)

**By Ed Spinazzola and
Kent Kammermeyer**

SUGAR BEETS are the only species of agricultural importance in their small family, which includes sugar and fodder beets and mangels. Several members of the family are common weeds. The wild beets from which cultivated forms were derived are sea-coast plants of Europe and Asia. Sugar beets were first recorded in Egypt during the Great Pyramid era.

Modern sugar beets are a hardy biennial vegetable that is grown commercially in a wide variety of temperate climates including the western and midwestern United States. During its first growing season, it produces a large 2- to 4-lb. storage root

PEGGY GREB, USDA AGRICULTURAL RESEARCH SERVICE

whose dry mass is 15 to 20 percent sugar by weight. If not harvested, during its second growing season the nutrients in this root are used to produce the plant's flowers and seeds. In commercial beet production, the root is harvested after the first growing season, when the root is at its maximum size.

ADAPTATION/MANAGEMENT

In most temperate climates, beets are planted in the spring and harvested in autumn. At the northern end of its range, short growing seasons (100 days) can still produce sugar beet crops. In warmer climates, sugar beets are a winter crop, being planted in autumn and harvested in the spring.

For deer, beets make a great attractant food plot. They can have a sugar content of 20 percent dry matter, a protein content of 10 percent, and they can produce up to 20 tons of beets per acre! Sugar beets are appropriate forage for the critical winter stress period. They have the highest digestibility (95 percent) of any forage.

It's possible that for a couple of years you may have to dig up a few beets for the deer until they discover that they like them. Soon, however, they will take quite well to planted crops. Also, advancing cool weather, which increases the sugar content in the roots, increases palatability to deer. Deer also eat the tops. Do not mow the tops of sugar beets, it encourages growth of new leaves, which decreases sugar content in the root. Spring-planted sugar beets grow well into November, with more than half of their volume above the soil surface for easy deer access.

Sugar beets are a very finicky crop. They prefer a medium to heavy loam soil and a steady supply of moisture, especially in late summer and early fall. This is reversed during their young growth stage, when they are susceptible to drowning. Sugar beet seedlings cannot compete with weeds, and repeated applications of herbicides may be necessary until full canopy closure.

VARIETIES/MANAGEMENT

Choose the heaviest soil (but not pure clay), the most level ground, and the lowest elevations for your sugar beet plots. There are a host of pests that attack sugar beets, from fungi to nematodes, and one way to stay ahead of them is a four-year rotation plan – grow sugar beets on a given plot for one year, then do not plant sugar beets in that same field again for three consecutive years. To have sugar beets every year, plan ahead for future rotations of sugar beets and make pH corrections to 6.5 up to 7.5 on several plots. Fertilize and lime according to a soil test.

To prepare a field for sugar beets in the North, spray with glyphosate (Roundup) in September followed by tillage two weeks later. The following spring, plant sugar beets soon after danger of killing frost has passed. However, just prior to spring seeding, spray again with Roundup to kill emerged weeds, wait two weeks then broadcast 300 to 400 lbs./acre of 19-19-19 and 25 lbs./acre of manganese sulfate. Till in the fertilizer with the blades set no deeper than 4 inches. Plant the sugar beet seeds (method described below). Around six to eight weeks later when plants reach near full canopy, broadcast 100 lbs/acre of urea (46-0-0) per acre. Sugar beets can be difficult to grow in the South, but they can be planted in September following the same procedures described above.

Sugar beet seeds differ in size and are available in pelletized form (seed hairs are trimmed and the surface coated with fungicide). The pelletized sugar-beet seeds, designed for improved germination and emergence, also improve seed flow in your broadcast spreader and broadcast accuracy rate. Broadcast about 8 lbs./acre. The emerging plants should average around a foot apart, which is ideal for most conditions.

Sugar beet seed should be covered around $\frac{1}{2}$- to $\frac{3}{4}$-inch deep, with firm seed-to-soil contact. Broadcasting seed on freshly tilled soil followed by a double cultipacking does the job.

To control grass in your sugar-beet plots, use a grass-selective herbicide at an early stage of weed growth. Broadleaf weed control is more difficult and expensive. Contact your local agricultural extension agent for advice.

If sugar beets sound like high-maintenance food plots, they are. However, Roundup Ready sugar beets are in the works, and this will change the picture completely. With Roundup Ready sugar beets, the exacting application of herbicide described above will be simplified, although the rest of the high standards for a successful sugar beet plot will still be there.

After a successful sugar beet crop, use the field for crops such as soybeans, clover/small grain mixes or buckwheat until you can rotate sugar beets onto the field again. These crops help build soil fertility and organic matter for the next rotation.

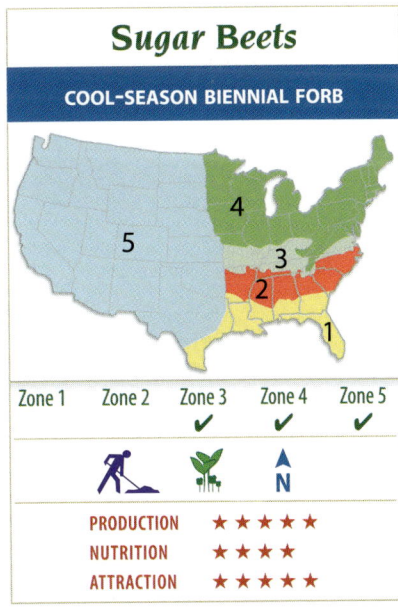

Sugar Beets

COOL-SEASON BIENNIAL FORB

Zone 1	Zone 2	Zone 3	Zone 4	Zone 5
		✔	✔	✔

PRODUCTION	★ ★ ★ ★ ★
NUTRITION	★ ★ ★ ★
ATTRACTION	★ ★ ★ ★ ★

285

DIRECTORY OF SERVICES

FOOD PLOT SEED

AMPAC Seed Company

32727 Hwy 99 E.
PO Box 318
Tangent, OR 97389
(866) 663-0129
scott@ampacseed.com
www.ampacseed.com

Wildlife Perfect Mixes™ are formulated for intense grazing by wildlife. AMPAC selects species and varieties that are adapted to each region. Our mixtures have been proven over the years by wildlife biologists, sportsmen, and deer farmers. **Wildlife Perfect seeds** are grazing type varieties that are high in protein. Attract the Wild!!

Cooper Feed and Seed

131 Eaton St.
Lawrenceville, GA 30045
(770) 963-2101
(770) 963-9477 fax
cooper@cooperseeds.com
www.cooperseeds.com

Plottoppers is the latest advancement in seed mixes and planting techniques for food plots. Plottoppers was created by Cooper Seeds with technical advice from Kent Kammermeyer, Certified Wildlife Biologist and QDMA Senior Technical Advisor with over 30 years of food plot experience. **Cooper Seeds** offers the finest seeds available with a sincere mission to help hunters nationwide.

Buck Busters Seed Co.

5152 Hwy 84
Vidalia, LA 71373
(318) 336-3503
(318) 336-3506 fax
sales@buckbusters.biz
www.buckbustersseedcompany.com

The Food Plot Co.

302 Western Ave.
Red Lion, PA 17356
(717) 244-8647
FoodPlots@aol.com

Deer Creek Seed

N7760 Flambeau Road
Ladysmith WI, 54848
(715) 532-9303
(715) 532-9305 fax
deercreekseed@hotmail.com
www.deercreekseed.com

FOOD PLOT SEED

Frigid Forage

10015 Aspen Ave. N.W.
Bemidji, MN 56601
(218) 751-0147
(218) 759-4656 fax
sales@sunrichfarm.com
www.frigidforage.com

Frigid Forage, the hardiest food plot forage in the land, was developed and is produced in our nation's ice box, northern Minnesota. Extremely **cold tolerant**, highly palatable and very nutritious to your deer. If you are tired of your food plots freezing out, Frigid Forage's Total Nutritional Program is essential for your management plan.

Hunter's Specialties

6000 Huntington CT N.E.
Cedar Rapids, IA 52402
(319) 395-0321
(319) 395-0326 fax
website@hunterspec.com
www.hunterspec.com

VITA-Rack Seed Mixtures are scientifically developed for maximum deer attraction. These dynamic mixtures aid in antler growth and overall herd health. When these premium high yielding seed turn to lush vibrant forage, they create a safe haven for whitetail deer.

Your Forests   Your Future

Plum Creek is dedicated to producing the highest quality pine & hardwood seedlings available for our customers with a commitment to providing exceptional service to meet our customer's individual needs.

Species:

Hardwoods: Autumn Olive, French Mulberry, Bald Cypress, Common Pear, Mayhaw, Persimmon, Southern Crabapple , Sweet Pecan, Sawtooth Oak (Gobbler), Sawtooth Oak,Cherrybark Oak,Laurel Oak, Live Oak, Northern Red Oak, Nuttall Oak , Overcup Oak ,Shumard Oak, Swamp Chestnut Oak , Water Oak ,White Oak, Willow Oak
Pines: Loblolly - Slash

Wildlife Package Available

Toll Free: 1-866-894-1072
www.plumcreektrees.com

PlumCreek

Osborne, Kansas
800-782-7311
Visit us on the web at
www.gostarseed.com
or e-mail us at
deer@gostarseed.com

Native Grass
HEADQUARTERS

Star Seed is your single resource for all of your native grass needs. They offer a complete line of native grass, wildflowers and CRP grasses for use in establishing food plots, game management, conservation programs, erosion control and prairie management. Contact us today at 1-800-782-7311.

POGUE
Agri Partners

287 Hwy 72 W. – P.O. Box 389 – Kenedy, TX 78119
830-583-3456   830-583-9843 fax
www.pogueagri.com

POGUE Agri Partners offers a full line of products to create and enhance a healthy wildlife habitat for both warm and cool season environments through adapted plant genetics.

Custom blending and pre-inoculated seed are available using our AGRICOAT™ coating process. Inform our expert staff of your geographical location and they will provide a wealth of field experience, education and knowledge relative to your choice of program.

Improving Wildlife Habitat — Now . . . And for the Future!

BUCK BUFFET FOOD PLOT

FOOD PLOT SEED

GENERAL DEER MANAGEMENT

Hunter's Specialties

6000 Huntington CT N.E.
Cedar Rapids, IA 52402
(319) 395-0321
(319) 395-0326 fax
website@hunterspec.com
www.hunterspec.com

The **VITA-Rack 26 Nutritional System** was developed for wildlife management. This superior formula has everything whitetails need to reach their full genetic potential. VITA-RACK 26 contains 26 vitamins and minerals essential to balanced nutrition.

Natural Resource Systems

P.O. Box 628
Atlanta, TX 75551
(903) 748-3851
(903) 796-8491 fax
rboitnott@nrsllc.com
www.nrsllc.com

Natural Resource Systems, LLC is a wildlife management consulting firm that produces **CheckStation Deer Management Software**. CheckStation is a computer program that allows hunters, landowners, and wildlife managers to enter deer harvest and observation data and create reports and graphs that provide important information for making deer management decisions.

Tecomate Wildlife Systems

111 Industrial Blvd.
Wrightsville, GA 31096
(478) 864-9108
(478) 864-9109 fax
bburley@theplotmaster.com
www.tecomate.com

FERTILIZERS & REPELLENTS

Messina Wildlife Mgmt.

55 Willow St., Suit 1
Washington, NJ 07882
(908) 320-7009
(908) 320-7088 fax
info@messinawildlife.com
www.MessinaWildlife.com

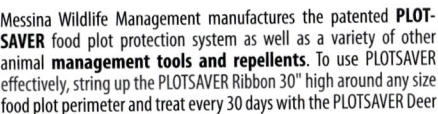

Messina Wildlife Management manufactures the patented **PLOTSAVER** food plot protection system as well as a variety of other animal **management tools and repellents**. To use PLOTSAVER effectively, string up the PLOTSAVER Ribbon 30" high around any size food plot perimeter and treat every 30 days with the PLOTSAVER Deer Repellent.

United Agri Products

7251 West 4th St.
P.O. Box 1286
Greeley, CO 80632-1286
(970) 356-4400
(856) 694-0462 fax
dave.bachinsky@uap.com
www.uap.com

United Agri Products (UAP) is the largest independent distributor of agriculture chemicals, seed and fertilizers in the United States and Canada. Our sales representatives can help you establish your food plots and maintain them for years to come. Please visit our web site to find your nearest location - **www.uap.com**.

SOIL & PLANT TESTING LABS

PlotRx.com

Do you expect the most ROBUST food plots? Get quick, reliable analysis of your soils in a laboratory with **thirty-years experience**. Indicate your choice of food plot species and we will customize the fertility plan in an **easy-reading report**. We also offer seed inoculants (use online code 'QFP 6').

TRACTORS & EQUIPMENT

B-I-H Enterprises, LLC.

P.O. Box 485
Leola, PA 17540
(717) 314-9909
(717) 556-0967 fax
dpberry@dejazzd.com
www.b-i-henterprises.com

The **Pulverized Lime Spreaders**, are ground driven and feature a precise gate opening that dispenses dry or damp lime. Be free to lime anytime! The **Ground Preparation Implements** consist of 4 ft. and 6 ft. models that are built rugged enough to till rocky soils and tough sod conditions. GroundBuster units can be pulled using your ATV, tractor or vehicle.

GroundHog Connections

#289 4002 Hwy 78, Suite 530
Snellville, GA 30039
(800) 566-1691
(678) 749-7781 fax
info@groundhogdiscplow.com
www.groundhogdiscplow.com

The **GroundHog by Tufline**. This next generation ATV disc plow uses the weight of ATV and driver to achieve an aggressive cut. Ideal for food plots, gardening, landscaping, and maintaining firebreaks and weed control. It is a rugged, **go-anywhere tool**: plows soggy bottomland to rocky hillsides and everything in between.

At $2.50/lb, the **BrushMaster** is
Cheaper than Steak but
Tougher than all get out!

QUALITY VEGETATIVE MANAGEMENT WILDLIFE SPECIALTY
BRUSHMASTER

Wildlife Specialty, Inc.
P.O. Box 1107, Yazoo City, MS 39194
(877) 647-2563 phone; (662) 746-6825 fax
www.amcomfg.com

Double offset tandem disc harrow. Blades are 1/4" thick plus front outside blades have a back up blade. Gangs have shock-bearing risers to give relief to the gangs when they encounter a stump. Bearings are re-greasable triple-lip sealed with Protect-O-Shield. Six to 10 foot width weighing 1600-3000 lbs.

The Firminator
By: Modern Habitat Solutions

(317) 336-7184
www.TheFirminator.com

"The Firminator" is a commercial-grade implement built to tackle the toughest conditions. It combines three vital tools on one rugged frame. "The Best Food Plot Implement on Earth" boasts an aggressive disc assembly, an agricultural-grade cultipacker, topped by the most precise, ground-driven seed metering system available.

WEEKEND WARRIOR
The original food plot people.

Tough Equipment for tough jobs

A COMPLETE LINEUP OF

SMALL PULL-BEHIND

AND 3-POINT HITCH

TILLAGE EQUIPMENT

WEEKEND WARRIOR
www.weekend-warrior.com • 866-539-8944

Manufactured for use with compact tractors and ATV's

TRACTORS & EQUIPMENT

Kolpin Powersports, Inc.

205 North Depot St.
Fox Lake, WI 53933
(877) 956-5746
(920) 928-6440 fax
customerservice@kolpinpowersports.com
www.kolpinpowersports.com

Kolpin Powersports, Inc. provides a full line of Food Plot and Landscaping implements for your ATV or UTV with the Kolpin/Dirtworks 3-Point Hitch System. Every implement mounts in seconds without the need for tools. Available implements include: **Disc Plow, Cultivator, Landscape Rake, Rear Blade, Box Blade Attachment and Fork Lift.**

WILDLIFE CONSULTANTS

Finger Lakes Food Plots

8572 Lawrence Gull
Wayland, NY 14572
(585) 613-5478
(585) 669-9434 home
craig@fingerlakesfoodplots.com
www.fingerlakesfoodplots.com

Phil Anderson Nutrition Consulting

1538 West Home Road
Emlenton, PA 16373
(724) 867-5876
admgt@csonline.net

Wildlife Plot Management

1160 BlueFeild Road
Lexington, SC 29073
(803) 755-7305
wildlifeplotmgmt@bellsouth.net

Educating the hunter-landowner through...

WHITETAIL ALLIANCE™
Research • Education • Stewardship

Wildlife Management Plans

Property Layout and Management

Turn-key Hunting Properties

Books, DVD's

Short Courses

Property Tours

Food Plot Products and Equipment

**www.NorthCountryWhitetails.com
315-331-6959**

Kent Kammermeyer Consulting

Over 30 years of experience in deer and food plot management specializing in quality deer management plans, maximizing protein in cool and warm season food plots, analysis of deer harvest data, habitat quality evaluations, and harvest recommendations per square mile. QDMA Technical Advisor. Award winner: "Biologist of the Year" (2000) and "Deer Management Career Achievement" (2005).

*www.deerclovers.com
(706) 805-7030
kentk40@yahoo.com*

WILDLIFE CONSULTANTS

Drop-Tine Wildlife Consulting

P.O. Box 780
Millville, PA 17846
(570) 458-0477
(570) 458-6477 fax
droptinewildlife@verizon.net

Drop-Tine remains on the cutting edge of deer management by employing advanced wildlife management techniques. We specialize in all aspects of deer management program design and implementation. **Drop-Tine offers** herd surveying, herd management, food plot design/installation, data collection, habitat management, harvest recommendations, GPS/GIS, property design/development, property acquisitions and hunting enhancement.

Corter's Game Enhancement Specialties

207 Snyder School Road
Nescopeck, PA 18635
(570) 336-0492
corters@bwkip.com

Whitetail Habitat Solutions, LLC

P.O. Box 536
Munising, MI 49862
(906) 387-3904
(906) 387-4148 fax

Coaching individuals to realize their property's habitat, herd, and buck age structure potential through consultation or seminar activities, including: Strategic property design, access, and stand position; food plot program establishment & efficiency; sanctuary area enhancement and protection; proven non-invasive mature buck holding and harvest techniques; and balanced herd management strategies.

jeff@whitetailhabitatsolutions.com
www.whitetailhabitatsolutions.com

Milliken Forestry Company

P.O. Box 23629
Columbia, SC 29224
(803) 788-0590
(803) 788-0596 fax
www.millikenforestry.com

MILLIKEN FORESTRY COMPANY, INC.

Good timber and good habitat can go together. For more than half a century, we've guided landowners in acquiring and improving timberland to meet goals as unique as their properties. We'll show you how your timberlands can reward you, and help you achieve that **balance of timber and wildlife**.

Westervelt Wildlife Services

(800) 281-7991
www.westervelt.com

With **over 50 years experience** and more than a million acres under management, Westervelt is recognized as the leading source for wildlife, food plot, and habitat management consultation in the Southeast. Let our experience go to work for you.

Woodlands & Wildlife Consultants

P.O. Box 1508
Fortson, GA 31808
(706) 568-8412
wildlife@woodlandsandwildlife.com
www.woodlandsandwildlife.com

Woodlands & Wildlife Consultants, LLC

W & WC provides an array of wildlife and forestry management services to its clients. Property management plans, intensive forest/habitat management practices, turn-key food plot management and specialized game management techniques are a few examples of how **our staff can help you** take your property/lease and your hunting to the next level.

WILDLIFE CONSULTANTS

Southern Wildlife & Land Consultants

2050 Howell Bridge Road
Ball Ground, GA 30107
(770) 737-5125
(770) 737-5135 fax
info@swlci.com
www.swlci.com

Trupe's Wildlife Management

RR 1 Box 114
RT 44 Sharon Center
Shinglehouse, PA 16748
(877) 806-6993 phone/fax
(814) 697-7723 phone/fax
(717) 314-1067 mobile
www.ezsowdeerfood.com

Wildlife Landscape Services

Brian Sheppard
631 Old Chipley Road
Pine Mountain, GA 31822
(706) 718-1690
(706) 668-4664 fax
bsheppar@bellsouth.net

HUNTING CLUB INSURANCE

THE EDITORS

Kent Kammermeyer was born and raised in Winsted, Connecticut, and harvested his first deer in 1966. Mentored by his friend Jim Zucco, he has been hunting and managing deer ever since. He graduated with a B.S. degree in wildlife management from the University of Connecticut in 1972 and received an M.S. in wildlife biology from The University of Georgia in 1975. During Kent's 30-year career with Georgia DNR's Wildlife Resources Division, he directly supervised six WMAs totaling 150,000 acres with 900 acres of food plots. For more than 25 years, he was chairman of the state's Deer Committee. Kent has published more than 50 scientific articles or abstracts and more than 300 popular articles, mostly on deer. Since 1999, he has published more than 60 plant "Species Profile" columns for *Quality Whitetails* magazine. In 2000, he received the Southeastern Director's Wildlife Biologist of the Year award. In 2005, he received the Career Achievement Award for outstanding contributions to white-tailed deer management in the Southeast. Kent and his wife of over 20 years, Freda, and daughter Vanda live on a 36-acre woodland paradise near Clermont, Georgia.

Karl V. Miller, Ph.D., grew up hunting deer in the forests of northern Pennsylvania where he learned woodsmanship skills from his father and grandfather. Karl is now a professor of wildlife ecology and management at The University of Georgia. He received a B.S. degree from The Pennsylvania State University in 1979, an M.S. degree from Ohio State University in 1981, and a Ph.D. in Forest Resources from The University of Georgia in 1985. In addition to teaching courses in forest and wildlife management, he has developed a multifaceted research program that includes investigations of the behavioral ecology, habitat requirements and management of white-tailed deer and on the impact of forest management practices on deer and other wildlife species. He is the co-editor of the book *Quality Whitetails–The Why and How of Quality Deer Management* and co-author of *Forest Plants of the Southeast and Their Wildlife Uses.* He has published more than 200 professional reports, publications and book chapters. Karl is married to a special woman and venison gourmet, Renee Miller, and has two young deer hunters, Shaun David and Timothy Raymond.

Lindsay Thomas Jr. was raised on a farm in southeast Georgia and introduced to deer hunting at an early age by his father. After earning a journalism degree at The University of Georgia, Lindsay went to work as an editor for *Georgia Outdoor News* magazine, where he spent much of his nine years on the staff researching and writing about Quality Deer Management, habitat improvement and food plots. In 2003 he joined QDMA as the Director of Publications and the editor of QDMA's *Quality Whitetails* magazine. As a hunter, he has been actively practicing all aspects of QDM for two decades. Lindsay and his wife Anne have three children – Jacob, Laurel and Julia.

OTHER CHAPTER AUTHORS

Craig Dougherty, Ph.D., is the chairman of the National Board of Directors of the Quality Deer Management Association and co-founder of NorthCountry Whitetails. He is the co-author with his son, Neil, of the book *Grow 'Em Right.*

Phil Freshley is a certified professional soil scientist, board certified soil classifier, registered forester and president of LandTec Southeast Inc., a consulting firm specializing in soil and water science issues. He has extensive experience with soil and landscape evaluation, hydrology, and soil nutrient cycling in the eastern United States.

Joe Hamilton is a wildlife biologist and the founder of the Quality Deer Management Association. During his nearly 20 years with the South Carolina Department of Natural Resources, Joe helped implement QDM practices on more than two million acres. In 2000, he was awarded the Deer Management Career Achievement Award from The Wildlife Society as well as an honorary lifetime appointment on the QDMA National Board of Directors.

Craig A. Harper, Ph.D., is an associate professor of wildlife management and the Extension Wildlife Specialist at the University of Tennessee. Craig develops wildlife-related programs for UT Extension and maintains an applied research program that concentrates on quality deer management, fire effects in upland hardwoods, timber stand improvement, native warm-season grasses, and food plot management. He is a certified wildlife biologist with The Wildlife Society and has published numerous articles, book chapters, and manuals related to his work.

W. Carroll Johnson III, Ph.D., is a research agronomist at the Coastal Plain Experiment Station in Tifton, Ga. Carroll conducts weed science and agronomic research on peanut, vegetable crops and organic crop production. Areas of research include integrated weed management systems, herbicide and fumigant application technology, ecology of weeds in the southeastern Coastal Plain, and use of alternate strategies to manage weeds without herbicides. During Carroll's 22-year career, he has published 46 articles in scientific journals, 34 popular press articles, and 11 Extension service bulletins. Carroll is also consulting agronomist and weed scientist with the Whitetail Institute of North America in Pintlala, Ala.

Brian Murphy is a wildlife biologist and has been the executive director of the Quality Deer Management Association since 1997. He has been involved in deer research and management for more than 20 years. Brian has written more than 100 popular and scientific articles and given nearly 500 lectures on deer biology and management.

Jim Wills Jr., Ph.D., is professor and coordinator of Power and Machinery Systems in the Biosystems Engineering and Environmental Science Department at The University of Tennessee. Jim works with farmers and equipment dealers to address questions regarding farm machinery, and he conducts 30 to 40 seminars a year on the use of specialized equipment, such as no-till drills. He is also an avid deer hunter and an experienced planter of food plots.

OTHER CONTRIBUTORS

Phil Anderson is a ruminant nutrition and management consultant. He is a former extension educator and a member of the American Registry of Professional Animal Scientists.

Bryan Kinkel is a wildlife and habitat consultant who specializes in small-land management, deer utilization of terrain and habitat, localized herd dynamics, and digital mapping.

Brian Sheppard is a food plot consultant and owner of Wildlife Landscape Services. He regularly contributes articles to *Quality Whitetails* on specialized food plot equipment and techniques.

Rans Thomas is a wildlife biologist and consultant and the manager of the Consulting Services division of Tecomate Wildlife Systems.

Grant Woods, Ph.D., is a research biologist and the president of Woods & Associates Inc., a wildlife management consulting company. Grant is a Charter Life Member of QDMA.

ABOUT QUALITY DEER MANAGEMENT

Quality Food Plots will be a reliable guide through many seasons of food plot management as you strive to produce better deer and better deer hunting. However, Quality Deer Management involves much more than food plots.

WHAT IS QDM?

Quality Deer Management (QDM) is a management philosophy/practice that strives to produce healthy, more natural deer herds with balanced adult sex ratios and increased numbers of older bucks. This approach typically involves protection of young bucks and active harvest of female deer to maintain herds within existing habitat conditions. The increased number of older bucks available for breeding often results in an earlier, more defined rut. In many cases, antler growth and body weights increase due to improved habitat conditions. A successful QDM program requires an increased knowledge of deer biology and active participation in management. This level of involvement extends the hunter's role from consumer to manager and often requires a change in hunting practices and mindset. Many landowners and hunters receive great satisfaction from the increased involvement with their deer herds that QDM offers.

THE HISTORY OF QDM

South Texas is the formal birthplace of QDM. In 1975, wildlife biologists Al Brothers and Murphy Ray Jr. published their landmark book, *Producing Quality Whitetails*, which formally defined this concept. The QDM approach was brought to the Southeast in the late 1970s and slowly gained acceptance. Throughout the 1980s and 1990s, QDM gained popularity throughout other portions of the whitetail's range. By 2000, dozens of states and many thousands of hunters had implemented QDM practices on millions of acres of private and public lands across the United States.

THE FOUR CORNERSTONES OF QDM

While QDM guidelines must be tailored to each property, there are four corner-stones to all successful QDM programs – herd management, habitat management, hunter management, and herd monitoring.

Herd Management. Determining the appropriate number of deer to harvest by sex and age is essential to every QDM program. In many areas, deer populations are at or above optimum levels, and active harvest of female deer is necessary. In fact, appropriate antlerless harvest often is the most important aspect of herd manage-ment. Another important aspect is restricting the harvest of young bucks. A reason-able starting point for most QDM programs is the protection of yearling bucks. Re-strictions are established on a property-specific basis according to hunter objectives, property size, habitat quality, neighboring management practices, and other factors. Several body and antler characteristics can be used to protect young bucks, although advice from a wildlife biologist is recommended to help determine which are most appropriate for your deer herd.

Habitat Management. Ensuring adequate nutrition is another important cornerstone of QDM. The diet of a healthy deer herd should contain a minimum of 16 percent protein and adequate levels of calcium, phosphorus and other important nutrients. Although whitetails can maintain themselves on lower-quality diets, antler development, body growth, and reproductive success suffer. Fortunately, several techniques are available to increase nutrition to desirable levels. Three common practices include natural vegetation management, food plots and supplemental feeding. Another effective method of improving available nutrition

BILL LEA

Hot Pursuit

When the ratio of adult bucks to adult does in a population is brought closer toward a balance through QDM, rut behaviors like chasing and features like rubs and scrapes become more prevalent, greatly increasing the satisfaction of participating hunters.

is by simply reducing the number of deer relative to the habitat's carrying capacity through the harvest of female deer. This technique may be the only viable option in areas where other nutritional improvement practices are not possible.

Hunter Management. Managing hunters is a critical yet often difficult aspect of QDM. Within most hunting groups, support for QDM varies. It is difficult to achieve the objectives of QDM without the support of all hunters on a given property. Education is the key. Hunters must fully understand the benefits and costs of QDM before they become active participants. Active participation in QDM requires an increased understanding of deer biology, ecology and behavior. Hunters must learn to distinguish fawns, does, yearling bucks, intermediate-aged bucks (2½ and 3½ years old), and mature bucks (4½ years and older). Knowledge leads to increased respect for the quarry and often a greater focus on the experience rather than the number or size of animals harvested.

Herd Monitoring. Herd monitoring, or data collection, is the final cornerstone of QDM. Two types of data are commonly collected – harvest data and observation data. Typical harvest data include sex, age, weight, antler measurements, and reproductive information. This information enables managers to determine management success and fine-tune their programs based on sound information. Observation data can be collected by hunters or with remote-sensing cameras. Because some bucks are protected from harvest, observation data can provide useful information not provided by harvest data.

To continue learning more about all aspects of QDM, consider becoming a member of the Quality Deer Management Association (QDMA). This book is only a small part of QDMA's ongoing mission to supply deer hunters with scientifically sound guidance on whitetail management. Read on to learn more about QDMA and the benefits of membership.

ABOUT THE QDMA

QDMA is a national nonprofit wildlife conservation organization and the leading advocate of the QDM philosophy. The QDMA was founded in 1988 in the South Carolina Lowcountry by wildlife biologist Joe Hamilton, author of the Foreword of this book. Responding to the call by Texas biologist and deer management pioneer Al Brothers for hunters to become active managers of whitetails, Joe saw a need for an organization that would bridge the knowledge gap between biologists and hunters. Joe was assisted by a group of Charter Life Members that included prominent names in whitetail research and management.

While the QDMA was originally founded as a state-based organization in South Carolina, widespread interest from other states and several foreign countries resulted in expansion to a national organization in 1991. In 1998, the QDMA moved its headquarters to Georgia and today is among the fastest growing conservation organizations

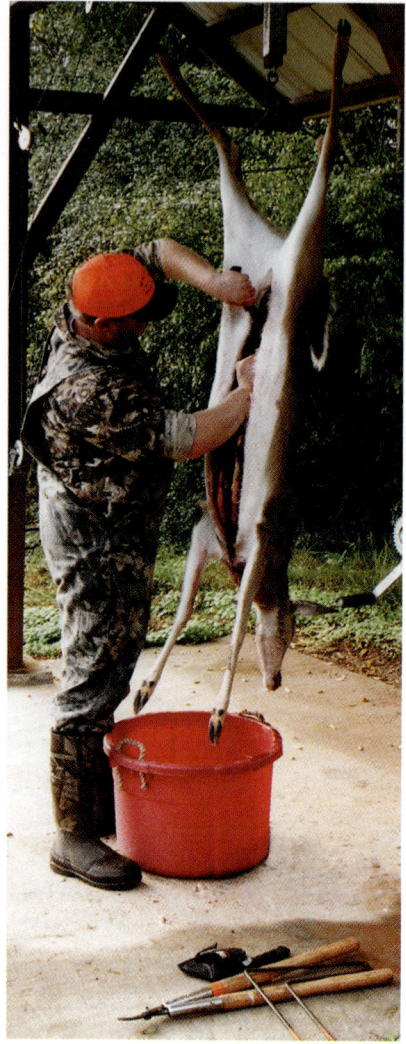

DEER RESEARCHER

QDM *practicioners must keep a finger on the pulse of their deer population in order to make adjustments to their management program. This is accomplished through collecting data, including age, weight and other harvest information as well as deer observations while hunting and by using infrared-triggered cameras.*

in the nation with members in all 50 states and several foreign countries. Among the QDMA's current members are hundreds of the nation's leading deer management professionals. Their collective knowledge enables the QDMA and its members to remain at the forefront of deer biology, research and management.

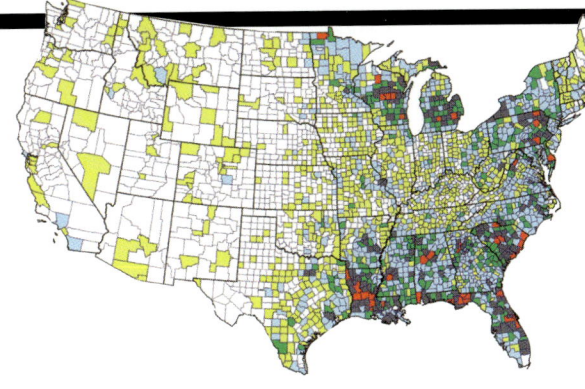

MAPPING GROWTH

By 2004, *when this county-by-county QDMA membership map was created, the organization's membership had spread throughout areas with strong whitetail populations.*

QDMA's PROUD HISTORY OF ACCOMPLISHMENTS

While many wildlife conservation organizations focus their efforts on habitat acquisition or species restoration, the QDMA's primary focus has always been on education, research and on-the-ground management. Here, the QDMA has achieved great success. Today, thousands of hunters and millions of acres of public and private lands are managed under QDM guidelines. The QDMA's relentless educational efforts, which include conducting hundreds of seminars annually and publishing numerous books, videos, posters, and other items, have substantially increased the understanding of and participation in QDM.

The QDMA has influenced the attitudes of millions of deer hunters and managers. The acronym "QDM," while still misunderstood by many, is now a household word. You cannot pick up a hunting magazine today without finding something on QDM. Likewise, while the QDMA's journal *Quality Whitetails* was the first publication to focus exclusively on herd and habitat management, just about every deer magazine today addresses these subjects.

The QDMA also has actively partnered with numerous state and federal agencies, forest products companies, conservation organizations and other groups to increase support for QDM. The QDMA was the first whitetail organization to join the Chronic Wasting Disease Alliance and is a proud supporter of numerous deer research projects conducted by state wildlife agencies and universities.

Preserving the deer-hunting heritage is also a priority for the QDMA. Each year the QDMA conducts numerous events for youth and women as well as supporting worthy organizations like Farmers and Hunters Feeding the Hungry, the Paralyzed Veterans Association and the Catch-A-Dream Foundation. The QDMA also supports state law enforcement agencies through donations of educational and law-enforcement items such as mechanized deer decoys.

> ## QDMA's MISSION
>
> The QDMA is dedicated to promoting sustainable, high-quality white-tailed deer populations, wildlife habitats and ethical hunting experiences through education, research and management in partnership with hunters, landowners, natural resource professionals and the public.

The QDMA's ongoing commitment to education and stewardship was formally recognized when it was awarded the prestigious "Group Achievement Award" from The Wildlife Society. The QDMA is the only whitetail organization ever to receive this coveted award.

QDMA Membership Benefits

The QDMA is a grassroots, membership-based organization open to anyone with an interest in the wise management of white-tailed deer and preservation of the deer-hunting heritage. By joining the QDMA, you will undertake a path toward becoming the most knowledgeable deer hunter and manager possible.

Quality Whitetails

Your membership entitles you to a subscription to *Quality Whitetails*, QDMA's acclaimed deer management journal. Each issue is filled with practical information on all aspects of deer biology, management, and habitat enhancement written by the nation's leading whitetail experts. *Quality Whitetails* gets to the meat of the subject so members in all regions can apply what they learn to improve their own deer hunting and management situations. In fact, most members keep every issue as future reference material. Just as this book, *Quality Food Plots*, covers every detail of food plot management in practical terms that any hunter can understand, *Quality Whitetails* covers all aspects of QDM.

QDMA members receive the journal Quality Whitetails *six times annually. Each issue contains reliable, practical information on deer and habitat management.*

Educational Events & Materials

Your membership provides access to the QDMA's experts through numerous educational events held annually throughout the nation. Each year, more than 200 seminars and field days are held throughout North America to allow QDMA members to learn directly from experienced wildlife biologists and managers as well as everyday landowners and hunters who have experienced QDM success. You also will gain access to the QDMA's extensive line of educational books, videos, maps, posters, and booklets, as well as discounts on commonly-used deer management products and services.

Branch Involvement

Your membership allows you to participate in a local QDMA Branch to promote the philosophy of QDM and the mission of the QDMA in your area and to unite like-minded sportsmen in this common goal. Like organized chapters of other conservation organizations, QDMA Branches help raise funds for their community, state and national efforts and spread awareness of QDMA. However, QDMA Branches are unique among conservation groups in that each Branch conducts at least one educational function annually – and often many more than one. These events include seminars, food plot field days, property tours, deer data collection stations and deer aging and scoring events. You can take advantage of this outreach by attending local Branch fundraisers and educational events, or you can become involved in helping your local Branch spread the word about Quality Deer Management. To get in touch with a Branch near you, visit www.QDMA.com.

ON A MISSION

QDMA Branches are unique among conservation groups in their educational mandate. This educational field day held at QDMA National Headquarters in 2006 was a joint effort of the Georgia Branches of QDMA. Here, QDMA's senior technical advisor Kent Kammermeyer, also an editor of Quality Food Plots, *leads a food plot seminar.*

THE REACH PROGRAM

In early 2006, the QDMA launched REACH – the most ambitious education and outreach program in its history. REACH stands for Research, Educate, Advocate, Certify and Hunt, and each area represents one of QDMA's five core mission areas. This program will provide numerous benefits to QDMA members and the whitetail resource.

Research – Sound deer management decisions require reliable information, and this information generally comes from research. Under REACH, QDMA will increase its involvement in all areas of white-tailed deer research, including biology, ecology, management, hunting, diseases and human dimensions. QDMA will help design, fund and coordinate practical research projects that increase knowledge and improve management.

Educate – QDMA has long been a recognized leader in educating hunters, landowners, wildlife professionals and the public on all aspects of whitetail biology and management. However, the types of information desired by these groups as well as the mechanisms to deliver this information are changing, and QDMA must keep pace. While QDMA will continue with existing educational activities, it will also pursue other delivery methods such as television, DVDs, and Internet-based learning modules and video downloads.

Advocate – Each year, there are countless threats to the future of deer hunting and management at the local, state and national levels. Due to QDMA's recent growth and strong support from the professional wildlife community, it is considered the most respected and influential whitetail organization in North America. As a result, QDMA has accepted the challenge to become the leading advocate for the wise management of white-tailed deer and the protection of our deer-hunting heritage.

Certify – Many QDMA members are dedicated to learning everything possible about QDM and how they can make their hunting properties true showcases of QDM principles. As a result, the QDMA has established individual and property certification programs to meet this demand. The end result of these programs will be more knowledgeable and effective deer managers and more properties with better deer and better deer hunting.

Hunt – In response to declines in hunter numbers, QDMA has developed an innovative mentored hunting program which, unlike programs which involve a one-time contact with a young hunter, matches a young person with a QDMA mentor for a minimum of one year. During this period, the mentor and first-time hunter will complete several required stages such as developing woodsmanship skills, hunting small game, hunting deer, and learning how to clean and prepare wild game. The goal of this program is to make more hunters, not simply to take more kids hunting.

Without question, REACH will strengthen QDMA's position as the nation's leading whitetail conservation organization.

The Future of Deer Hunting and Management

The QDMA's early days were devoted to convincing hunters, landowners, and even many biologists that QDM could work and hunter attitudes could change. Thousands of success stories later, this is no longer the most difficult task. In more recent

Home, Sweet Home

In 2005, QDMA *moved into its permanent National Headquarters near Athens, Georgia, on a 23-acre property that will serve as a base for future growth as well as a field education center.*

302

years, new challenges have surfaced. Whitetail populations have skyrocketed, hunter numbers have declined, hunter attitudes have changed, society's respect for deer has declined, and diseases have threatened some deer herds. Collectively, these issues are more difficult, complex, and important than at any time in history. Now, more than ever, whitetail hunters must unite in a collective effort to ensure that whitetail hunting and management remain an integral part of wildlife management in the future. The QDMA has faced each new challenge head-on and will continue to do so while pursuing our mission to become the most respected, most influential, and most effective whitetail conservation organization in the world.

If you share these goals and the desire to improve whitetail herds and hunting experiences for yourself and future generations of sportsmen, join QDMA today.

INDEX TO SIDEBARS, GRAPHS & MAPS

INDEX

NOTES

NOTES

NOTES

NOTES